Vue.js 2 Cookbook

Build modern, interactive web applications with Vue.js

Andrea Passaglia

BIRMINGHAM - MUMBAI

Vue.js 2 Cookbook

First published: April 2017

Production reference: 1200417

Published by Packt Publishing Ltd.
Livery Place
35 Livery Street
Birmingham
B3 2PB, UK.

ISBN 978-1-78646-809-3

www.packtpub.com

Credits

Author

Andrea Passaglia

Reviewer

Bogdan-Alin Bâlc

Commissioning Editor

Ashwin Nair

Acquisition Editor

Siddharth Mandal

Content Development Editors

Narendrakumar Tripathi

Mohammed Yusuf Imaratwale

Technical Editor

Sushant S Nadkar

Copy Editor

Shaila Kusanale

Project Coordinator

Ritika Manoj

Proofreader

Safis Editing

Indexer

Aishwarya Gangawane

Graphics

Jason Monteiro

Production Coordinator

Aparna Bhagat

About the Author

Andrea Passaglia was born in Genoa, in northern Italy. Interested about technology since his parents gave him a toy computer when he was a boy, he started studying web technologies at an early age. After obtaining his master's degree in computer engineering he worked on the design and implementation of web interfaces for companies of various sizes and in different industries (healthcare, fashion, tourism, and transport).

In 2016 he moves in the silicon valley of Europe to tackle new problems in the banking industry at the Edgeverve Dublin Research and Development Labs.

A backend technologist by trade, Vue.js is his first tool to bring to life his creations when it comes to the frontend.

Andrea is married to a lovely Russian girl from Siberia and they often cook together mixing culinary traditions.

I would like to thank Packt for giving me the opportunity to write this book--Narendra Tripathi, Smeet Thakkar, Siddharth Mandal, and the whole team for being so professional and supporting. A big thank you to Bogdan Bâlc for his attention to detail, and all the people that helped me with reviewing the book; I'm talking to Alesya Kholodova, Eamon McNamee, and Yomi Eluande. Thank you guys for your practical suggestions and useful additions to the book.

Support from my colleagues at the lab was invaluable, to you guys goes my gratitude for always asking "How's the book going?" It really meant a lot to me.

Thanks to my wife for constantly pushing me to write every day and everywhere; thanks to my family for your love and support.

About the Reviewer

Bogdan is a team lead with a passion for frontend technologies. He has worked on JavaScript for the past 8 years, from the emergence of jQuery and Ajax to modern full-fledged MVC frameworks. When he is not fiddling with some new JavaScript challenge, he spends his time playing sports and games with friends, and watching sports and movies.

Nowadays he channels most of his efforts into making WE3 Interactive one of the most successful and creative startups in Cluj.

He is so passionate about Vue.js that he has already helped publish another awesome book written by Olga Filipova: *Learning Vue.js.*

www.PacktPub.com

For support files and downloads related to your book, please visit www.PacktPub.com.

Did you know that Packt offers eBook versions of every book published, with PDF and ePub files available? You can upgrade to the eBook version at www.PacktPub.com and as a print book customer, you are entitled to a discount on the eBook copy. Get in touch with us at service@packtpub.com for more details.

At www.PacktPub.com, you can also read a collection of free technical articles, sign up for a range of free newsletters and receive exclusive discounts and offers on Packt books and eBooks.

https://www.packtpub.com/mapt

Get the most in-demand software skills with Mapt. Mapt gives you full access to all Packt books and video courses, as well as industry-leading tools to help you plan your personal development and advance your career.

Why subscribe?

- Fully searchable across every book published by Packt
- Copy and paste, print, and bookmark content
- On demand and accessible via a web browser

Customer Feedback

Thanks for purchasing this Packt book. At Packt, quality is at the heart of our editorial process. To help us improve, please leave us an honest review on this book's Amazon page at https://www.amazon.com/dp/1786468093.

If you'd like to join our team of regular reviewers, you can e-mail us at customerreviews@packtpub.com. We award our regular reviewers with free eBooks and videos in exchange for their valuable feedback. Help us be relentless in improving our products!

Con amore infinito, tuo figlio Andrea

Table of Contents

Preface

Vue.js 2 is a minimal but powerful framework. It will empower you to quickly prototype small applications, and it won't get in the way when structuring large frontend systems. This is a cookbook and every paragraph is a recipe; just as with a regular cookbook, you can quickly skip to the recipe that interests you or read it cover to cover to become a great chef. All the recipes (except a handful) represent working Vue apps, so at the end of the exercise you are never left empty handed. When I wrote them, I tried to give meaningful examples and sprinkle some fun where possible. All the recipes are slightly different when it comes to doing the same thing, so that you will learn something new even when implementing very similar recipes.

This book took about 6 months to write, and even in this short amount of time I had to go back and update pictures and the API that changed, as well as add new concepts. Still, many recipes are imbued with the everlasting concepts of reusability and good engineering, so I like to think that some parts of this will remain with you, the reader, as useful techniques to reuse in your apps.
Finally, while I made sure to complement every chapter with plenty of picture to illustrate the desired output, I think it is paramount for you to actually type and try out the recipes while learning.
Have fun building great things!

What this book covers

Chapter 1, *Getting Started*, is where you create your first Vue application and get familiar with the most common features and development tools.

Chapter 2, *Basic Vue.js Features*, is where you effortlessly build lists and forms, and learn how to style them.
Chapter 3, *Transitions and Animations*, where you learn how transitions and animations work to bring more life to your apps. You will also integrate with external CSS libraries.

Chapter 4, *Components!*, is where you realize everything in Vue is a component and you can exploit this to reduce duplication and reuse your code.

Chapter 5, *Communicate with the Internet*, is where you make your first AJAX call and create forms and a full fledged REST client (and server!).

Chapter 6, *Single Page Applications*, is where you use vue-router to create static and dynamic routes to create a modern SPA.

Chapter 7, *Unit Testing and End-To-End Testing*, is where you learn to create professional software by adding Karma, Chai, Moka, Sinon.JS, and nightwatch to make sure you can refactor your app with confidence.

Chapter 8, *Organize + Automate + Deploy = Webpack*, is where you actually publish your accurately crafted components to npm and learn how Webpack and Vue play together in the process.

Chapter 9, *Advanced Vue.js*, is where you explore directives, plugins, functional components, and JSX.

Chapter 10, *Large Application Patterns with Vuex*, is where you structure your application with tested patterns using Vuex to make sure your apps are maintainable and performant.

Chapter 11, *Integrating with External Frameworks*, is where you build four different applications with Vue and Electron, Firebase, Feathers, and Horizon.

What you need for this book

To follow along with this book, you'll need a computer with an Internet connection. You can choose to work online on Chrome to complete the recipes. At some point, you will need at least a text editor; I highly recommend Microsoft Visual Studio Code for this job.

Who this book is for

This book has been tested on people who didn't even know JavaScript. They were able to pick up Vue by reading the first chapter! Going forward, you will find concepts that are more and more advanced and, even if you are familiar with Vue 2, you will probably find some trick you didn't know about or some wise suggestion that will help you along the way.

This book, if followed from cover to cover, will turn you into a proficient Vue developer. On the other hand, if you already are, it provides a good reference for many different features and techniques that may come in handy from time to time. Finally, this book is also a valid migration guide if you have already experimented with Vue 1 and you feel overwhelmed by change.

Sections

In this book, you will find several headings that appear frequently (Getting ready, How to do it, How it works, There's more, and See also).

To give clear instructions on how to complete a recipe, we use these sections as follows:

Getting ready

This section tells you what to expect in the recipe, and describes how to set up any software or any preliminary settings required for the recipe.

How to do it…

This section contains the steps required to follow the recipe.

How it works…

This section usually consists of a detailed explanation of what happened in the previous section.

There's more…

This section consists of additional information about the recipe in order to make the reader more knowledgeable about the recipe.

See also

This section provides helpful links to other useful information for the recipe.

Conventions

In this book, you will find a number of text styles that distinguish between different kinds of information. Here are some examples of these styles and an explanation of their meaning.

Code words in text, database table names, folder names, filenames, file extensions, pathnames, dummy URLs, user input, and Twitter handles are shown as follows: "I'm going to update the `ChasePlayerComponent` class that already exists in the `EngineTest` project."

A block of code is set as follows:

```
new Vue({
  el: '#app',
  methods: {
    vueSubmit() {
      console.info('fake AJAX request')
    }
  }
})
```

When we wish to draw your attention to a particular part of a code block, the relevant lines or items are set in bold:

```
data: {
 userId: 1,
 title: '',
 body: '',
 response: '...'
}
```

Any command-line input or output is written as follows:

```
npm install axios
```

New terms and **important words** are shown in bold. Words that you see on the screen, for example, in menus or dialog boxes, appear in the text like this: "Open Webstorm and create a new **Empty Project**"

Warnings or important notes appear in a box like this.

Tips and tricks appear like this.

Reader feedback

Feedback from our readers is always welcome. Let us know what you think about this book-what you liked or disliked. Reader feedback is important for us as it helps us develop titles that you will really get the most out of.

To send us general feedback, simply e-mail feedback@packtpub.com, and mention the book's title in the subject of your message.

If there is a topic that you have expertise in and you are interested in either writing or contributing to a book, see our author guide at www.packtpub.com/authors.

Customer support

Now that you are the proud owner of a Packt book, we have a number of things to help you to get the most from your purchase.

Downloading the example code

You can download the example code files for this book from your account at http://www.packtpub.com. If you purchased this book elsewhere, you can visit http://www.packtpub.com/support and register to have the files e-mailed directly to you.

You can download the code files by following these steps:

1. Log in or register to our website using your e-mail address and password.
2. Hover the mouse pointer on the **SUPPORT** tab at the top.
3. Click on **Code Downloads & Errata**.
4. Enter the name of the book in the **Search** box.
5. Select the book for which you're looking to download the code files.
6. Choose from the drop-down menu where you purchased this book from.
7. Click on **Code Download**.

Once the file is downloaded, please make sure that you unzip or extract the folder using the latest version of:

- WinRAR / 7-Zip for Windows
- Zipeg / iZip / UnRarX for Mac
- 7-Zip / PeaZip for Linux

The code bundle for the book is also hosted on GitHub at `https://github.com/PacktPubl ishing/Vuejs-2-Cookbook`. We also have other code bundles from our rich catalog of books and videos available at `https://github.com/PacktPublishing/`. Check them out!

Errata

Although we have taken every care to ensure the accuracy of our content, mistakes do happen. If you find a mistake in one of our books--maybe a mistake in the text or the code-- we would be grateful if you could report this to us. By doing so, you can save other readers from frustration and help us improve subsequent versions of this book. If you find any errata, please report them by visiting `http://www.packtpub.com/submit-errata`, selecting your book, clicking on the **Errata Submission Form** link, and entering the details of your errata. Once your errata are verified, your submission will be accepted and the errata will be uploaded to our website or added to any list of existing errata under the Errata section of that title.

To view the previously submitted errata, go to `https://www.packtpub.com/books/conten t/support` and enter the name of the book in the search field. The required information will appear under the **Errata** section.

Piracy

Piracy of copyrighted material on the Internet is an ongoing problem across all media. At Packt, we take the protection of our copyright and licenses very seriously. If you come across any illegal copies of our works in any form on the Internet, please provide us with the location address or website name immediately so that we can pursue a remedy.

Please contact us at `copyright@packtpub.com` with a link to the suspected pirated material.

We appreciate your help in protecting our authors and our ability to bring you valuable content.

Questions

If you have a problem with any aspect of this book, you can contact us at `questions@packtpub.com`, and we will do our best to address the problem.

1

Getting Started with Vue.js

In this chapter the following recipes will be covered:

- Writing Hello World with Vue.js
- Writing lists
- Creating a dynamic and animated list
- Reacting to events such as clicks and keystrokes
- Choosing a development environment
- Formatting your text with filters
- Debugging your application with mustaches (for example, a JSON filter)
- X-raying your application with Vue developer tools
- Upgrading to Vue.js 2

Introduction

Vue is a very powerful framework but one of its strengths is that it is very lightweight and easy to pick up. As a matter of fact, in the first recipe you will build a simple but functioning program in minutes, with no setup required.

In this chapter, you will learn lists which will help you create web pages where an element is repeated (like a catalog). Furthermore, you will build an interactive page with event listeners.

Some development environments are presented so you can choose the one that suits you better; you will use some debugging tricks that will give you a head start when developing your own code and better insight to kill bugs in your apps.

Please note that, at the time of writing, ES5 is the most well supported standard for JavaScript in browsers. In this chapter, I will use ES5 so you can follow along even if your browser does not support the newer ES6. Remember though that in following chapters ES6 will be used. By now, Chrome is compatible with most ES6 important constructs, but in general you should use **Babel** to make your app compatible with older browsers. Refer to the recipe *How to use Babel to compile from ES6* in `Chapter 8`, *Organize + Automate + Deploy = Webpack*, when you are ready to use Babel.

Writing Hello World with Vue.js

Let's create the simplest possible program in Vue.js, the obligatory Hello World program. The objective here is to get our feet wet with how Vue manipulates your webpage and how data binding works.

Getting Ready

To complete this introductory recipe, we will only need the browser. That is, we will use JSFiddle to write our code:

If you have never used JSFiddle, don't worry; you are about to become an expert frontend developer and using JSFiddle will become a handy tool in your pocket:

1. Head your browser to `https://jsfiddle.net`:

    You will be presented with a blank page divided into quadrants. The bottom-left is where we will write our JavaScript code. Going clockwise, we have an HTML section, a CSS section, and finally our preview of the resulting page.

    Before beginning, we should tell JSFiddle that we want to use the Vue library.

2. In the top-right part of the JavaScript quadrant, press the cogwheel and select Vue 2.2.1 from the list (you should find more than one version, "edge" refers to the latest version and at the time of writing corresponds to Vue 2).

We are now ready to write our first Vue program.

How to do it...

1. In the JavaScript section, write:

    ```
    new Vue({el:'#app'})
    ```

2. In the HTML quadrant, we create the `<div>`:

    ```
    <div id="app">
      {{'Hello ' + 'world'}}
    </div>
    ```

3. Click the **Run** button in the upper-left corner; we see the page greeting us with **Hello world**:

How it works...

`new Vue({el:'#app'})` will instantiate a new Vue instance. It accepts an options object as a parameter. This object is central in Vue, and defines and controls data and behavior. It contains all the information needed to create Vue instances and components. In our case, we only specified the `el` option which accepts a selector or an element as an argument. The `#app` parameter is a selector that will return the element in the page with `app` as the identifier. For example, in a page like this:

```
<!DOCTYPE html>
<html>
  <body>
    <div id="app"></div>
  </body>
</html>
```

Everything that we will write inside the `<div>` with the ID as `app` will be under the scope of Vue.

Now, JSFiddle takes everything we write in the HTML quadrant and wraps it in body tags. This means that if we just need to write the `<div>` in the HTML quadrant, JSFiddle will take care of wrapping it in the body tags.

It's also important to note that placing the `#app` on the `body` or `html` tag will throw an error, as Vue advises us to mount our apps on normal elements, and its the same thing goes for selecting the `body` in the `el` option.

The mustaches (or handlebars) are a way to tell Vue to take everything inside them and parse it as code. The quotes are a normal way to declare a literal string in JavaScript, so Vue just returns the string concatenation of `hello` and `world`. Nothing fancy, we just concatenated two strings and displayed the result.

There's more

We can leverage that to do something more interesting. If we were aliens and we wanted to greet more than one world at a time, we could write:

```
We conquered 5 planets.<br/>
{{'Hello ' + 5 + ' worlds'}}
```

We may lose track of how many worlds we conquer. No problem, we can do math inside the mustaches. Also, let's put `Hello` and `worlds` outside brackets:

```
We conquered {{5 + 2}} planets.<br/>
Hello {{5 + 2}} worlds
```

Having the number of worlds as raw numbers inside the mustaches is just messy. We are going to use data binding to put it inside a named variable inside our instance:

```
<div id="app">
  We conquered {{countWorlds}} planets.<br/>
  Hello {{countWorlds}} worlds
</div>

new Vue({
  el:'#app',
  data: {
    countWorlds: 5 + 2
  }
})
```

This is how tidy applications are done. Now, every time we conquer a planet, we have to edit only the `countWorlds` variable. In turn, every time we modify this variable, the HTML will be automatically updated.

Congratulations, you completed your first step into the Vue world and are now able to build simple interactive applications with reactive data-binding and string interpolation.

Writing lists

The desire to produce lists almost seems to be an innate part of human nature. There is a deeply satisfying feeling that one obtains by watching a well ordered list marching down the computer screen.

With Vue, we are given the tools to make lists of any kind with a stunning appearance and maximum ease.

Getting Ready

For this recipe we are going to use basic data-binding, if you follow the very first recipe you are already familiar with it.

How to do it...

We are going to build lists in a couple of different ways: with a range of numbers, with an array, and finally with an object.

Range of numbers

To start off with lists, set up your JSFiddle like in the preceding recipe, adding Vue.js as a framework. Select **Vue 2.2.1** (or **Vue (edge)**):

1. In the JavaScript section, write:

```
new Vue({el:'#app'})
```

2. And in the HTML write:

```
<div id="app">
  <ul>
    <li v-for="n in 4">Hello!</li>
  </ul>
</div>
```

This will result in a list with *Hello!* written four times. In a few seconds your first list is complete, nice job!

We can write a countdown with this technique--in the HTML, replace the content of the `<div>` with the following:

```
<div id="app">
  <ul>
    <li v-for="n in 10">{{11-n}}</li>
    <li>launch missile!</li>
  </ul>
</div>
```

Arrays

1. In the HTML, to achieve the same result, edit the list to reflect the following:

```
<ul>
    <li v-for="n in [10,9,8,7,6,5,4,3,2,1]">{{n}}</li>
    <li>launch missile!</li>
</ul>
```

Although this list is identical to the previous one, we shouldn't put literal arrays in HTML markup.

2. We're better off with a variable that contains the array. Edit the preceding code to match the following:

```
<ul>
    <li v-for="n in countdown">{{n}}</li>
    <li>launch missile!</li>
</ul>
```

3. Then put the array countdown in the JavaScript:

```
new Vue({
  el:'#app',
  data: {
    countdown: [10,9,8,7,6,5,4,3,2,1]
  }
})
```

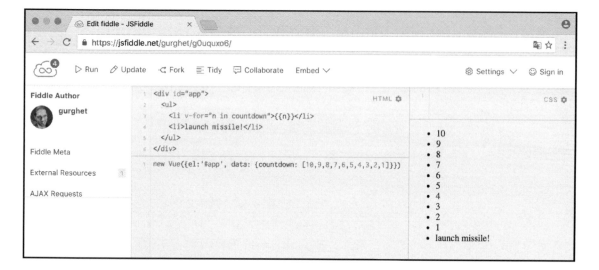

Arrays with index notation

When enumerating an array, we also have access to the index, represented by the variable i in the following code:

1. The HTML becomes:

```
<div id="app">
  <ul>
    <li v-for="(animal, i) in animals">
      The {{animal}} goes {{sounds[i]}}
    </li>
  </ul>
</div>
```

2. In the code part, write:

```
new Vue({
  el: '#app',
```

```
    data: {
      animals: ['dog', 'cat', 'bird'],
      sounds: ['woof', 'meow', 'tweet']
    }
  })
```

Objects

The preceding example can be refactored to match animal names and their sounds so that an accidental misalignment of the index will not affect our list.

1. The HTML becomes:

```
<div id="app">
  <ul>
    <li v-for="(sound, name) in animals">
      The {{name}} goes {{sound}}
    </li>
  </ul>
</div>
```

2. And we need to create the `animals` object in the JavaScript:

```
new Vue({
  el: '#app',
  data: {
    animals: {
```

```
              dog: 'woof', cat: 'meow', bird: 'tweet'
          }
       }
    })
```

How it works...

The workings of lists are quite simple; here is a little more explanation on the syntax.

Range of numbers

The variable n is in scope inside the `<li>` tag. To prove it to yourself, you can quickly build a countdown list as follows:

```
<ul>
  <li v-for="n in 10">{{11 - n}}</li>
  <li>launch missile!</li>
</ul>
```

We write 11 instead of 10 because enumeration in Vue is 1-indexed; this means that n in 10 will start to count from 1, not from 0 like someone might expect, and go up to 10. If we want our countdown to start from 10, then we have to put 11. The last number will be 10, so we'll have 1 as the last number before the missile is launched.

What `v-for="n in 10"` does is call **enumeration**; specifically we are enumerating a range of numbers (1 to 10).

Arrays

Vue allows us to enumerate arrays too. The general syntax is as follows:

```
v-for="(element, index) in array"
```

As seen, the index and parenthesis can be omitted if all we want are the array elements.

This form of enumeration is guaranteed to be ordered. In other words, the ordered sequence of elements in the array will be the same you will see on the screen; this is not the case when enumerating objects.

Objects

The syntax is `v-for="(value, property)"` and if you want you can also squeeze in the index with `v-for="(value, property, index)"`. The latter is not recommended though since, as already said, the order in which properties are enumerated is not fixed. In practice, in most browsers, the order is the same as the insertion order but this is not guaranteed.

Creating a dynamic and animated list

In Vue most data is reactive. In practice this means that if something is going to change in our view-model, we will see the results immediately. This is what lets you concentrate on the app itself, leaving aside all the drawing logic. In this recipe, we are also going to acknowledge some limitations of this system.

Getting Ready

To complete this recipe, you should know how to use basic data-binding (introduced in the very first recipe) and how to create lists (second recipe).

How to do it...

In the previous recipe we built a list for a countdown for a missile launch:

```
<div id="app">
  <ul>
    <li v-for="n in countdown">{{n}}</li>
    <li>launch missile!</li>
  </ul>
</div>

new Vue({
  el:'#app',
  data: {
    countdown:
      [10,9,8,7,6,5,4,3,2,1]
  }
})
```

Wouldn't it be great if it was animated? We can tweak the JavaScript to add numbers to countdown as seconds pass:

1. Copy the preceding code in the HTML and JavaScript sectors of JSFiddle, with the exception that we will fill the countdown ourselves, so set it to an empty array.

   To get hold of the countdown variable we must pass the variable through the Vue instance itself.

2. Assign the Vue instance to a variable for later reference:

   ```
   var vm = new Vue({
     el:'#app',
     data: {
       countdown: []
     }
   })
   ```

   This way we can use vm to access the Vue instance.

3. Initialize the countdown from 10:

   ```
   var counter = 10
   ```

4. Set up a function that repeatedly adds the number of remaining seconds to the now empty countdown array:

   ```
   setInterval(function () {
     if (counter > 0) {
       vm.countdown.push(counter--)
     }
   }, 1000)
   ```

How it works...

What we are going to do is get a reference of the countdown array and fill it with decrementing numbers with the help of setInterval.

We are accessing countdown through the vm variable we set in the line vm.countdown.push(counter--), so our list will get updated every time we add a new number to the array.

This code is very simple, just note that we must use the `push` function to add elements to the array. Adding elements with the square brackets notation will not work:

```
vm.countdown[counter] = counter-- // this won't work
```

The array will get updated, but this way of assignment will skip Vue's reactive system due to how JavaScript is implemented.

There's more

Running the code now will add countdown numbers one at a time; great, but what about the final element `launch missile`? We want that to appear only at the end.

To do that here is a little hack we can do directly in HTML:

```
<ul>
  <li v-for="n in countdown">{{n}}</li>
  <li>{{ countdown.length === 10 ? 'launch missile!' : '...' }}</li>
</ul>
```

This solution is not the best we can do; learn more in the recipe on `v-show`.

We just learned that we cannot add elements to a reactive array with the brackets notation if we want it to update in the view. This is true also for the modification of elements using brackets and for manually changing the length of the array:

```
vm.reactiveArray[index] = 'updated value' // won't affect the view
vm.reactiveArray.length = 0 // nothing happens apparently
```

You can overcome this limitation using the splice method:

```
vm.reactiveArray.splice(index, 1, 'updated value')
vm.reactiveArray.splice(0)
```

Reacting to events such as clicks and keystrokes

A fundamental part of every application is the interaction with the user. Vue has shorthand to intercept most user events and connect them to relevant actions.

Getting Ready

To successfully complete this recipe, you should know how to create a list. If you don't, check out recipe *Filtering a list with a computed property* in Chapter 2, *Basic Vue.js Features*.

How to do it...

The following bit of code shows how to react to a click event:

1. Fill in the following HTML:

```
<div id="app">
  <button v-on:click="toast">Toast bread</button>
</div>
```

2. As for the JavaScript, write the following:

```
new Vue({el:'#app', methods:{toast(){alert('Tosted!')}}})
```

3. Run the code! An event listener will be installed on the button.
4. Click the button and you should see a popup that says **Toasted!**

How it works...

Running the preceding code will install an event handler on the button. The syntax is v-on:DOMevent="methodEventHandler". The handler must be a method, that is, a function in the methods option. In the preceding example, toast is the handler.

Two-way data binding

The v-on attribute will have you covered in most cases, especially if the event comes from the element. On the other hand, it may sometimes be too verbose for some tasks.

For example, if we had a textbox and we wanted to update a variable with the content of the textbox and ensure that the textbox always has an updated value of the variable (which is called **two-way data binding**), we would have to write a couple of handlers.

Instead, this operation is carried out by the v-model attribute, as the following code shows:

```
<div id="app">
  <button v-on:click="toast">Toast bread</button>
  <input v-model="toastedBreads" />
  Quantity to put in the oven: {{toastedBreads}}
</div>

new Vue({
  el: '#app',
  methods: {
    toast () {
      this.toastedBreads++
    }
  },
  data: {
    toastedBreads: 0
  }
})
```

Play a little with this application and notice how no handler is necessary to keep the textbox in sync. Every time toastedBreads is updated, the text will update too; conversely, every time you write a number, the quantity gets updated as well.

There's more

If you followed the first recipe in this chapter, you'll remember how we greeted a variable number of worlds; we can make the experience more interactive. Let's build a list of planets we'd like to greet:

```
<div id="app">
  <ul>
    <li v-for="world in worlds">{{world}}</li>
  </ul>
</div>

new Vue({
  el: '#app',
  data: {
    worlds: ['Terran', 'L24-D', 'Ares', 'New Kroy', 'Sebek', 'Vestra']
  }
})
```

We want to be able to keep track of newly conquered worlds and delete the ones we destroy. This means adding and removing elements from the list. Consider the following HTML:

```
<ul>
  <li v-for="(world, i) in worlds">
    {{world}}
    <button @click="worlds.splice(i, 1)">Zap!</button>
  </li>
</ul>
<input v-model="newWorld"/>
<button @click="worlds.push(newWorld)">Conquer</button>
```

Here the @ symbol is the shorthand for v-on: Let's examine the modifications:

- We added a button to remove the planet (we needed to write out the index in the v-for)
- We placed a textbox that is bound to the data variable newWorld
- We placed a corresponding button that adds what's inside the textbox to the list

Running this code will work. But if you look at the console, you will see a warning when you update the text field:

```
[Vue warn]: Property or method "newWorld" is not defined on the instance
but referenced during render. Make sure to declare reactive data properties
in the data option. (found in root instance)
```

This is because we never declared newWorld in our Vue instance, but that's easy to fix:

```
new Vue({
  el: '#app',
  data: {
    worlds: ['Terran', 'L24-D', 'Ares', 'New Kroy', 'Sebek', 'Vestra'],
    newWorld: ''
  }
})
```

Choosing a development environment

We are going to explore some different styles of developing, from the naive JSFiddle approach, to a more robust approach with WebStorm support. Since we want to use libraries to add new functionalities to our software, I'll provide you with a guide to add them regardless of whichever method of development you choose.

How to do it...

I will start from the simplest method and then present you some more involved methods for bigger projects.

Just the browser

There are a series of websites such as JSFiddle that let you write a Vue application right from the browser (CodePen and JS Bin among others) and those are very good to test new functionalities and try recipes in this book. On the other hand, they are too limited in terms of code organization to develop anything more. In first recipe of this chapter, this style of development is used so please refer to that to learn how to develop with only the browser. In general, you should take what you learn by doing the recipes this way and transfer it into more structured projects, depending on what you are developing.

Adding dependencies with just the browser

Every time I mention an external library, you will search for the relative `.js` file on the Internet, preferably distributed by a CDN, and add it to the left menu of JSFiddle. Let's try with moment.js.

1. Open a new JSFiddle (point your browser to `https://jsfiddle.net/`).
2. In another tab, search for `momentjs CDN` in your favorite search engine.
3. The first result should lead you to a CDN website with a list of links; you should eventually find something like
   `https://somecdn.com/moment.js/X.X.X/moment.js` where the X represents the version number.
4. Copy the link you found and go back to JSFiddle.
5. In the **External Resources** section in the left sidebar, paste your link and press *Enter*.

For many libraries this is sufficient; some libraries do not support this and you will have to include them in your JSFiddle in some other way.

TextEditor

The rawest way to be up and running is with a text editor and a browser. This is totally legitimate for simple, self contained components.

There are plenty of text editors from which to choose these days. One I like to use is Microsoft Visual Studio Code (`https://github.com/Microsoft/vscode`). There is little difference if you use another, is just so happens that Code has a plugin for Vue:

1. Create a new file called `myapp.html`, in which we write:

```
<!DOCTYPE html>
<html>
  <head>
    <title>Vue.js app</title>
  </head>
  <body>
    <div id="app">
      {{'hello world'}}
    </div>
    <script
      src="https://cdnjs.cloudflare.com/ajax
      /libs/vue/2.0.0/vue.js">
    </script>
    <script>
      new Vue({el:'#app'})
    </script>
  </body>
</html>
```

2. Open the file you just created in a browser.

Vue gets downloaded from `https://cdnjs.com/` and the text `hello world` should appear (without mustaches--if you see the mustaches, chances are something's gone wrong so check the console for errors).

This approach resembles the JSFiddle one: we have an HTML part, a JavaScript part, and a CSS part on the top. We are just bringing everything under our control. Also, this way we can use Vue developer tools (check out the recipe *X-raying your application with Vue developer tools* for an introduction of those).

Adding dependencies with a TextEditor

Adding external libraries in this configuration means simply adding another `<script>` entry to your file and setting the source attribute to the respective link. If we wanted to add `moment.js`, we look for the library in the same way as explained before and we add the following snippet to our page:

```
<script src="https://somecdn.com/moment.js/X.X.X/moment.js "></script>
```

Please note that you have to paste the link you found instead of the fake one mentioned in the preceding snippet.

Node package manager (npm)

The canonical way to work with Vue projects, and the one officially supported by the Vue community, involves the use of npm and in particular an npm package named `vue-cli`.

If you are not familiar with npm, put it on your list of things to do, especially if you plan to develop with JavaScript extensively.

Briefly stated, npm is a tool to organize and share your code, beyond using other people's code in your projects. More formally, it's a package manager for everything JavaScript. We will use some basic commands now and some more advanced later in the book, but you are invited to learn more by yourself:

1. Install npm. As it's bundled in Node.js, the best route to follow is to install Node.js directly. You will find instructions at `https://nodejs.org/en/download/`.
2. After you install npm, open a command line and type `npm install -g vue-cli`; this will install `vue-cli`. The `-g` options stands for globally and it means that wherever you are, you can type `vue` and it will run the program.
3. Create a new directory that will act as a workspace. We will put all of our projects inside it.
4. Type `vue list`; we get all the available templates from the official Vue template repository--other templates can be used from other sources.

The `simple` template will create a page similar to what we have done a few paragraphs before. I invite you to run `vue init simple` and check it out; spot the difference between that and what we have done. What we are doing now instead is a step further. We are going to use a more involved template that includes a bundler. There is one for `webpack` and `browserify`; we are going with the first.

If you are not familiar with `webpack` or `browserify` they are programs to control the build process of JavaScript programs from sources and assets (images, css files, and others) to customized bundles. For example, for a single `.js` file:

1. Type `vue init webpack-simple` and the program will ask you some questions on how you would like your project to be. If you don't know how to answer, press *Enter* to go with the default.

   We could have chosen in an equivalent way the `browserify-simple` template; those are two different libraries to achieve the same results.

2. Once the scaffolding is complete, type `npm install`. This will take care of downloading and installing all the npm packages we need to write our Vue app.

   After this, you'll have a functioning demo application already in place.

3. Type `npm run dev` to run your application. Further instruction, will appear on the screen and will tell you to visit a specific web address, but there is a good chance that your browser will be opened automatically.

4. Point the browser at the specified address. You should be able to see the demo application right away.

Exploring the source files created by `vue-cli`, you will find two notable files. The first file is the entry point for your application, `src/main.js`. It will contain something like the following:

```
import Vue from 'vue'
import App from './App.vue'

new Vue({
  el: '#app',
  render: h => h(App)
})
```

This code was loaded in the `index.html` page you just saw. It just tells the main Vue instance to load and render the `App` component in an element selected by `#app` (the element with the attribute `id="app"`, a `<div>` in our case).

The `App.vue` file you will find is a self contained way you can write Vue components. You will find more on components in other recipes, but for now think of it as a way you can further divide your application to keep it more ordered.

The following code is different from what you'll find in the official template but it summarizes the general structure:

```
<template>
  <div id="app">
    <img src="./assets/logo.png">
    <h1>\{{ msg }}</h1>
  </div>
</template>
<script>
export default {
  data () {
    return {
      msg: 'Hello Vue 2.0!'
    }
  }
}
</script>
<style>
body {
  font-family: Helvetica, sans-serif;
}
</style>
```

You can see that having code divided into HTML, JavaScript, and CSS is a recurring pattern. In this file we can see something similar to what we saw in JSFiddle in the first recipes.

In the `<template>` tag we put our HTML, in the `<script>` tag JavaScript code and we use the `<style>` tag to add some styling to our application.

After running `npm run dev`, you can try to edit the `msg` variable in this file; the webpage will reload the component automatically after saving your modifications.

Adding dependencies with npm

To add external libraries in this configuration you simply type `npm install` followed by the name of the library. Then in your code you use it with something along the lines of the following:

```
import MyLibrary from 'mylibrary'
```

We can import `moment.js` with the following command:

```
npm install moment
```

Then in our JavaScript we add the following lines:

```
import moment from 'moment'
```

IDE

If you have a very big project, chances are you are already using tools such as IntelliJ or Webstorm. In this case, I suggest you stick to the embedded console for most of the work and only use features such as syntax highlighting and code completion. This is because developer tools are still immature for Vue and you will probably spend more time configuring your tools than actually programming:

1. Open Webstorm and create a new **Empty Project**:

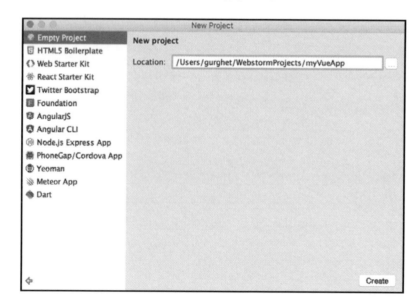

2. In the bottom-left corner you should be able to open up the console or **Terminal**:

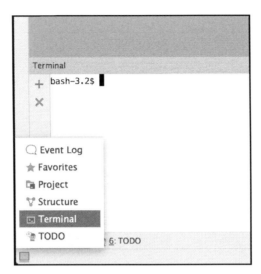

3. From this prompt you should be able to work with npm exactly as explained in the previous paragraph. Read it if you haven't yet. In our case, we are going to suppose Node is installed and vue-cli is also installed.

4. Type `vue init simple` and answer the questions; you should end up with something similar to this:

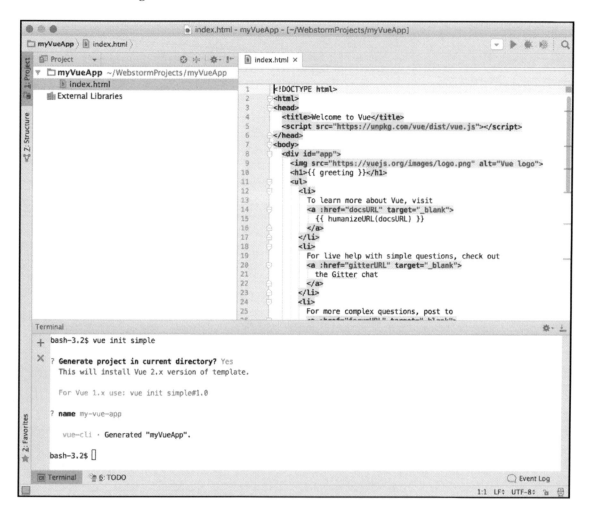

5. Open the `index.html` file by double-clicking it.
6. Hover over the top-right corner of the `index.html` file, and you should see the browser icons; click one:

```
e</title>
/unpkg.com/vue/dist/vue.js"></script>


vuejs.org/images/logo.png" alt="Vue logo">
</h1>


about Vue, visit
URL" target="_blank">
RL(docsURL) }}


with simple questions, check out
```

7. Your sample application is up and running!

Wrap up

You can see more of how this works in dedicated recipes. Here I wanted you to have an overview of the possibilities for developing with Vue. For quick prototypes, you can definitely go with JSFiddle. When you need your own environment or you need to use Vue developer tools but not much more, using just a text editor can be acceptable. For the majority of serious projects though, you should familiarize yourself with npm, webpack, or Browserify and use vue-cli to scaffold your new projects.

Formatting your text with filters

The first version of Vue came bundled with some text filters that helped format text and solve some common problems.

In this new version, there are no built-in filters (except the equivalent of the JSON filter covered in the next recipe). I think this is because it's very easy to write your own filter and also very easy to find online libraries that do a much better job in specialized situations. Finally, filters have somewhat changed purpose: they are more for post-processing now and less for actual filtering and sorting arrays.

To demonstrate how easy it is to create a filter, we will recreate a filter of the old version of Vue: capitalize.

Getting Ready

You don't need any particular knowledge to complete this recipe.

How to do it...

Sometimes we have some strings floating around in our variables like labels. When we put them in the middle of a sentence they work fine, but on the other hand they don't look very good at the beginning of a sentence or bullet point.

We want to write a filter that will capitalize whatever string we put into it. If, for example, we want the string `hello world` to start with a capital `H`, we'd like to be able to write:

```
{{'hello world' | capitalize }}
```

If we try to run this as HTML in a Vue app, it will complain [Vue warn]: Failed to resolve filter: capitalize.

Let's create the filter and add it to Vue's internal list of filters:

1. Write the following JavaScript to register a filter and instantiate Vue:

```
Vue.filter('capitalize', function (string) {
  var capitalFirst = string.charAt(0).toUpperCase()
  var noCaseTail = string.slice(1, string.length)
    return capitalFirst + noCaseTail
})
new Vue({el:'#app'})
```

2. In the HTML section, write:

```
{{'hello world' | capitalize }}
```

3. Run your code and notice how the text now reads **Hello world**.

How it works...

The pipe sign indicates that the following is the name of a filter; in our case capitalize is not in Vue's list of filters, hence the warning. Vue will print the string as is.

What Vue will do before even starting is register our filter (with Vue.filter) in its asset library. Vue has an the internal filters object and will create a new entry: capitalize. Every time it sees the pipe symbol it will look for a corresponding filter. Remember to write it before the actual instantiation of a Vue instance because otherwise Vue will not find it.

The working of the filter is very basic JavaScript, in fact, a better way to write this filter with ES6 would be:

```
Vue.filter('capitalize', function (string) {
  var [first, ...tail] = string
  return first.toUpperCase() + tail.join('')
})
```

If you are not familiar with ES6, here is a brief explanation. The second line is called a **destructuring** assignment of string; in particular we are interpreting string as an array of characters, separating the first character into first and putting all the other characters in tail. This is a faster way to assign different parts of an array to multiple variables. The other thing that may seems mysterious is that join(''). Since tail is now an array of characters, we need some means to re-join the single letters into a compact string. The argument of join represents a separator between the single characters. We don't want any, so we pass an empty string.

In the next chapter, you will find more recipe for filters and cover other real use cases.

Debugging your application with mustaches (for example, a JSON filter)

In the previous recipe, we had a complete overview of filters and we said that Vue comes with no built-in filters except for an equivalent of the JSON filter. This filter was very useful and, while its considered not really orthodox to debug with it, sometimes it just makes your life easier. Now we have it straight away without even writing it.

How to do it...

To see it in action, we can simply display the value of an object in our Vue instance.

1. Write the following JavaScript:

```
new Vue({
  el: '#app',
  data: {
    cat: {
      sound: 'meow'
    }
  }
})
```

This just creates a cat object in our code with a string inside.

2. Write the following HTML:

```
<p>Cat object: {{ cat }}</p>
```

3. Run your app and notice how the `cat` object is outputted in all it's beauty, just like `JSON.stringify`.

How it works...

Cat will display the content of the `cat` object. In the old Vue, to get this result we had to write `{{ cat | json }}`.

A thing to be wary of is loops in our objects. If our object contains a circular reference, and you wrap it in mustaches, this will not work. These objects are more common than you would think. HTML elements, for example, are JavaScript objects that contain references to a parent node; the parent node in turn contains a reference to its children. Any such tree structure would cause the mustaches to print an infinite description of the object. When you actually do it, Vue simply throws an error and refuses to work. The error you would see in the console is actually thrown by the internal method used to print the `JSON.stringify` object.

A practical situation in which using mustaches could be useful is when the same value is changed in several places, or when you want to quickly check the content of a variable. Mustaches can be useful even for demonstrational purposes, as it's clear from the usage you will see in this book.

X-raying your application with Vue developer tools

Using mustaches is a quick way to display the content of an object. However it has some limitations; one of them outlined in the previous recipe is that, out of the box, it breaks when dealing with objects that contain circular references. A tool that doesn't present this limitation when inspecting internal variables and that sports many more debugging features is Vue developer tools. There's a Chrome extension that will help you at every step of development, visualizing the state of your components, where they are in the page, and more. It's also deeply integrated with **Vuex** (covered in later recipes) and has a time machine feature that lets you rewind the event flow directly from the browser.

Getting Ready

To install it, you just have to download the extension from the **Chrome Web Store** in the extensions category. Just look for **Vue.js devtools** and you'll find it right away, press the **ADD TO CHROME** button, and you're set to go:

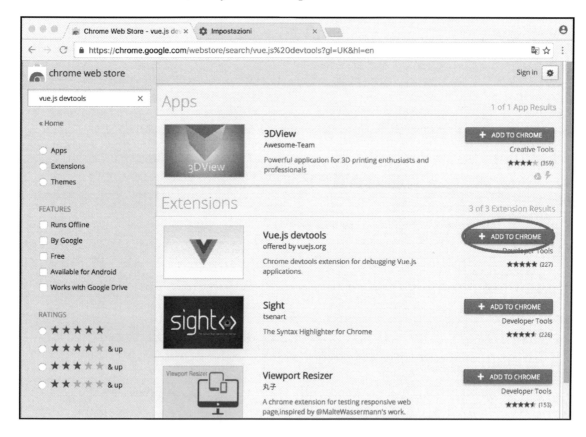

Unfortunately you won't be able to use it in some configurations; particularly it currently doesn't seem to work in `iframe` environments and JSFiddle is one of them, so to see it you have to at least use the *one page approach* outlined in the *Choosing a development environment* recipe.

.

How to do it...

1. Access the **Developer Tools** of Chrome (Usually with *cmd* + *opt* + *I* or *Ctrl* + *Shift* + *I*) and you will see a new tab at the end that says **Vue**. Clicking it will bring forth the developer tools.

 To make it work for pages opened via the `file://` protocol, you need to check **Allow access to file URLs** for this extension in Chrome's extension management panel.

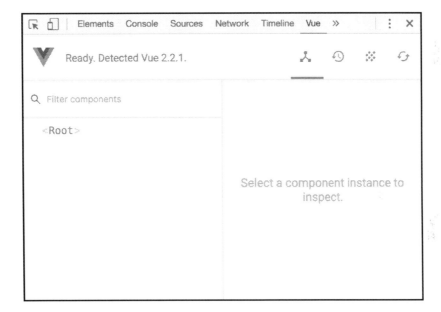

You will be presented with a hierarchical tree of components laid out in your page and by selecting them you will be able to see all the variables in depth and in real time.

2. Click on the various objects in the three to see details:

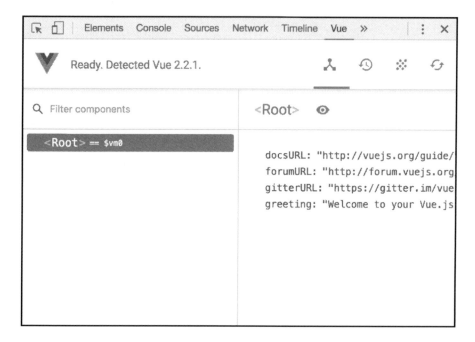

Also, you will see a useful button: the **inspect DOM** button (the eye) will scroll the page to where the element is and will show you the DOM representation in the Chrome developer tools. Furthermore, when you click on a component (root in the illustration) you will have a variable like $vm0 available to be used in the console. For example, you can execute methods or inspect variables.

3. Click on the root component and write the following in the console to explore the $vm0.docsUrl property:

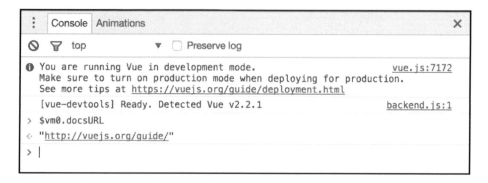

Upgrading to Vue.js 2

If you need to upgrade your Vue app to version 2, most of your code is good to go. There are a couple of features though that need some modifications. Some are simple renaming, some are more involved.

How to do it...

To give your migration a head start; Chris Fitz (a member of the Vue core team) created a little helper app that will scan your code and guide you in the migration:

1. Install Vue Migration Helper with the following npm command:

```
npm install -g git://github.com/vuejs/vue-migration-helper.git
```

2. Navigate to your app folder.
3. Run the program with the following command:

```
vue-migration-helper
```

All the lines in which a change is necessary will be highlighted. Once you are finished updating, or if you still have doubts, you should take a look at the official documentation migration page at `https://rc.vuejs.org/guide/migration.html`.

How it works...

Reading through the documentation will help you understand the critical points that need to be updated. Here I will provide you a rationale for some of the most challenging modifications.

Deprecation of $broadcast, $dispatch, and the events option

Both methods `$broadcast` and `$dispatch` are now merged in the `$emit` method with the same syntax as the old version. Unfortunately, replacing every instance of `$broadcast` and `$dispatch` with `$emit` is not guaranteed to always work because the pattern used to manage events is a little different now.

In Vue 1, you had events follow a path either downward (for $broadcast) or upward (for $dispatch), and horizontally (for $emit) through the hierarchical tree.

To be honest, I never liked having two (three if you count the old $emit) methods for emitting events. It was confusing even in the smallest contexts because you had to ask yourself *is this event for parents or children?* Most of the time it was not that important of a distinction, you just wanted your method to fire. But there is no such thing as a free lunch; we have to add a moving part to our system to make everything work in the new paradigm.

Now all events should pass through one or more central hubs. The role of this central hubs can be taken by a Vue instance since they implement the necessary interface.

When emitting an event consumed by v-on, you're good to go by replacing $broadcast with $emit, since the event doesn't have to travel far. On the other hand, if you are defining an interface for a component in terms of events, you will have to say goodbye to the events option since it will not work anymore. This is the direct consequence of having all the events passing through a hub--the events option wouldn't know where to register all the events. This is the trade off for having a single emitting method: it fires in every direction but only in a precise piping.

Let's say you have a dedicated empty Vue instance that will act as an event hub:

```
var eventBus = new Vue()
```

If you are writing a teapot component and you want to register the brew event, you will write in the created hook something like the following:

```
new Vue({
  el: '#app',
  components: {
   comp1: {
        template: '<div/>',
        created () {
        eventBus.$on('brew', () => {
        console.log('HTTP Error 418: I'm a teapot')
        })
      }
    },
    comp2: {
        template: '<div/>',
        created () {
        eventBus.$emit('brew')
      }
    }
  }
})
```

And with the HTML:

```
<div id="app">
  <comp1></comp1>
  <comp2></comp2>
</div>
```

Every time the `brew` event is emitted with `eventBus.$emit('brew')`, the console will output a message.

 As you can see, this example is not very scalable. You cannot register a lot of events in the created hook and then expect to easily keep track of what they do and in which hub they are registered. For these more involved scenarios, the suggested way to proceed is to use Vuex, introduced in later recipes.

Any component you'll write can act as an event hub. You also have the API methods `$off` which deletes listeners, and `$once`, which listens for an event but only once.

Deprecation of array filters

If you had a lot of filtered `v-for` lists, I have bad news for you. Even if in the wild the most common use for filters was with `v-for`, the community chose to remove this feature. The reason is mainly because having a lot of filters, often piped together, was hard to reason about and thus to maintain.

The new recommended way to filter a list is with a computed property. Luckily for you, we have an entire recipe on how to do that. See the recipe *Filtering a list with a computed property* in the next chapter.

Deprecation of Vue.config.delimiters

Custom delimiters are not at the component level. If you want, you can have two different components using different delimiters.

This is fairly easy to upgrade and allows you to write components intended to be used inside other template engines:

```
<div id="app">
  {!msg!}
</div>

new Vue({
```

```
el: '#app',
data: {
  msg:'hello world'
},
delimiters: ['{!','!}']
})
```

Renaming of life cycle hooks

Life cycle have now a more consistent naming that will help with remembering their names in the long run:

Old hook	New hook
init	beforeCreate
created	created
beforeCompile	created
no equivalent	beforeMount
compiled	mounted
ready	mounted
attached	no equivalent
detached	no equivalent
no equivalent	beforeUpdate
no equivalent	updated

2
Basic Vue.js Features

In this chapter, the following recipes will be covered:

- Learning how to use computed properties
- Filtering a list with a computed property
- Sorting a list with a computed property
- Formatting currencies with filters
- Formatting dates with filters
- Displaying and hiding an element conditionally
- Adding styles conditionally
- Adding some fun to your app with CSS transitions
- Outputing raw HTML
- Creating a form with checkboxes
- Creating a form with radio buttons
- Creating a form with a select element

Introduction

In this chapter, you will find all the building blocks needed to develop a fully functional, interactive, self-contained Vue application. In the first recipe, you will create computed properties that encapsulate the logic you can use to create a more semantic application; you will then explore some more text formatting with filters and the v-html directive. You will create a graphically appealing application with the help of conditional rendering and transitions. Finally, we will build some form elements such as checkboxes and radio buttons.

From now on, all recipes will be written exclusively with ES6. At the time of this writing, if you are using Chrome 9x and JSFiddle to follow along, they should work seamlessly; if you are integrating this code into a bigger project, remember to use Babel (for more information, check out the *Using Babel to compile from ES6* recipe in `Chapter 8`, *Organize + Automate + Deploy = Webpack*).

Learning how to use computed properties

Computed properties are data in Vue components that depend on some calculation on other, more primitive data. When this primitive data is reactive, the computed properties are up-to-date and reactive themselves. In this context, primitive is a relative term. You can certainly build computed properties based on other computed properties.

Getting ready

Before venturing to prepare this recipe, be sure to familiarize yourself with the `v-model` directive and the `@event` notation. You can complete the *React to events like clicks and keystrokes* recipe in the preceding chapter if you are unsure.

How to do it...

A simple example will clarify what a computed property is:

```
<div id="app">
  <input type="text" v-model="name"/>
  <input type="text" id="surname" value='Snow'/>
  <button @click="saveSurname">Save Surname</button>
  <output>{{computedFullName}}</output>
</div>

let surname = 'Snow'
new Vue({
  el: '#app',
  data: {
    name: 'John'
  },
  computed: {
    computedFullName () {
      return this.name + ' ' + surname
    }
  },
```

```
methods: {
  saveSurname () {
    surname = this.$el.querySelector('#surname').value
  }
}
})
```

Running this example will display two input fields: one for the name and one for the surname, and one button specifically to save the surname. Examining the JavaScript code will reveal that while the name is declared in the data section of our object, the surname is declared at the beginning, external to our Vue instance. This implies that it will not be picked up by Vue as a reactive variable. We can check that while editing; the name affects the computed value, editing the surname does not, even if the surname variable itself is actually changed, as we can check in the browser console:

1. **Run** the app on JSFiddle; you will see both John and Snow in the input fields and, as a result of computedFullName, you will see the following:

2. Type Johnny instead of John and you will see the computed property changing in real time. This is because the variable name is reactive:

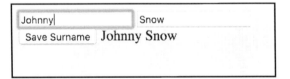

3. Type `Rain` instead of `Snow` then click on **Save Surname**. Nothing will happen because the `surname` is not reactive. It will not trigger an update on the view. Let's check whether it was indeed saved:

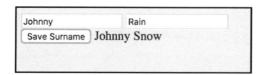

4. Replace `Johnny` with `John`. The surname in the computed property instantly becomes "Rain". That's because changing the first name triggered an update for the computed property:

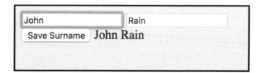

We just experimentally verified that, although changes in variables are saved to memory, no view refresh is triggered when non-reactive variables are edited.

It is worth noting that the same limitation applies here for reactivity--if the variable is an array, changing the elements with bracket notation won't work, deleting an element without using `$remove` won't work either. For other limitations of computed properties, you should check out the official documentation at `https://vuejs.org/v2/guide/computed.html`.

There's more...

In the following text, by the word dependencies I refer to variables that are reactive and are used inside a computed property. When a dependency is changed, the computed property is calculated.

Computed properties are not meant for memorizing data, but you can define a setter in case it makes more sense to set a value directly instead of indirectly manipulating it through its dependencies. Moreover, if a computed property returns an object, it will be a new object every time, not a modified version of the previous one. Lastly, the computed property will not be called if all the dependencies haven't changed.

This caching mechanism and defining a setter are analyzed in the following sections.

Caching computed properties

While functions inside the methods option are executed every time we call them, functions in computed are cached based on the dependencies, which in turn are defined by everything reactive found inside the function.

In the next recipe, composing computed properties is explored, but you can easily imagine how you can have very heavy calculations on a computed property:

```
computed: {
  trillionthDigitOfPi () {
    // hours of computations and terabytes later...
    return 2
  }
}
```

Then, you can use the same property over and over, without the need for re-evaluation at every usage:

```
unnecessarilyComplexDoubler (input) {
  return input * this.trillionthDigitOfPi
}
```

Every time we call this function, we just fetch the cached value of `trillionthDigitOfPi`; there is no need for calculations again.

Computed setters

Sometimes, we have a computed property that really represents a clear object in our model, and it feels cleaner to simply edit it directly than to modify its dependencies.

In the context of a table factory, we would like to specify the number of tables or the number of legs we will build:

```
<div id="app">
  <label>Legs: <input v-model="legCount" type="range"></label><br>
  <label>Tops: <input @input="update" :value="tableCount"></label><br>
  <output>
    We are going to build {{legCount}} legs
    and assembly {{tableCount}} tables.
  </output>
</div>
```

Our state is only determined by `legCount`, and the number of tables is determined automatically. Create a new Vue instance:

```
new Vue({
  el: '#app',
  data: {
    legCount: 0
  }
}
```

To know the number of tables, we have the `tableCount` computed property:

```
computed: {
  tableCount: {
    get () {
      return this.legCount / 4
    },
    set (newValue) {
      this.legCount = newValue * 4
    }
  }
}
```

The `get` part is, as usual, the value of the property at any time, the setter allows us to set the number of tables directly (and the number of legs indirectly). We can then write the `update` method that is triggered whenever we change the number of tables:

```
update (e) {
  this.tableCount = e.target.value
}
```

Filtering a list with a computed property

With the earlier version of Vue, filters were used in the `v-for` directives to only extract some values. They are still called filters, but they are not used in this sense anymore. They are relegated to the role of post-processing for text. To be honest, I never really understood how to use filters in Vue 1 with lists, but that won't be a problem in version 2 because the only proper way to filter a list is to use computed properties.

With this recipe, you will be able to filter your list from the simplest to-do list to the most complex bills-of-materials of a spaceship.

Getting ready

You should have some familiarity with Vue lists and know the basics of computed properties; if you don't, the *Writing lists* and *Learning how to use computed properties* recipes will get you covered.

How to do it...

To get started with this recipe, we need an example list from which to filter our favorite elements. Let's suppose we work for the *ACME Research and Development Laboratory*, and we are in charge of reproducing some experiment in any field we want. We may choose an experiment from the following list:

```
data: {
  experiments: [
    {name: 'RHIC Ion Collider', cost: 650, field: 'Physics'},
    {name: 'Neptune Undersea Observatory', cost: 100, field: 'Biology'},
    {name: 'Violinist in the Metro', cost: 3, field: 'Psychology'},
    {name: 'Large Hadron Collider', cost: 7700, field: 'Physics'},
    {name: 'DIY Particle Detector', cost: 0, field: 'Physics'}
  ]
}
```

Let's print the list right away using a simple `<ul>` element:

```
<div id="app">
  <h3>List of expensive experiments</h3>
  <ul>
    <li v-for="exp in experiments">
      {{exp.name}} ({{exp.cost}}m €)
    </li>
  </ul>
</div>
```

If you are not a big fan of physics, you may want to filter out physics experiments from this list. To do this, we create a new variable that will hold only `nonPhysics` experiments. This variable will be a computed property:

```
computed: {
  nonPhysics () {
    return this.experiments.filter(exp => exp.field !== 'Physics')
  }
}
```

Also, of course, we now want the list to draw an element from here:

```
<li v-for="exp in nonPhysics">
  {{exp.name}} ({{exp.cost}}m €)
</li>
```

If we start the program now, only the non-physics experiments are shown in the list:

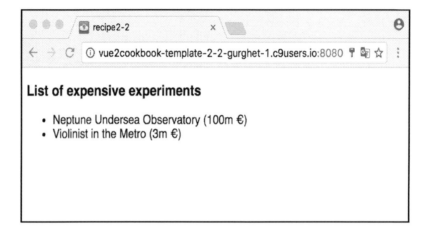

How it works...

The `nonPhysics` computed property will contain a copy of our array with the processing specified inside. It will simply check for experiments with fields that are not `Physics` and pass the new array to be rendered as a list.

As you can see, the filtering is totally arbitrary. We could take, instead of the word `Physics`, a word from a variable that in turn is taken from a textbox:

```
<input v-model="term"> // HTML

// inside the Vue instance
data: {
  term: ''
},
computed: {
  allExceptTerm () {
    return this.experiments
      .filter(exp => exp.field.indexOf(this.term) === -1)
  }
}
```

There's more...

It turns out we'd like to reproduce such experiments but we are on a budget; anything over 3,000,000 euro is off limits for us. Let's build a filter for that:

```
lowCost () {
   return this.experiments.filter(exp => exp.cost <= 3)
}
```

If we use this filter instead of the previous one, we still have the *Do-It-Yourself Particle Detector* physics experiment lying around. Since we don't like physics, we'd like to combine the two filters.

In the old version of Vue, you could just pipe the two filters inside v-for; here, we will move the computed properties we just created down in the methods aisle and turn them into pure functions:

```
methods: {
   nonPhysics (list) {
      return list.filter(exp => exp.field !== 'Physics')
   },
   lowCost (list) {
      return list.filter(exp => exp.cost <= 3)
   }
}
```

This way, the filters are composable; we can use them both in the v-for in the following way:

```
<li v-for="exp in nonPhysics(lowCost(experiments))">
   {{exp.name}} ({{exp.cost}}m € )
</li>
```

Another way to put less logic in the HTML would be to encapsulate everything in a dedicated computed property:

```
filteredExperiments () {
   return this.lowCost(this.nonPhysics(this.experiments))
}
```

The HTML becomes as follows:

```
<li v-for="exp in filteredExperiments">
   {{exp.name}} ({{exp.cost}}m € )
</li>
```

At last, the only element remaining on the list after all this filtering is the *Violinist in the Metro* and, to be fair, 3 millions is the cost of the violin, not of the whole experiment.

Sorting a list with a computed property

Ordering inside a `v-for` with a filter is another thing that was considered for removal in Vue 1 and didn't survive in the current version.

Sorting a list with a computed property offers much more flexibility and we can implement any custom logic for ordering. In this recipe, you will create a list with some numbers within; we will sort the list using them.

Getting ready

To complete this recipe, you just require some familiarity with lists and computed properties; you can brush up on them with the *Writing lists* and *Learning how to use computed properties* recipes.

How to do it...

Let's write a list of the largest dams in the world.

First, we need an HTML table with three columns (**Name, Country, Electricity**):

```
<div id="app">
<table>
  <thead>
    <tr>
      <th>Name</th>
      <th>Country</th>
      <th>Electricity</th>
    </tr>
  </thead>
  <tbody>
  </tbody>
</table>
</div>
```

Also, we need the JavaScript of the Vue instance, which, for now, only contains a small database of dams, their location, and how much electricity they generate:

```
new Vue({
  el: '#app',
  data: {
    dams: [
        {name: 'Nurek Dam', country: 'Tajikistan', electricity: 3200},
        {name: 'Three Gorges Dam', country: 'China', electricity: 22500},
        {name: 'Tarbela Dam', country: 'Pakistan', electricity: 3500},
        {name: 'Guri Dam', country: 'Venezuela', electricity: 10200}
    ]
  }
})
```

Inside the `<tbody>` tag, we put a `v-for` that will simply iterate the list of dams we just created:

```
<tr v-for="dam in dams">
  <td>{{dam.name}}</td>
  <td>{{dam.country}}</td>
  <td>{{dam.electricity}} MegaWatts</td>
</tr>
```

This renders to the following table:

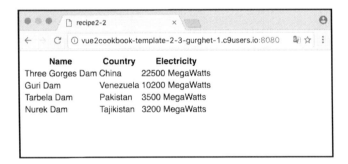

We want to sort these dams by installed electricity power. To do this, we will create a computed property, `damsByElectricity`, that will return an ordered set of dams:

```
computed: {
  damsByElectricity () {
    return this.dams.sort((d1, d2) => d2.electricity - d1.electricity);
  }
}
```

After adding the computed property, we just have to write `damsByElectricity` instead of dams in the HTML. Everything else remains the same and will behave the same:

```
<tr v-for="dam in damsByElectricity">
  <td>{{dam.name}}</td>
  <td>{{dam.country}}</td>
  <td>{{dam.electricity}} MegaWatts</td>
</tr>
```

How it works...

The computed property we just created, `damsByElectricity`, will return an array that will be a sorted clone of `this.dams`. As always with computed properties, the result will be cached (or memorized); every time we need the result, if the original list is not changed, the function will not be called and the cached result will be returned.

The `sort` function accepts two parameters: two members of the list. The return value must be a positive number if the second member is after the first or a negative number if the opposite is true.

The order we obtain with `d2.electricity - d1.electricity` is descending; if we want an ascending order, we have to commute the two operands or multiply them by *-1*.

There's more...

We can expand on our list by binding a click event on a field in the table header to reverse the ordering so that when we click on `Electricity`, it will sort the dams the other way around.

We will use conditional styling; if you are not familiar with it, you will be after completing the *Adding styles conditionally* recipe.

To make it clear which way we are ordering, we should introduce two CSS classes:

```
.ascending:after {
  content: "25B2"
}

.descending:after {
  content: "25BC"
}
```

Here, the content is the Unicode representation of an arrow pointing up for ascending and pointing down for descending.

First, we should keep track of the order with a variable order that will be 1 when ascending and -1 when descending:

```
data: {
  dams: [
    // list of dams
  ],
  order: 1 // means ascending
},
```

The conditional styling is a simple ternary operator. Check the *Adding styles conditionally* recipe for more on conditional styling:

```
<th>Name</th>
<th>Country</th>
<th v-bind:class="order === 1 ? 'descending' : 'ascending'"
    @click="sort">Electricity</th>
```

Here, the `sort` method is defined as follows:

```
methods: {
  sort () {
    this.order = this.order * -1
  }
}
```

The last thing we need to do is edit the `damsByElectricity` computed property to take the order in to account:

```
damsByElectricity () {
  return this.dams.sort((d1, d2) =>
    (d2.electricity - d1.electricity) * this.order);
}
```

This way, the order will be reversed when order is -1, representing an ascending order:

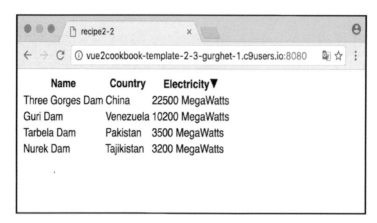

Formatting currencies with filters

Formatting currencies in Vue 1 was somewhat limited; we will be using the excellent accounting.js library to build a much more powerful filter.

Getting ready

The basics of filtering are explored in the *Formatting your text with filters* recipe; where you build a basic filter ensure that you complete that, then come back here.

How to do it...

Add accounting.js to your page. Refer to http://openexchangerates.github.io/accounting.js/ for more details on how to do it. If you are using JSFiddle though, you can just add it as an external resource to the left menu. You can add a link to CDN, which is serving it, for example, https://cdn.jsdelivr.net/accounting.js/0.3.2/accounting.js.

This filter will be extremely simple:

```
Vue.filter('currency', function (money) {
  return accounting.formatMoney(money)
})
```

You can try it out with a one-liner in HTML:

```
I have {{5 | currency}} in my pocket
```

It will default to dollars, and it will print I have $5.00 in my pocket.

How it works...

When you add accounting.js to your page in JSFiddle or manually in your page (or with an import), you make object accounting available. This way, you can use external libraries in your filter (and everywhere else in your code).

There's more...

Currency often ends up in tables and they need to be aligned; let's see how that will work out. We begin with this HMTL table:

```
<div id="app">
<table>
  <thead>
    <tr>
      <th>Item</th>
      <th>Price</th>
    </tr>
  </thead>
  <tbody>
    <tr v-for="item in inventory">
      <td>{{item.name}}</td>
      <td>{{item.price}}
    </td>
  </tr>
  </tbody>
</table>
</div>
```

We are iterating an inventory that, of course, we need to specify in our JavaScript:

```
new Vue({
  el:'#app',
  data: {
    inventory: [
      {name: 'tape measure', price: '7'},
      {name: 'stamp', price: '0.01'},
      {name: 'shark tooth', price: '1.5'},
```

```
        {name: 'iphone', price: '999'}
      ]
    }
  })
```

At this point, we have a table with the prices rendered on the page, but there is no currency symbol, no consistency in the number of digits after the decimal point, and no alignment.

We plan to use our filter to help us add all three of these.

Before moving on, the most astute readers may have noted that I used strings to represent the prices. Why not numbers? This is because numbers in JavaScript are floating points; in other words, they are not accurate because the number of decimal digits "floats."

If we have a kitten key chain on sale for 0.83 euros and we have a kitty 50% discount on that, we should sell it for 0.415 euros. Since 0.5 cents do not exist, we will perform some rounding.

A client surfs our online shop and is amazed by our kitty discounts. He buys 3. If you do the math, that would result in 1.245 euros; we apply the `Math.round` function on it and that should result in 1.25 euros. We can check it with this code:

```
Math.round(1.245 * 100) / 100
// output: 1.25
```

However, consider that we code all our calculations:

```
var kittenKeychain = 0.83
var kittyDiscount = 0.5
var discountedKittenKeychain = kittenKeychain * kittyDiscount
var boughtKeychains = discountedKittenKeychain * 3
Math.round(boughtKeychains * 100) / 100
// outputs: 1.24
```

We lost one cent in the process. Imagine having a big application processing thousands of such transactions, or imagine that this was not a price but an exchange rate. Imagine you have to return this result to the backend and the calculations don't match up. The errors can accumulate and the final number can diverge significantly. This is just a small example, but there is more that can go wrong with floating point numbers when used with money.

Using strings (or integers) to represent currencies gives you the level of precision that you want.

Using our previous filter will introduce the dollar sign and two numbers after the decimal point, but we will still be short of the alignment we want. We should add a new style to our CSS:

```
.price {
  text-align: right
}
```

Assigning the class price to the price column will ensure alignment on the point. Here's the complete code:

```
<div id="app">
<table>
  <thead>
    <tr>
      <th>Item</th>
      <th>Price</th>
      </tr>
  </thead>
  <tbody>
    <tr v-for="item in inventory">
      <td>{{item.name}}</td>
      <td class="price">{{item.price | dollars}}</td>
    </tr>
  </tbody>
</table>
</div>
```

Here's the code for the JavaScript:

```
Vue.filter('dollars', function (money) {
  return accounting.formatMoney(money)
})
new Vue({
  el:'#app',
  data: {
    inventory: [
      {name: 'tape measure', price: '7'},
      {name: 'stamp', price: '0.01'},
      {name: 'shark tooth', price: '1.5'},
      {name: 'iphone', price: '999'}
    ]
  }
})
```

Formatting dates with filters

Sometimes you need a slightly more powerful filter than a basic one. You have to use similar filters many times, but every time with a slight variation. Having too many filters can create confusion. This example with dates will illustrate the problem and the solution.

Getting ready

Before moving ahead, make yourself more comfortable with filters by going through the *Formatting your text with filters* recipe in Chapter 1, *Getting started with Vue.js* ; if you already know filters, keep reading.

How to do it...

Let's say we are curating an interactive page to learn history. We have our Vue instance with the following JavaScript code:

```
new Vue({
  el:'#app',
  data: {
    bastilleStormingDate: '1789-07-14 17 h'
  }
})
```

In our data, we have a date written informally as a string in our instance data. Our HTML can contain a timeline of the French Revolution and, at some point, can contain the following:

```
<div id="app">
  The Storming of the Bastille, happened on {{bastilleStormingDate | date}}
</div>
```

We need a filter capable of completing the sentence. For this, one possible library is the excellent moment.js and, for our purposes, we'll choose the localized version: https://cdnjs.cloudflare.com/ajax/libs/moment.js/2.14.1/moment-with-locales.js.

After adding the library, write the following filter:

```
Vue.filter('date', function (date) {
  return moment(date).format('LL')
})
```

This will display a nicely formatted date: `The Storming of the Bastille, happened on July 14, 1789.`

What if we want a multi-language site and we would like the date to be formatted in French? The `moment.js` library is great with locales; in fact, let's write the same text in French:

```
La prise de la Bastille, survenue le {{bastilleStormingDate | date}}
```

We have to amend our filter with the following:

```
Vue.filter('date', function (date) {
  moment.locale('fr')
  return moment(date).format('LL')
})
```

Our result is `La prise de la Bastille, survenue le 14 juillet 1789`, nice! We don't want to hard-code the language in every page though. It's much better to add a parameter in our filter. We want to be able to pass a variable to the filter with the language, like this:

```
La prise de la Bastille, survenue le {{bastilleStormingDate | date('fr')}}
```

To achieve this, we have to add a second parameter to the filter declaration:

```
Vue.filter('date', function (date, locale) {
  moment.locale(locale)
  return moment(date).format('LL')
})
```

This way, we can pass the language in a parameter through a variable in the page, for example, depending on the selected language.

Displaying and hiding an element conditionally

Displaying and hiding an element on a web page is fundamental to some designs. You could have a popup, a set of elements that you want to display one at a time, or something that shows only when you click on a button.

In this recipe, we will use conditional display and learn about the important `v-if` and `v-show` directives.

Getting ready

Before venturing into this recipe, ensure that you know enough about computed properties or take a look at the *Filtering a list with a computed property* recipe.

How to do it...

Let's build a ghost that is only visible at night:

```
<div id="ghost">
  <div v-show="isNight">
    I'm a ghost! Boo!
  </div>
</div>
```

The `v-show` guarantees that the `<div>` ghost will be displayed only when `isNight` is `true`. For example, we may write as follows:

```
new Vue({
  el: '#ghost',
  data: {
    isNight: true
  }
})
```

This will make the ghost visible. To make the example more real, we can write `isNight` as a computed property:

```
new Vue({
    el: '#ghost',
    computed: {
      isNight () {
        return new Date().getHours() < 7
    }
  }
})
```

If you load this program in JSFiddle, you will see the ghost only after midnight and before 7:00. If you really can't wait to see the ghost, you can cheat and insert a time in the night, for example:

```
return (new Date('4 January 03:30')).getHours() < 7
```

How it works...

The `v-show` directive evaluates the `isNight` computed property and puts a `display:` `none` in the element `style` attribute.

This means that the element is completely rendered by Vue; it's just invisible, like a ghost.

The other directive for displaying elements conditionally is the `v-if` directive. The behavior is the same as that of `v-show` except that you won't find the element in the DOM at all. When `v-if` evaluates to `true`, the element will be added dynamically, no element styling involved. To try it, just replace the `v-show` with `v-if`:

```
<div id="ghost">
  <div v-if="isNight">
    I'm a ghost! Boo!
  </div>
</div>
```

In general, if it makes no difference, using `v-show` is better because it requires fewer resources in the long run. On the other hand, if you are not even sure that some elements will appear on the page, using `v-if` will let your users save some CPU time (you never know when your app will go viral and have millions of users; you can save a lot of energy by choosing the right one!).

On a side note, don't wait in front of the page until midnight. Nothing will happen. Computed properties are re-evaluated only when reactive properties inside them change. In this case, we have a `Date` that is not reactive and, thus, will not trigger any update.

Adding styles conditionally

One great feature of modern web page architecture is the ability to pack tons of display logic in CSS. This means you can have a very clean and expressive HTML and still create impressive interactive pages via CSS.

Vue is particularly good at expressing relationships between HTML and CSS and allows you to encapsulate complex logic in easy-to-use functions.

In this recipe, we will explore the basics of styling with Vue.

How to do it...

We will build a text area that warns you when you are reaching the maximum allowed number of characters:

```
<div id="app">
  <textarea
    v-model="memeText"
    :maxlength="limit">
  </textarea>
  {{memeText.length}}
</div>
```

The text written inside will be bound to the memeText variable and the length of our text is written at the end via mustaches.

We want to change the background color when only 10 characters are left. For this, we have to bake a little CSS class warn:

```
.warn {
  background-color: mistyrose
}
```

We will use this class on the textarea to signal the imminent alt on writing. Let's take a look at our JavaScript:

```
new Vue({
  el: '#app',
  data: {
    memeText: 'What if I told you ' +
              'CSS can do that',
    limit: 50
  }
})
```

This is just our model; we want to add a function, longText, that will evaluate to true whenever we reach 40 characters (10 characters away from 50):

```
computed: {
  longText () {
    if (this.limit - this.memeText.length <= 10) {
        return true
    } else {
        return false
    }
  }
}
```

Now everything is in place to actually add the warn style conditionally. To do this, we have two options: **object syntax** and **array syntax**. Let's first try with the object syntax:

```
<div id="app">
  <textarea
    v-model="memeText"
    :class="{ warn: longText }"
    :maxlength="limit">
  </textarea>
  {{memeText.length}}
</div>
```

This means that, whenever `longText` evaluates to `true` (or in general to a truthy), the class warn will be added to the `textarea`.

How it works...

If you try to write past the 39 characters in the text area, the background will turn misty rose. The general object syntax for *n* classes is as follows:

```
:class="{ class1: var1, class2: var2, ..., classn: varn }"
```

There are, however, a couple of alternatives to this syntax. First of all, you don't need to write the full object in the HTML; you can also bind to an object. The general way to do it is as shown:

```
<div :class="classes"></div> // in HTML

// in your Vue instance
data: {
  classes: {
    warn: true
  }
}
```

At this point, manipulating the classes object will add or remove the warn class from the `<div>`. An even more clever way to bind is to a computed property that itself returns an object:

```
<div :class="classes"></div>

computed: {
  classes () {
    return {
      warn: true
```

```
        }
      }
    }
```

And, of course, it's much easier to put some custom logic inside the computed property:

```
computed: {
  classes () {
    const longText = this.limit - this.memeText.length <= 10
    return {
      warn: longText
    }
  }
}
```

Adding some fun to your app with CSS transitions

Transitions are effects that can be applied when elements are inserted, updated, and removed from the DOM.

For this recipe, we will build a little riddle for our friends to enjoy. When they want to know the solution, it will appear with a fading transition.

Getting ready

To complete this lesson, you should already know conditional display and conditional rendering. The *Displaying and hiding an element conditionally* recipe will teach you how to do that.

How to do it...

Let's set up the riddle in our HTML:

```
<div id="app">
  <article>
    They call me fruit.<br>
    They call me fish.<br>
    They call me insect.<br>
    But actually I'm not one of those.
    <div id="solution" @click="showSolution = true">
```

```
    I am a <span id="dragon" v-show="showSolution">Dragon</span>
  </div>
  </article>
</div>
```

The Vue instance is initialized very easily; you just have to write the following:

```
new Vue({
    el: '#app',
  data: {
    showSolution: false
  }
})
```

In the CSS, we want to make clear that the `<div>` solution can be clicked on, and so we add the following rule:

```
#solution {
  cursor: pointer;
}
```

At this point the application works, but you will see the **Dragon** immediately. We want to add a touch of class to our riddle and make the dragon appear with a fading effect.

We need two CSS classes; the first class will be applied for one tick when the solution appears:

```
.fade-enter {
  opacity: 0
}
```

The second one will be persistent after the first one:

```
.fade-enter-active {
  transition: opacity .5s;
}
```

Finally, we wrap the solution in a transition:

```
I am a <transition name="fade">
  <span id="dragon" v-show="showSolution">Dragon</span>
</transition>
```

How it works...

The name of the transition is the first word of the CSS class selectors (fade), and Vue will look for them based on whether the element is appearing or disappearing from the screen. If no name is specified and only <transition> is used, Vue will use the transition name, v for CSS.

In our case, the dragon that was previously invisible is appearing and so, fade-enter will be applied for a tick (a tick is a cycle for refreshing the view, but you can think of it as a frame in an animation). This means the <span> will be effectively invisible at the beginning because the opacity will be set to 0.

After that, the fade-enter class will be removed and fade-enter-active, which was attached to fade-enter, is now the only class remaining. The opacity will go to 1 in half a second as you can see from the rules of the class. Where is 1 specified? It's the default value.

The complete set of classes Vue will look for in transitions are as follows:

- name-enter: This is the starting class for enter; it is applied before an element is inserted, and removed after one frame.
- name-enter-active: This is the persistent class for enter. It is applied before an element is inserted and is removed when the transition/animation finishes. Use this to define the features of the transition, such as duration and easing.
- name-enter-to: This is the ending class for enter. It is applied when name-enter is removed.
- name-leave: This is the starting class for leave. It is applied when leave transition is triggered and is removed after one frame.
- name-leave-active: This is the persistent class for leave. It is applied when leave transition is triggered and is removed when the transition/animation finishes.
- name-leave-to: This replaces name-leave.

Here, name is the name of your transition (v where no name is specified).

There's more...

Transitions are cool, but there is a tree that is blocking our view in this recipe and it's ruining the transition's reputation; to follow along, consider the following HTML:

```
<div id="app">
  <p>
    Transitions are awesome, careful<br/>
    please don't use them always.
  </p>
  <transition name="fade">
    <img id="tree"
      src="http://i.imgur.com/QDpnaIE.png"
      v-show="show"
      @click="show = false"/>
  </transition>
</div>
```

A little bit of CSS is as follows:

```
#tree {
  position: absolute;
  left: 7.5em;
  top: 0em;
  cursor: pointer;
}

.fade-leave-active {
  transition: opacity .5s;
  opacity: 0
}
```

Finally, a simple Vue instance is required:

```
new Vue({
    el: '#app',
  data: {
    show: true
  }
})
```

When we run the application, this is what we get:

Clicking on the tree reveals the real message.

Outputting raw HTML

Sometimes you need to insert HTML content, such as line breaks (`<br>`), in your application data. This can be easily achieved with the `v-html` directive.

In this recipe, we will build a thank-you note.

Getting ready

For this recipe, you don't need any special knowledge, but we will build upon some basic Vue functionalities; if you completed a recipe in this or the last chapter, you are good to go.

How to do it...

Let's say you have a friend John. You want to prepare a formatted thank-you note before receiving a gift, but you don't know what he'll be giving you yet. You prewrite three texts:

```
new Vue({
    el: '#app',
  data: {
    htmlTexts: [
    'Dear John,<br/>thank you for the <pre>Batman vs Superman</pre> DVD!',
    'Dear John,<br/>thank you for <i>Ghostbusters 3</i>!',
    'Dear John,<br/>thanks, <b>Gods of Egypt</b> is my new favourite!'
    ]
  }
})
```

Consider that you were to output this variable directly in mustaches, as shown:

```
<div id="app">
  {{htmlTexts[0]}}
</div>
```

The problem is that, in this case, you would get plain text and all the HTML gibberish:

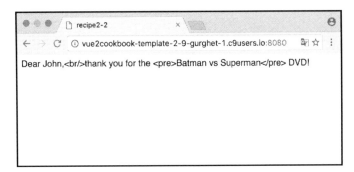

This is not what you're looking for; you would like your thank-you letter well formatted following the HTML tags.

What you need to do is use the v-html directive, as shown:

```
<div id="app" v-html="htmlTexts[0]">
</div>
```

This way, the HTML tags won't be escaped by Vue and will be interpreted as is in our component:

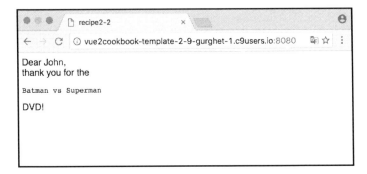

How it works...

Outputting raw HTML in general is very dangerous. Explaining web security is beyond the scope of this book, but just to get the idea, imagine that you have a comments section in your website, and that someone puts an <img> in a comment. If you were to interpret that as HTML and display it to other users, you could make your users download an image they don't necessarily want; if the image is not yours, you may be charged for bandwidth you didn't plan. Now you can expand this reason. If a user puts a <script> in the comment, this poses a greater risk as scripts can do almost anything.

Vue, by default, avoids the problem altogether by not letting you output HTML by default; that's why we need the special v-html directive to see it. This said, always ensure that you are in full control of the content you are outputting.

There's more...

There is another way to output raw HTML; it is advanced, but it's much cleaner and maintainable, especially if you have a component that depends heavily on HTML formatting.

In these more contrived cases, you can opt for **functional components** that are covered in detail in the *Create a functional component* recipe in Chapter 9, *Advanced Vue.js - Directives, Plugins and Render Functions,* but here you will find an example that is an extension of what we have just done.

The HTML you should write is as follows:

```
<div id="app">
  <thanks gift="Batman" decoration="strong"></thanks>
</div>
```

You can already see that the intent is clear: to write a thank-you note for the batman gift using the HTML <strong> as decoration. The JavaScript to create the <thanks> component is as follows:

```
Vue.component('thanks', {
    functional: true,
  render: function (createElement, context) {
    let decoratedGift =
      createElement(context.props.decoration, context.props.gift)
    return createElement('p', ['Dear John, thanks for ', decoratedGift])
  },
  props: {
```

```
      gift: String,
      decoration: String
   }
})
```

Of course, you will need the Vue instance as well.

Creating a form with checkboxes

Asking for user input is fundamental in today's web apps. Presenting the user with multiple choices makes the interface more fun to use and is necessary for structured input.

In this recipe, you will learn how to create checkboxes by building a confirmation page for your own print shop!

Getting ready

We already know how data binding works in Vue, so you are good to go. Otherwise go back to the first recipe, collect 200, and then proceed to the *React to events like clicks and keystrokes* recipe in `Chapter 1`, *Getting started with Vue.js*, to learn more about the `v-model` directive.

How to do it...

Let's suppose you have to set up a Martian printing shop with three different printers:

- Monochrome printer
- Plasma Color printer
- 3D DNA Clone printer

The confirmation page will basically be just a form:

```
<div id="app">
  <form>
    <!-- list of printers go here -->
  </form>
</div>
```

Instead of name, we will use `v-model` to bind our model to the view:

```
<label>
```

```
    <input type="checkbox" v-model="outputPrinter" value="monochrome"/>
    Monochrome
</label>
```

Every `<input>` checkbox with the same `v-model` will participate in a reactive array that will be updated in real time. Let's declare this array in the Vue instance:

```
new Vue({
    el:'#app',
  data:{
    outputPrinter: []
  }
})
```

This is just a regular array. All the selected printers will be inserted and removed automatically from the array. Here's the complete HTML:

```
<div id="app">
  <form>
    <fieldset>
      <legend>What printers you want to use?</legend>
      <label>
        <input type="checkbox" v-model="outputPrinter" value="monochrome"/>
        Monochrome</label><br>
      <label>
        <input type="checkbox" v-model="outputPrinter" value="plasma"/>
        Plasma Color</label><br>
      <label>
        <input type="checkbox" v-model="outputPrinter" value="cloner"/>
        3D DNA Cloner</label><br>
      <input type="submit" value="Print now"/>
    </fieldset>
  </form>
</div>
```

This will result in a form like the following:

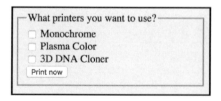

Put `{{ outputPrinter }}` somewhere inside your app in a `<div>` tag and see for yourself the array changing in real time while selecting printers.

How it works...

If you check the first and last printer, the array will look like this:

```
outputPrinter: ['monochrome', 'cloner']
```

You can than use this array to send it via AJAX to a web service or to further build upon it.

Checkboxes in Vue are just regular `<input>` elements, the only difference being that we don't really need the name attribute used in traditional forms. That's because we won't have a second page to submit our values (the page that normally reads the value using the name attributes).

There's more...

To reach this "second page" I was talking about, just click on the submit button. This is the default behavior and, in our case it's not what we want; since we usually don't like having to change page when dealing with Vue, I will show you how to prevent it.

Modern websites tend to give feedback for your action on the same page, sometimes without interrupting your workflow (what if you want to clone another five or six creatures in the same session?)

Let's turn it into something more useful. First of all, we have to prevent the button default action, which is to change page; for this, we use the prevent modifier:

```
<input type="submit" value="Print now" @click.prevent="printHandler"/>
```

The `printHandler` will be a method in our Vue instance that will get us some feedback. You are free to add whatever you want as a handler, perhaps a popup that tells you that printing is in progress; maybe you can just go back to the home page.

In this example, we will just check whether the button works with an alert popup:

```
methods: {
  printHandler () {
    let printers = this.outputPrinter
    alert('Printing with: ' +
      (printers.length ? printers.join(', ') : 'none') + '.')
  }
}
```

Creating a form with radio buttons

Radio buttons let you choose only one option among many. When the user selects a radio button, any previously selected radio button is deselected. A common example of its use is when you are creating a registration form and you choose between male and female.

Getting ready

This recipe will resemble the *Creating a form with checkboxes* recipe because we are using a similar technique. I suggest you to complete both the recipes to become a black belt in Vue forms.

How to do it...

First of all, we need something to choose from, so we write an array in our Vue instance:

```
new Vue({
  el: '#app',
  data: {
    genders: ['male', 'female', 'alien'],
    gender: undefined
  }
})
```

We will use the variable gender (singular) to hold the value of the chosen option. From here, we can set up a form in just a few lines:

```
<div id="app">
  <form>
    <fieldset>
      <legend>Choose your gender</legend>
      <label>
        <input type="radio" v-model="gender" value="male"/>
        Male
      </label><br>
      <label>
        <input type="radio" v-model="gender" value="female"/>
        Female
      </label> <br>
      <label>
        <input type="radio" v-model="gender" value="alien"/>
        Alien
      </label>
```

```
    </fieldset>
  </form>
</div>
```

You can run the app and it will work; however, you need to add a mustache after the form to see what is happening :

```
<div>
  Choosen gender: '{{ gender }}'
</div>
```

This way, you can see how clicking on the radio buttons affects the internal data:

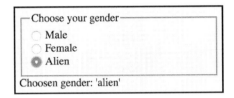

How it works...

Here we just inserts three radio buttons. Since they all have `v-model="gender"`, they logically belong to the same group. This means that only one of the values can be selected at any given time. We can have as many groups as we want in the same form.

There's more...

In this recipe, the value of the radio buttons was completely fixed:

```
<input type="radio" v-model="gender" value="male"/>
```

We can change the `value="male"` to make it reactive using `v-bind:value`. This binds the value to whatever variable we pass to it. For example, let's say we have an array of genders in our model:

```
genders: ['male', 'female']
```

We can rewrite the preceding radio button like this:

```
<input type="radio" v-model="gender" :value="genders[1]"/>
```

Here, `:value` is a shorthand for `v-bind:value`.

To put what we have learned into practice, let's build a simple game.

Suppose you are a farmer, and you start with zero animals in your farm. Every day, there are new animals on sale at the animal market. You can only buy one on any given day. We can express this choice with radio buttons!

So we have an animals array in our model, an animal variable that will contain our choice for the day, and a farm array (initially empty) that will represent our hoarding. We add a little randomness with the `i` variable to hold a random number representing the available animals for the day:

```
data:{
  animals: ['🐑', '🐔', '🐖'],
  animal: undefined,
  farm: [],
  i: 0
}
```

I used emojis to represent the animals because they are super fun to use. If you don't know where to find them, just copy and paste them from `http://emojipedia.org/` and look for animals.

We can start from the same HTML we used at the beginning; we just need to change the legend:

```
<legend>Today's animals</legend>
```

At this point we should add a list of animals from which to choose, but we want it to be dynamic, that is, a different pair of animals for every day:

```
<label>
  <input type="radio" v-model="animal" :value="animals[i]"/>
  {{animals[i]}}
</label><br>
<label>
  <input type="radio" v-model="animal" :value="animals[i+1]"/>
  {{animals[i+1]}}
</label><br>
```

This means that the value (and the label) of the radio button will change as the `i` variable is changed.

The only thing remaining is a way to buy the animal, add it to the farm, and wait for the next day. We will summarize all this in a submit button:

```
<input type="submit" value="Add to Farm" @click.prevent="addToFarm"/>
```

Here, the `addToFarm` method is defined by the following:

```
addToFarm () {
    if (this.animal === undefined) { return }
    this.farm.push(this.animal)
    this.i = Math.floor(Math.random() * (this.animals.length - 1))
  this.animal = undefined
}
```

Don't do anything if the animal was not chosen; otherwise, add the animal to the farm, draw a random number for the next day, and reset the selection. To see your farm, add this to your HTML:

```
<div>
  Your farm is composed by {{ farm.join(' ') }}
</div>
```

Your app will look like this:

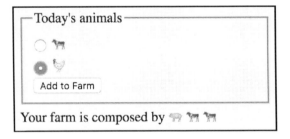

Creating a form with a select element

Select elements or "drop-down lists" are used in a form when radio buttons won't cut it, either because there are too many choices or because they always take the same space no matter how many options.

Getting ready

I suggest you complete a recipe on data binding or forms before delving into the world of select elements. The *Creating a form with radio buttons* recipe will make you familiar with radio buttons, which have a function similar to select elements.

How to do it...

In this recipe, we will create a simple country selector. I will start by writing the selector without the help of Vue, just to brush up on HTML. First, create a `form` in which to put the `select` element:

```
<form>
  <fieldset>
    <legend>Choose your country</legend>
      <!-- here goes the select element -->
  </fieldset>
</form>
```

Inside the `fieldset`, write the code for the `select` element:

```
<select>
  <option>Japan</option>
  <option>India</option>
  <option>Canada</option>
</select>
```

Run the application. There you have a working select element right from the start. The anatomy is pretty simple. Every `<option>` will lengthen the list of things to choose from.

For now, there is not much to be done with this element. Let's bind the chosen country to a variable with Vue. You have to edit your HTML:

```
<select v-model="choosenCountry">
```

Now, you have to add `choosenCountry` to your model:

```
new Vue({
    el:'#app',
  data:{
    choosenCountry: undefined
  }
})
```

Don't forget to surround the form with `<div id="app">` or it won't be picked up by Vue.

Run the application now; you will notice that, whereas earlier the drop-down started with **Japan** already selected, now it's obeying our initialization in the code.

This means that, initially, no country will be selected. We can add a mustache to see the current status of the variable:

```
<div>
  {{chosenCountry}}
</div>
```

The country selector will look like this:

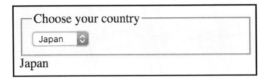

How it works...

When you bind a `<select>` element with `v-model`, the selected option will populate the bound variable.

Note that, if you set a value for your options, the variable will take it instead of what is written within the tags. For example, you can write as follows:

```
<select>
  <option value="1">Japan</option>
  <option value="2">India</option>
  <option value="7">Canada</option>
</select>
```

This ensures that you have every country bound to a numeric value.

There's more...

Often, countries and cities are arranged in hierarchical ways. This means that we need two or more select elements to pin down a user birth place, for example. In this paragraph, we will explore a little bit of hierarchical selection with multiple drop-down menus. Since there are too many cities in the world, I will use a biological equivalent and we will select from animals:

```
clans: {
  mammalia: {
    'have fingers': {
      human: 'human',
      chimpanzee: 'chimpanzee'
    },
    'fingerless': {
      cat: 'cat',
      bear: 'bear'
    }
  },
  birds: {
    flying: {
      eagle: 'eagle',
      pidgeon: 'pidgeon'
    },
    'non flying': {
      chicken: 'chicken'
    }
  }
}
```

We will call the top level a `clan`, the second level a `type` and the last will be an animal. I know it's an unorthodox way of classifying animals, but it will work for this example.

Let's add the two variables that will hold the state to our Vue model:

```
clan: undefined,
type: undefined
```

We can now add the first `select` element:

```
<select v-model="clan">
  <option v-for="(types, clan) in clans">{{clan}}</option>
</select>
```

This will create a drop-down menu with the following:

- Mammalia
- Birds

The variable types don't really do anything in this particular case.

We would like to populate a second drop-down with the `type` of a particular `clan`:

```
<select v-model="type">
  <option v-for="(species, type) in clans[clan]">{{type}}</option>
</select>
```

When the variable clan has a value, this select element will let you choose the type of animal. Consider that we add a third select for the species though:

```
<select>
  <option v-for="(animals, species) in
clans[clan][type]">{{species}}</option>
</select>
```

It will cause an error in our program because `clans[clan]` is undefined and Vue will try to evaluate it. To correct this, we may want the third select element to appear only when the first and the second have a value. For this, we can use the `v-show` directive, but the problem is that Vue renders the elements with `v-show`, and only after rendering, will it hide them. This means that the error will still be thrown.

The right way is to use `v-if`, which prevents the rendering of the element if the condition inside is not satisfied is, as follows:

```
<select v-if="clans[clan]">
  <option v-for="(animals, species) in
clans[clan][type]">{{species}}</option>
</select>
```

Go ahead and choose your favorite animal hierarchically!

3
Transitions and Animations

In this chapter, the following recipes will be covered:

- Integrating with third-party CSS animation libraries such as animate.css
- Adding your own transition classes
- Animating with JavaScript instead of CSS
- Transitioning on the initial render
- Transitioning between elements
- Letting an element leave before the enter phase in a transition
- Adding entering and leaving transitions for elements of a list
- Transitioning elements that move in a list
- Animating the state of your components
- Packaging reusable transitions into components
- Dynamic transitions

Introduction

This chapter contains recipes related to transitions and animations. Vue has its own tags for dealing with transitions intended for when an element enters or leaves the scene: `<transition>` and `<transition-group>`. You will learn all about them and how to use them to give your customers a better user experience.

Vue transitions are pretty powerful in that they are completely customizable and can easily combine JavaScript and CSS styling while having very intuitive defaults that will let you write less code in case you don't want all the frills.

You can animate a great deal of what happens in your components even without transition tags since all you have to do is bind your state variables to some visible property.

Finally, once you have mastered everything that there is to know about Vue transitions and animations, you can easily package these in layered components and reuse them throughout your application. This is what makes them not only powerful, but also easy to use and maintain.

Integrating with third-party CSS animation libraries such as animate.css

Graphical interfaces not only need to be usable and easy to understand; they should also provide affordability and be pleasant to use. Having transitions can help a great deal by giving cues of how a website works in a fun way. In this recipe, we will examine how to use a CSS library with our application.

Getting ready

Before starting, you can take a look at `https://daneden.github.io/animate.css/`, as shown, just to get an idea of the available animations, but you don't really need any special knowledge to proceed:

How to do it...

Imagine that you are creating an app to book taxis. The interface we will create will be simple and fun.

First of all, add the `animate.css` library to the list of dependencies (refer to the *Choosing a development environment* recipe to learn how to do it).

To proceed, we need our usual wrapper:

```
<div id="app">
</div>
```

Inside, we will put a button to call for a taxi:

```
<button @click="taxiCalled = true">
  Call a cab
</button>
```

You can already tell that we will use the `taxiCalled` variable to keep track of whether the button has been pressed or not.

Let's add an emoji that will confirm to the user when the taxi is called:

```
<p v-if="taxiCalled">🚕</p>
```

At this point, we can add some JavaScript:

```
new Vue({
  el: '#app',
  data: {
    taxiCalled: false
  }
})
```

Run the application and you will see the taxi appear instantly when you press the button. We are a cool taxi company, so let's make the taxi drive to us with a transition:

```
<transition
  enter-active-class="animated slideInRight">
  <p v-if="taxiCalled">🚕</p>
</transition>
```

Now run your application; if you call the taxi, it will get to you by sliding from the right:

The taxi will slide from right to left, as shown:

How does it work...

Every transition applies four classes. Two are applied when the element enters the *scene* and the other two are applied when it leaves:

Name	Applied when	Removed when
v-enter	Before the element is inserted	After one frame
v-enter-active	Before the element is inserted	When transition ends
v-enter-to	After one frame	When transition ends
v-leave	Transition starts	After one frame
v-leave-active	Transition starts	When transition ends
v-leave-to	After one frame	When transition ends

Here, the initial *v* stands for the name of your transition. If you don't specify a name, *v* will be used.

> While the beginning of the transition is a well-defined instant, the end of the transition is a bit of work for the browser to figure out. For example, if a CSS animation loops, the duration of the animation will only be one iteration. Also, this may change in future releases, so keep this in mind.

In our case, we wanted to provide a third-party v-enter-active instead of writing our own. The problem is that our library already has a different name for the class of the animation we want to use (slideInRight). Since we can't change the name of the class, we tell Vue to use slideInRight instead of looking for a v-enter-active class.

To do this, we used the following code:

```
<transition enter-active-class="animated slideInRight">
```

This means that our v-enter-active is called animated slideInRight now. Vue will append those two classes before the element is inserted and drop them when the transition ends. Just note that animated is a kind of helper class that comes with animate.css.

Adding your own transition classes

If your application is rich in animations and you would like to reuse your CSS classes in other projects by mixing and matching them, this is the recipe for you. You will also understand an important technique for performant animations, called **FLIP (First Last Invert Play)**. While the latter technique is normally triggered automatically by Vue, we will implement it manually to get a better understanding of how it works.

Getting ready

To complete this recipe, you should understand how CSS animations and transitions work. This is out of the scope of this book, but you can find a good primer at `http://css3.bradshawenterprises.com/`. This website is also great because it will explain when you can use animations and transitions.

How to do it...

We will build an interface for a taxi company (similar to the preceding recipe) that will enable users to call a taxi at the click of a button and will provide a nice animated feedback when the taxi is called.

To code the button, write the following HTML:

```
<div id="app">
  <button @click="taxiCalled = true">
    Call a cab
  </button>
  <p v-if="taxiCalled">🚕</p>
</div>
```

Then, you initialize the `taxiCalled` variable to `false`, as shown in the following JavaScript:

```
new Vue({
  el: '#app',
  data: {
    taxiCalled: false
  }
})
```

At this point, we will create our own custom transition in CSS:

```css
.slideInRight {
  transform: translateX(200px);
}

.go {
  transition: all 2s ease-out;
}
```

Wrap your car emoji in a Vue transition:

```html
<transition
  enter-class="slideInRight"
  enter-active-class="go">
  <p v-if="taxiCalled">🚕</p>
</transition>
```

When you run your code and hit the **Call a cab** button, you will see a taxi stopping by.

How it works...

When we click on the button, the `taxiCalled` variable turns `true` and Vue inserts the taxi into your page. Before actually doing this, it reads the classes you specified in `enter-class` (in this case, only `slideInRight`) and applies it to the wrapped element (the <p> element with the taxi emoji). It also applies the classes specified in `enter-class-active` (in this case, only go).

The classes in `enter-class` are removed after the first frame, and the classes in `enter-class-active` are also removed when the animation ends.

The animation created here follows the FLIP technique that is composed of four points:

- **First (F)**: You take the property as it is in the first frame of your animation; in our case, we want the taxi to start somewhere from the right of the screen.
- **Last (L)**: You take the property as it is in the last frame of your animation, which is the taxi at the left of the screen in our case.
- **Invert (I)**: You invert the property change you registered between the first and last frame. Since our taxi moved to the left, at the final frame it will be at say -200 pixel offset. We invert that and set the `slideInRight` class to have transform as `translateX(200px)` so that the taxi will be at +200 pixel offset when it appears.

- **Play (P)**: We create a transition for every property we have touched. In the taxi example, we use the transform property and so, we use `writetransition: all 2s ease-out` to tween the taxi smoothly.

This technique is used automatically by Vue under the cover to make transitions work inside the `<transition-group>` tag. More on that in the *Adding entering and leaving transition for elements of a list* recipe.

Animating with JavaScript instead of CSS

It's a common misconception that animating with JavaScript is slower and that animations should be done in CSS. The reality is that if used correctly, animation in JavaScript can have similar or superior performance. In this recipe, we will create an animation with the help of the simple but powerful **Velocity.js** (`http://velocityjs.org/`) library:

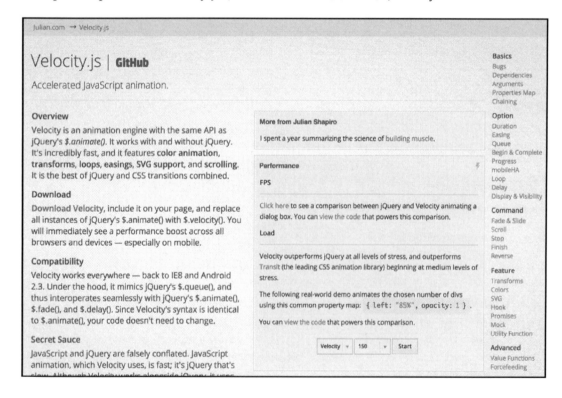

Getting ready

This recipe, while it presupposes no knowledge of the Velocity library, assumes that you are quite familiar with animations either in CSS or with JavaScript libraries, such as jQuery. If you've never seen a CSS animation and you want a speedy introduction, just complete the two preceding recipes and you should be able to follow along.

How to do it...

We're still looking for the perfect transition for a taxi company (the same as in the preceding recipe) that will entertain our clients while waiting for a taxi. We have a button to call a cab and a little taxi emoji that will appear when we make a reservation.

Before anything else, add the Velocity library as a dependency to your project--https://cd njs.cloudflare.com/ajax/libs/velocity/1.2.3/velocity.min.js.

Here is the HTML to create the skeleton of our interface:

```
<div id="app">
  <button @click="taxiCalled = true">
    Call a cab
  </button>
  <p v-if="taxiCalled">🚕</p>
</div>
```

Our Vue model is very simple and consists only of the `taxiCalled` variable:

```
new Vue({
  el: '#app',
  data: {
    taxiCalled: false
  }
})
```

Create the animation by wrapping the little taxi in a Vue transition:

```
<transition
  @enter="enter"
  :css="false"
>
<p v-if="taxiCalled">🚕</p>
</transition>
```

The enter method will be called as soon as the taxi emoji is inserted at the press of a button.

The enter method, which you have to add to your Vue instance, looks like this:

```
methods: {
    enter (el) {
        Velocity(el,
        { opacity: [1, 0], translateX: ["0px", "200px"] },
        { duration: 2000, easing: "ease-out" })
    }
}
```

Run your code and press the button to book your taxi!

How it works...

As you may have noted, there is no CSS in your code. The animation is purely driven by JavaScript. Let's dissect our Vue transition a little:

```
<transition
  @enter="enter"
  :css="false"
>
  <p v-if="taxiCalled">🚕</p>
</transition>
```

Although this is still a transition that could use CSS, we want to tell Vue to shut down the CSS and save precious CPU cycles by setting :css="false". This will make Vue skip all the code related to CSS animation and will prevent CSS from interfering with our pure JavaScript animation.

The juicy part is in the @enter="enter" bit. We are binding the hook that triggers when the element is inserted in to the enter method. The method itself is as follows:

```
enter (el) {
    Velocity(el,
      { opacity: [1, 0], translateX: ["0px", "200px"] },
      { duration: 2000, easing: "ease-out" }
    )
}
```

Here, we are calling the Velocity library. The el parameter is passed for free by Vue, and it refers to the element that was inserted (in our case, the <p> element containing the emoji of the car).

The syntax of the Velocity function is as illustrated:

```
Velocity( elementToAnimate, propertiesToAnimate, [options] )
```

Other syntaxes are possible, but we will stick to this one.

In our call to this function, we passed our paragraph element as the first argument; we then said that the opacity should change from 0 to 1 and, at the same time, the element should move from a starting position of 200 pixels on the x axis toward its origin. As options, we specified that the animation should last for two seconds and that we want to ease the animation near the end.

I think everything is pretty clear maybe except how we are passing the opacity and translateX parameters.

This is what Velocity calls **forcefeeding**--we are telling Velocity that the opacity should start from 0 and go to 1. Likewise, we are telling Velocity that the translateX property should start at 200 pixels, ending at 0 pixels.

In general, we can avoid passing arrays to specify the initial value for the properties; Velocity will calculate how to transition.

For example, we could have had the following CSS class:

```
p {
   opacity: 0;
}
```

If we rewrite the Velocity call as follows:

```
Velocity(el,
   { opacity: 1 }
)
```

The car will slowly appear. Velocity queried the DOM for the initial value of the element and then transitioned it to 1. The problem with this approach is that since a query to the DOM is involved, some animations could be slower, especially when you have a lot of concurrent animations.

Another way we can obtain the same effect as force-feeding is by using the begin option, like so:

```
Velocity(el,
   { opacity: 1 },
   { begin: () => { el.style.opacity = 0 } }
)
```

This will set the opacity to zero just before the animation begins (and hence, before the element is inserted). This will help in slower browsers in which forcefeeding will still display a flash of the car before bringing it all the way to the right and starting the animation.

The possible hooks for JavaScript animations are summarized in this table:

Attribute	Description
@before-enter	This function is called before the element is inserted.
@enter	This function is called when the element is inserted.
@after-enter	This function is called when the element is inserted and the animation is finished.
@enter-cancelled	This function is called when the animation is still in progress, but the element has to leave. If you use Velocity you can do something like `Velocity(el, "stop")`.
@before-leave	This function is called before the leave function is triggered.
@leave	This function is called when the element leaves.
@after-leave	This function is called when the element leaves the page.
@leave-cancelled	This is called in case the element has to be inserted before the leave call is finished. It works only with v-show.

Just be reminded that these hooks are valid for any library, not just Velocity.

There's more...

We can try another take with this interface by implementing a cancel button. If the user booked a cab by mistake, hitting cancel will delete the reservation, and it will be apparent by the fact that the little taxi emoji disappears.

First, let's add a cancel button:

```
<button @click="taxiCalled = false">
  Cancel
</button>
```

That was easy enough; now we add our leave transition:

```
<transition
  @enter="enter"
  @leave="leave"
  :css="false"
>
  <p v-if="taxiCalled">🚕</p>
</transition>
```

That brings us to our leave method:

```
leave (el) {
  Velocity(el,
    { opacity: [0, 1], 'font-size': ['0.1em', '1em'] },
    { duration: 200})
}
```

What we are doing is making the emoji disappear while scaling it down.

If you try to run your code, you will encounter some problems.

When you click on the cancel button, what should happen is the leave animation should start and the taxi should become smaller and eventually disappear. Instead, nothing happens and the taxi disappears abruptly.

The reason the cancel animation doesn't play as planned is because since the animation is written in JavaScript instead of CSS, Vue has no way to tell when the animation is finished. In particular, what happens is that Vue thinks that the leave animation is finished before it even starts. That is what makes our car disappear.

The trick lies in the second argument. Every hook calls a function with two arguments. We have already seen the first, el, which is the subject of the animation. The second is a callback that when called, tells Vue that the animation is finished.

We will leverage the fact that Velocity has an option called `complete`, which expects a function to call when the animation (from the Velocity perspective) is complete.

Let's rewrite our code with this new information:

```
leave (el, done) {
  Velocity(el,
    { opacity: [0, 1], 'font-size': ['0.1em', '1em'] },
    { duration: 200 })
}
```

Adding the done arguments to our function lets Vue know that we want a callback to call when the animation is finished. We don't need to explicitly use the callback as Vue will figure it out by itself, but since it's always a bad idea to rely on default behaviors (they can change if they are not documented), let's call the done function when the animation is finished:

```
leave (el, done) {
  Velocity(el,
  { opacity: [0, 1], 'font-size': ['0.1em', '1em'] },
  { duration: 200, complete: done })
}
```

Run your code and press the **Cancel** button to cancel your taxi!

Transitioning on the initial render

With the `appear` keyword, we are able to package transition for elements when they are first loaded. This helps the user experience in that it gives the impression that the page is more responsive and faster to load when you apply it to many elements.

Getting ready

This recipe doesn't assume any particular knowledge, but if you have completed at least the *Adding some fun to your app with CSS transitions* recipe, it will be a piece of cake.

How to do it...

We will build a page about the American actor Fill Murray; no, not Bill Murray. You can find more information about him at `http://www.fillmurray.com`. We will use images from this site to fill our page about him.

In our HTML, let's write a header as the title of our page:

```
<h1>
  The Fill Murray Page
</h1>
```

After the title, we will place our Vue application:

```
<div id="app">
  <img src="https://fillmurray.com/50/70">
```

```
<p>
  The internet was missing the ability to
  provide custom-sized placeholder images of Bill Murray.
  Now it can.
</p>
</div>
```

Which when rendered in a browser would appear like the following:

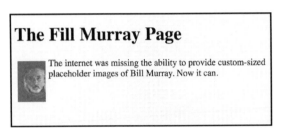

Our page is very plain right now. We want the Fill Murray picture to fade in. We have to wrap it inside a transition:

```
<transition appear>
  <img src="https://fillmurray.com/50/70">
</transition>
```

The following are the CSS classes:

```
img {
  float: left;
  padding: 5px
}
.v-enter {
  opacity: 0
}
.v-enter-active {
  transition: opacity 2s
}
```

Running our page now will make the image appear slowly, but it will also move the text. To fix it, we have to specify the image size in advance:

```
<transition appear>
  <img src="https://fillmurray.com/50/70" width="50" height="70">
</transition>
```

This way, our browser will set aside some space for the image that will appear slowly.

How it works...

The `appear` directive in the `transition` tag will make the components appear for the first time with an associated transition (if it is found).

There are many possible ways to specify a transition on the first rendering of the component. In all cases, the `appear` directive must be specified.

The first things Vue will look for when this directive is present are JavaScript hooks or CSS classes specified in the tag:

```
<transition
  appear
  @before-appear="customBeforeAppearHook"
  @appear="customAppearHook"
  @after-appear="customAfterAppearHook"
  appear-class="custom-appear-class"
  appear-active-class="custom-appear-active-class"
>
  <p>My element</p>
</transition>
```

After that, if a name is specified, Vue will look for an entrance transition for that element:

```
<transition appear name="myTransition">
  <p>My element</p>
</transition>
```

The preceding code will look for classes named as follows:

```
.myTransition-enter {...}
.myTransition-enter-active {...}
```

Vue will look for the default CSS classes for the element insertion (`v-enter` and `v-enter-active`) if everything else fails. Incidentally, this is what we have done in our recipe.

Relying on these defaults is not a good practice; here, we have done it just as a demonstration. You should always give names to your transitions.

Maybe it's worth mentioning why we had to add the width and height to our image. The reason is that when we specify an image URL in our HTML, the browser doesn't know the size of the image in advance, so it doesn't reserve any space for it by default. Only by specifying the size of the image in advance, the browser is able to correctly compose the page even before an image is loaded.

Transitioning between elements

Everything on a web page is an element. You can easily make them appear and disappear, thanks to Vue `v-if` and `v-show` directives. With transitions, you can easily control how they appear and even add magic effects. This recipe explains how to do it.

Getting ready

For this recipe, you should have some familiarity with Vue transitions and how CSS works. This is easily achieved if you complete the *Adding some fun to your app with CSS transitions* recipe from `Chapter 2`, *Basic Vue.js Features*.

How to do it...

Since we talked about magic, we will turn a frog into a princess. The transformation itself will be a transition.

We will instantiate a button that, when pressed, will represent a kiss to the frog:

```
<div id="app">
  <button @click="kisses++">Kiss!</button>
</div>
```

Every time the button is pressed, the variable kisses increases. The variable will be initialized to zero, as the following code shows:

```
new Vue({
   el: '#app',
  data: {
   kisses: 0
  }
})
```

Next, we need the frog and the princess that we will add immediately after the button:

```
<transition name="fade">
  <p v-if="kisses < 3" key="frog">frog</p>
  <p v-if="kisses >= 3" key="princess">princess</p>
</transition>
```

The fade transition is the following CSS:

```
.fade-enter-active, .fade-leave-active {
  transition: opacity .5s
}
.fade-enter, .fade-leave-active {
  opacity: 0
}
```

To make it work properly, we need a last CSS selector to add:

```
p {
  margin: 0;
  position: absolute;
  font-size: 3em;
}
```

If you run the application and click enough times the kiss button, you should see your frog turn into a princess:

This transition will have a fade effect:

The frog emoji will turn into a princess emoji:

How it works...

When we wrote the two elements, we used the `key` attribute specifying who is the frog and who is the princess. This is because, Vue optimization system will kick in otherwise. It will see that the content of the two elements can be swapped without swapping the elements themselves and no transition will ensue since the element was the same and only the content changed.

If we remove the `key` attribute, we can see for ourselves that the frog and the princess will change, but without any transition:

```
<transition name="fade">
  <p v-if="kisses < 3">frog</p>
  <p v-if="kisses >= 3">princess</p>
</transition>
```

Consider that we use two different elements, as shown:

```
<p v-if="kisses < 3" >frog</p>
<span v-if="kisses >= 3">princess</span>
```

Also, we modify our CSS selector for <p> accordingly:

```
p, span {
  margin: 0;
  position: absolute;
  font-size: 3em;
  display: block;
}
```

Now if we launch our application again, everything works without using any `key` attribute.

Using keys is generally recommended even when not necessary, like in the preceding case. This is especially true when items have a different semantic meaning. There are a couple of reasons for this. The main reason is that when multiple people work on the same line of code, modifying the `key` attribute will not break the application as easily as switching a `span` element back into a `p` element, which will ruin the transition as we just saw.

There's more...

Here, we cover two subcases of the preceding recipe: switching between more than two elements and binding the `key` attribute.

Transitioning between more than two elements

We can expand on the recipe we just completed in a straightforward manner.

Let's suppose that if we kiss the princess too many times, she will turn into Santa Claus, which may or may not be appealing, depending on your age I guess.

First, we add the third element:

```
<transition name="fade">
  <p v-if="kisses < 3" key="frog">frog</p>
  <p v-else-if="kisses >= 3 && kisses <= 5" key="princess">princess</p>
  <p v-else key="santa">santa</p>
</transition>
```

We can launch the application immediately and when we kiss the princess/frog more than five times, Santa will appear with the same fading transition:

Using this setup, we are limited in using the same transition we used between the first two elements.

There is a workaround for this explained in the *Dynamic transitions* recipe.

Setting the key attribute dynamically

We don't have to write the key for all our elements if we already have some data available. Another way we could write the same app, but without repeating the element is as follows:

```
<transition name="fade">
  <p :key="transformation">{{emoji}}{{transformation}}</p>
</transition>
```

This, of course, means that we have to provide a sensible value for the `transformation` and `emoji` variables, depending on the number of kisses.

To do this, we will tie them to computed properties:

```
computed: {
  transformation () {
    if (this.kisses < 3) {
      return 'frog'
    }
    if (this.kisses >= 3 && this.kisses <= 5) {
      return 'princess'
    }
    if (this.kisses > 5) {
      return 'santa'
    }
  },
  emoji () {
    switch (this.transformation) {
      case 'frog': return '🐸'
      case 'princess': return '👸'
      case 'santa': return '🎅'
    }
  }
}
```

We traded off some complexity in the template for some more logic in our Vue instance. This can be good in the long run if we expect more complex logic in the future or if the number of transformation rises.

Letting an element leave before the enter phase in a transition

In the *Transitioning between elements* recipe, we explored how to make transition between two elements. The default behavior of Vue is to start the transition of the element that is entering at the same time that the first element is leaving; this is not always desirable.

You will learn about this important corner case and how to work around it in this recipe.

Getting ready

This recipe builds on top of the transitioning between two elements and solves a specific problem. If you don't know what we are talking about, go back one recipe and you'll be on track in no time.

How to do it...

First, you will see the problem if you have not encountered it yet. Next, we'll see what Vue offers us to solve it.

The two elements problem

Let's create a carousel effect for our website. The user will view one product at a time and then he will swipe to the next product. To swipe to the next product the user will need to click a button.

First, we need our list of products in the Vue instance:

```
new Vue({
  el: '#app',
  data: {
    product: 0,
    products: ['umbrella', 'computer', 'ball', 'camera']
  }
})
```

In our HTML, we will only need a button and the view of an element:

```
<div id="app">
  <button @click="product++">next</button>
  <transition name="slide">
    <p :key="products[product % 4]">{{products[product % 4]}}</p>
  </transition>
</div>
```

The modulo 4 (product % 4) is only because we want to start all over again when the list of products finishes.

To set up our sliding transition, we will need the following rules:

```
.slide-enter-active, .slide-leave-active {
  transition: transform .5s
}
.slide-enter {
  transform: translateX(300px)
}
.slide-leave-active {
  transform: translateX(-300px);
}
```

Also, to make everything look good, we finish up with the following:

```
p {
  position: absolute;
  margin: 0;
  font-size: 3em;
}
```

If you run the code now, you will see a nice carousel:

Now, let's try to remove the position: absolute from the last rule:

```
p {
  margin: 0;
  font-size: 3em;
}
```

If you try your code now, you will see a weird jumping from the products:

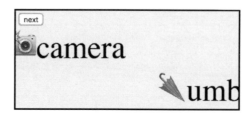

This is the problem we are trying to solve. The second transition starts before the first product has left. If the positioning is not absolute, we will see some weird effects.

Transition modes

To fix this problem, we will change the transition mode. Let's modify the `<transition>` code:

```
<transition name="slide" mode="out-in">
  <p :key="products[product%4]">{{products[product%4]}}</p>
</transition>
```

Now run your program and you will see the products taking a little more time before sliding inside the screen. They are waiting for the previous item to go away before entering.

How it works...

To recapitulate, you have two different ways to manage transitions between components in Vue. The default way is to start the *in* transition at the same time with the *out* transition. We can make that explicit with the following:

```
<transition mode="in-out">
  <!-- elements -->
</transition>
```

We can change this default behavior by waiting for the *out* part to be finished before starting the *in* animation. We achieved it with the following:

```
<transition mode="out-in">
  <!-- elements -->
</transition>
```

While the former is useful when elements have the absolute style position, the latter is more relevant when we really need to wait to have a clear way before putting more stuff on the page.

Absolute positioning won't care about having elements on top of each other because they don't follow the flow of the page. On the other hand, static positioning will append the second element after the first, making the transition awkward if both the elements are shown at the same time.

Adding entering and leaving transitions for elements of a list

We've already seen animated lists in the *Creating a dynamic, animated list* recipe; here, we will try to add a visual way to suggest that an element is added or removed from the list. This can add a lot to UX since you have an opportunity to suggest to the user why an element was added or removed.

Getting ready

As said, if you have completed the *Creating a dynamic, animated list* recipe, you are ready to go. Maybe some familiarity with CSS and transition will help. If you feel like this is needed, just browse the other recipes in this chapter.

How to do it...

We'll build a syllabus to study programming. When we are done with a topic, we'll feel relieved and we want to incorporate that feeling in our app by making the topic float away from the syllabus as we learn it.

The data of the list will be in our Vue instance:

```
new Vue({
  el: '#app',
  data: {
    syllabus: [
      'HTML',
      'CSS',
      'Scratch',
      'JavaScript',
```

```
        'Python'
    ]
  }
})
```

The list will be printed in our HTML with the following code:

```
<div id="app">
  <h3>Syllabus</h3>
  <ul>
    <li v-for="topic in syllabus">
      {{topic}}
    </li>
  </ul>
</div>
```

When we press a button, we want the topic to disappear from the list. For this to happen, we need to modify the code we have written.

First, let's add a **Done** button before each topic:

```
<li v-for="topic in syllabus">
  <button @click="completed(topic)">Done</button>{{topic}}
</li>
```

Here, the completed method will look like this:

```
methods: {
  completed (topic) {
    let index = this.syllabus.indexOf(topic)
    this.syllabus.splice(index, 1)
  }
}
```

Running the code now will reveal a simple application for checking off the topics we already studied. What we want though is an animation that will make us feel relieved.

For that, we need to edit the container of our list. We remove the <ul> tag and, instead, tell the <transition-group> to compile to a <ul> tag:

```
<transition-group tag="ul">
  <li v-for="topic in syllabus" :key="topic">
    <button @click="completed(topic)">Done</button>{{topic}}
  </li>
</transition-group>
```

Note that we also added a key to each list element according to the topic. The last thing we need is adding the transition rules to our CSS:

```
.v-leave-active {
  transition: all 1s;
  opacity: 0;
  transform: translateY(-30px);
}
```

Now, the subjects will disappear with transition on clicking the **Done** button, as shown:

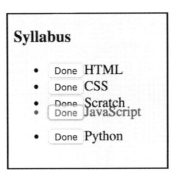

How it works...

The `<transition-group>` tag represents a container for a group of elements that will be displayed at the same time. By default, it represents the `<span>` tag, but by setting the tag attribute to `ul`, we made it represent an unordered list.

Every element in the list must have a unique key or the transitions won't work. Vue will take care of applying a transition to every element that enters or leaves.

Transitioning elements that move in a list

In this recipe, you will build a list of elements that move according to how the list changes. This particular animation is useful when you want to tell your user that something has changed and the list is now updated accordingly. It will also help the user identify the point in which the element was inserted.

Getting ready

This recipe is a little advanced; I would suggest you to complete some of the recipes in this chapter if you are not very familiar with transitions in Vue. If you can complete the *Adding entering and leaving transitions for elements of a lists* recipe without much difficulty, you are good to go.

How to do it...

You will build a little game--a bus station simulator!

Whenever a bus--represented by its emoji--leaves the station, all the other buses will drive a little ahead to take its place. Every bus is identified by a number, as you can see from the Vue instance data:

```
new Vue({
  el: '#app',
  data: {
    buses: [1,2,3,4,5],
    nextBus: 6
  }
})
```

Whenever a new bus arrives, it will have a progressive number assigned. We want a new bus to leave or go every two seconds. We can achieve this by hooking a timer when our component is mounted on screen. Immediately after data, write the following:

```
mounted () {
  setInterval(() => {
    const headOrTail = () => Math.random() > 0.5
    if (headOrTail()) {
      this.buses.push(this.nextBus)
      this.nextBus += 1
    } else {
      this.buses.splice(0, 1)
    }
  }, 2000)
}
```

The HTML of our app will look like this:

```
<div id="app">
  <h3>Bus station simulator</h3>
  <transition-group tag="p" name="station">
    <span v-for="bus in buses" :key="bus">🚌</span>
```

```
    </transition-group>
  </div>
```

To make the buses move around, we need to specify some CSS rules under the prefix station:

```css
.station-leave-active, .station-enter-active {
  transition: all 2s;
  position: absolute;
}

.station-leave-to {
  opacity: 0;
  transform: translateX(-30px);
}

.station-enter {
  opacity: 0;
  transform: translateX(30px);
}

.station-move {
  transition: 2s;
}

span {
  display: inline-block;
  margin: 3px;
}
```

Launching the app now will result in an orderly queue of buses in which one leaves or arrives every two seconds:

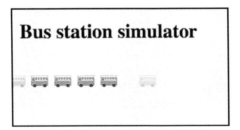

How it works...

The core of our app is the `<transition-group>` tag. It manages all the buses identified by their key:

```
<transition-group tag="p" name="station">
  <span v-for="bus in buses" :key="bus">🚌</span>
</transition-group>
```

Whenever a bus enters or leaves the scenes, a FLIP animation (see the *Adding your own transition classes* recipe) will be automatically triggered by Vue.

To fix ideas, let's say we have buses [1, 2, 3] and bus 1 leaves the scene. What happens next is that the properties of the first bus's `<span>` element will be memorized before the animation actually starts. So we may retrieve the following object describing the properties:

```
{
  bottom:110.4375
  height:26
  left:11
  right:27
  top:84.4375
  width:16
}
```

Vue does this for all the elements keyed inside the `<transition-group>` tag.

After this, the `station-leave-active` class will be applied to the first bus. Let's briefly review what the rules are:

```
.station-leave-active, .station-enter-active {
  transition: all 2s;
  position: absolute;
}
```

We note that the position becomes absolute. This means that the element is removed from the normal flow of the page. This in turn means that all the buses behind him will suddenly move to fill the space left blank. Vue records all the properties of the buses at this stage also and this is considered the final frame of the animation. This frame is not actually a real displayed frame; it is just used as an abstraction to calculate the final position of the elements:

Vue will calculate the difference between the final frame and the starting frame and will apply styles to make the buses appear in the initial frame even if they are not. The styles will be removed after one frame. The reason the buses slowly crawl to their final frame position instead of immediately moving in their new position is that they are span elements and we specified that any transform style (the one used by Vue to fake their position for one frame) must be transitioned for two seconds:

```
.station-move {
  transition: 2s;
}
```

In other words, at frame -1, the three buses are all in place and their position is recorded.

At frame 0, the first bus is removed from the flow of the page and the other buses are instantaneously moved behind it. In the very same frame, Vue records their new position and applies a transform that will move the buses back to where they were at frame -1 giving the appearance that nobody moved.

At frame 1, the transform is removed, but since we have a transition, the buses will slowly move to their final position.

Animating the state of your components

In computers, everything is a number. In Vue, everything that is a number can be animated in one way or other. In this recipe, you will control a bouncy ball that will smoothly position itself with a tween animation.

Getting ready

To complete this recipe, you will need at least some familiarity with JavaScript. The technicalities of JavaScript are out of the scope of this book, but I will break the code down for you in the *How it works...* section, so don't worry too much about it.

How to do it...

In our HTML, we will add only two elements: an input box in which we will enter the desired position of our bouncy ball and the ball itself:

```
<div id="app">
  <input type="number">
  <div class="ball"></div>
</div>
```

To properly render the ball, write this CSS rule and it will appear on the screen:

```
.ball {
  width: 3em;
  height: 3em;
  background-color: red;
  border-radius: 50%;
  position: absolute;
  left: 10em;
}
```

We want to control the bar *Y* position. To do that, we will bind the `top` property of the ball:

```
<div id="app">
  <input type="number">
  <div class="ball" :style="'top: ' + height + 'em'"></div>
</div>
```

Height will be part of our Vue instance model:

```
new Vue({
    el: '#app',
    data: {
      height: 0
    }
})
```

Now, since we want the ball to animate in the new position whenever the `enteredHeight` changes, one idea would be to bind the `@change` event of the input element:

```
<div id="app">
  <input type="number" @input="move">
  <div class="ball" :style="'top: ' + height + 'em'"></div>
</div>
```

The move method will be the one responsible for taking the current height of the ball and slowly transitioning it to the specified value.

Before doing this, you will add the **Tween.js** library as a dependency. The official repository is at `https://github.com/tweenjs/tween.js`. You can add the CDN link specified in the **README.md** page if you are using JSFiddle.

Add the move method after adding the library, like this:

```
methods: {
  move (event) {
    const newHeight = Number(event.target.value)
    const _this = this
    const animate = (time) => {
      requestAnimationFrame(animate)
      TWEEN.update(time)
    }
    new TWEEN.Tween({ H: this.height })
      .easing(TWEEN.Easing.Bounce.Out)
      .to({ H: newHeight }, 1000)
      .onUpdate(function () {
        _this.height = this.H
      })
      .start()
    animate()
  }
}
```

Try to launch the app and see the ball bounce while you edit its height:

When we change the height, the position of the ball also changes:

How it works...

The general principle here is that you have a state for an element or component. When the state is numeric in nature, you can "tween" (from between) from one value to the other following a specific curve or acceleration.

Let's break down the code, shall we?

The first thing we do is to take the specified new height for the ball and save it to the newHeight variable:

```
const newHeight = Number(event.target.value)
```

In the next line, we are also saving our Vue instance in a _this helper variable:

```
const _this = this
```

The reason we do so will be clear in a minute:

```
const animate = (time) => {
  requestAnimationFrame(animate)
  TWEEN.update(time)
}
```

In the preceding code, we are wrapping all of our animation in a function. This is idiomatic to the Tween.js library and identifies the main loop we will use to animate. If we have other tweens, this is the place to trigger them:

```
new TWEEN.Tween({ H: this.height })
  .easing(TWEEN.Easing.Bounce.Out)
  .to({ H: newHeight }, 1000)
  .onUpdate(function () {
    _this.height = this.H
  })
  .start()
```

This is the API call to our library. First, we are creating an object that will hold a copy of the height value in lieu of our component. Normally, here you put the object that represents the state itself. Due to Vue limitations (or Tween.js limitations), we are using a different strategy; we are animating a copy of the state and we are syncing the true state for every frame:

```
Tween({ H: this.height })
```

The first line initializes this copy to be equal to the current actual height of the ball:

```
easing(TWEEN.Easing.Bounce.Out)
```

We choose the easing to resemble a bouncy ball:

```
.to({ H: newHeight }, 1000)
```

This line sets the target height and and the number of milliseconds the animation should last for:

```
onUpdate(function () {
  _this.height = this.H
})
```

Here, we are copying the height of the animation back to the real thing. As this function binds this to the copied state, we are forced to use ES5 syntax to have access to it. This is why we had a variable ready to reference the Vue instance. Had we used the ES6 syntax, we would not have any way to get the value of H directly.

Packaging reusable transitions into components

We may have a signature transition in our website that we want to reuse throughout the user funnel. Packaging transition into components can be a good strategy if you are trying to keep your code organized. In this recipe, you will build a simple transition component.

Getting ready

Following this recipe makes sense if you have already worked your way through transition with Vue. Also, since we are working with components, you should at least have an idea of what they are. Skim through the next chapter for a primer on components. In particular, we will create a functional component, the anatomy of which is detailed in the *Creating a functional component* recipe.

How to do it...

We will build a signature transition for a news portal. Actually, we will use a premade transition in the excellent magic library (`https://github.com/miniMAC/magic`), so you should add it to your project as a dependency. You can find the CDN link at `https://cdnjs.com/libraries/magic` (go to the page to find the link, don't copy it as a link).

First you will build the website page, then you will build the transition itself. Lastly, you will just add the transition to different elements.

Building the basic web page

Our web page will consist of two buttons each that will display a card: one is a recipe and the other is the last breaking news:

```
<div id="app">
  <button @click="showRecipe = !showRecipe">
    Recipe
  </button>
  <button @click="showNews= !showNews">
    Breaking News
  </button>
  <article v-if="showRecipe" class="card">
    <h3>
      Apple Pie Recipe
    </h3>
    <p>
      Ingredients: apple pie. Procedure: serve hot.
    </p>
  </article>
  <article v-if="showNews" class="card">
    <h3>
      Breaking news
    </h3>
```

```
  <p>
    Donald Duck is the new president of the USA.
  </p>
  </article>
</div>
```

The cards will have their unique touch, thanks to the following CSS rule:

```
.card {
  position: relative;
  background-color: FloralWhite;
  width: 9em;
  height: 9em;
  margin: 0.5em;
  padding: 0.5em;
  font-family: sans-serif;
  box-shadow: 0px 0px 10px 2px rgba(0,0,0,0.3);
}
```

The JavaScript part will be a very simple Vue instance:

```
new Vue({
  el: '#app',
  data: {
    showRecipe: false,
    showNews: false
  }
})
```

Running this code will already display your web page:

Building the reusable transition

We decided that our website will feature a transition whenever a card is displayed. Since we intend to reuse the animation with everything in our website, we'd better package it in a component.

Before the Vue instance, we declare the following component:

```
Vue.component('puff', {
  functional: true,
  render: function (createElement, context) {
    var data = {
      props: {
        'enter-active-class': 'magictime puffIn',
        'leave-active-class': 'magictime puffOut'
      }
    }
    return createElement('transition', data, context.children)
  }
})
```

The `puffIn` and `puffOut` animations are defined in `magic.css`.

Using our transition with the elements in our page

Now, we will just edit our web page to add the `<puff>` component to our cards:

```
<div id="app">
  <button @click="showRecipe = !showRecipe">
    Recipe
  </button>
  <button @click="showNews = !showNews">
    Breaking News
  </button>
  <puff>
    <article v-if="showRecipe" class="card">
      <h3>
        Apple Pie Recipe
      </h3>
      <p>
        Ingredients: apple pie. Procedure: serve hot.
      </p>
    </article>
  </puff>
  <puff>
    <article v-if="showNews" class="card">
```

```
      <h3>
        Breaking news
      </h3>
      <p>
        Donald Duck is the new president of the USA.
      </p>
    </article>
  </puff>
</div>
```

The cards will now appear and disappear when pressing the button with a "puff" effect.

How it works...

The only tricky part in our code is building the `<puff>` component. Once we have that in place, whatever we put inside will appear and disappear according to our transition. In our example, we used an already made transition. In the real world, we may craft a seriously complex animation that can be difficult to apply every time in the same manner. Having it packaged in a component is much easier and maintainable.

Two things make the `<puff>` component work as a reusable transition:

```
props: {
  'enter-active-class': 'magictime puffIn',
  'leave-active-class': 'magictime puffOut'
}
```

Here, we specify the classes the component must adopt when entering and leaving; there is nothing too special here, we have already done it in the *Integrating with third-party CSS animation libraries such as animate.css* recipe.
At the end we return the actual element:

```
return createElement('transition', data, context.children)
```

This line creates the root of our element that is a `<transition>` tag with only one child-- `context.children`. This means that the child is unspecified; the component will put as child whatever actual child is passed in the template. In our examples, we passed some cards that were promptly displayed.

Dynamic transitions

In Vue, a constant theme is reactivity and, of course, transitions can be dynamic because of that. Not only the transition themselves, but all their properties can be bound to reactive variables. This gives us a lot of control on which transition to use at any given moment.

Getting ready

This recipe builds on top of the *Transitioning between elements* recipe. You don't need to go back if you already know about transitions, but if you feel like you're missing something, it might be a good idea to complete that first.

How to do it...

We will transform a frog into a princess with some kisses, but if we kiss too much the princess will turn into Santa. Of course, we are talking about emojis.

Our HTML setup is very simple:

```
<div id="app">
  <button @click="kisses++">💋Kiss!</button>
  <transition :name="kindOfTransformation" :mode="transformationMode">
    <p :key="transformation">{{emoji}}{{transformation}}</p>
  </transition>
</div>
```

Just note that most of the attributes here are bound to variables. Here is how the JavaScript unfolds.

First, we will create a simple Vue instance with all of our data:

```
new Vue({
el: '#app',
  data: {
    kisses: 0,
    kindOfTransformation: 'fade',
    transformationMode: 'in-out'
  }
})
```

The fade transformation we are referring to is the following CSS:

```
.fade-enter-active, .fade-leave-active {
  transition: opacity .5s
}
.fade-enter, .fade-leave-active {
  opacity: 0
}
```

The variables transformation and emoji are defined by two computed properties:

```
computed: {
  transformation () {
    if (this.kisses < 3) {
      return 'frog'
    }
    if (this.kisses >= 3 && this.kisses <= 5) {
      return 'princess'
    }
    if (this.kisses > 5) {
        return 'santa'
    }
  },
  emoji () {
    switch (this.transformation) {
      case 'frog': return '🐸'
      case 'princess': return '👸'
      case 'santa': return '🎅'
    }
  }
}
```

While we are using the fade transition between the frog and the princess, we want something else between the princess and the frog. We will use the following transition classes:

```
.zoom-leave-active, .zoom-enter-active {
  transition: transform .5s;
}

.zoom-leave-active, .zoom-enter {
  transform: scale(0)
}
```

Now, since we bound the name of the transition to a variable, we can easily switch that programmatically. We can do that by adding the following highlighted lines to the computed property:

```
transformation () {
  if (this.kisses < 3) {
    return 'frog'
  }
  if (this.kisses >= 3 && this.kisses <= 5) {
    this.transformationMode = 'out-in'
    return 'princess'
  }
  if (this.kisses > 5) {
    this.kindOfTransformation = 'zoom'
    return 'santa'
  }
}
```

The first added line is to avoid having an overlap while the zoom transition starts (more on that in the *Letting an element leave before the enter phase in a transition* recipe).

The second added line switches the animation to "zoom".

To make everything appear the right way, we need one more CSS rule:

```
p {
  margin: 0;
  position: absolute;
  font-size: 3em;
}
```

This is much nicer.

Now run the app and see how the two different transitions are used dynamically:

As the number of kisses increase, the princess zooms out:

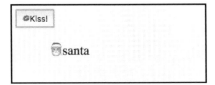

With this, the Santa zooms in:

How it works...

If you understand how reactivity works in Vue, there is not much to add. We bound the name of the transition to the `kindOfTransformation` variable and switched from fade to zoom in our code. We also demonstrated that the other attributes of the `<transition>` tag can be changed on the fly as well.

4
All About Components

In this chapter, the following recipes will be covered:

- Creating and registering a component
- Passing data to your components with props
- Making components talk to each other
- Making components talk with Vuex
- Reading a child's state
- Using components in your own components
- Using mixins in your components
- Content distribution with slots
- Single file components with Webpack
- Loading your components asynchronously
- Having recursive components
- Reusable component checklist

Introduction

Vue is very appealing to designers because of its very close relationship with raw HTML and CSS. However, Vue is also attractive to frontend engineers because it has very sound engineering. The main characteristic of Vue architecture is how everything can be discretize as a component.

Having components all the way down makes your program, no matter how big, workable in isolated chunks. You can always add a new one without affecting others, and you can always throw away what you don't need, being sure that nothing will break.

Actually, this will be the ideal situation. The truth is that writing well isolated (loosely coupled) components is not always straightforward. There might be the case that two components are meant to work together or they have a specific way to communicate with each other.

If you follow the recipes in this chapter with attention and dedication, you will take mostly the good sides of components, and you will learn how to avoid some common pitfalls.

Creating and registering a component

The first step in dealing with components is to create one. Once the component is registered, we need to tell a Vue instance about it so that it can use the component. In this recipe, you will build your first component.

Getting ready

In this recipe, we will not use any particular knowledge. If you're starting off, my only suggestion is to take a look at the recipes in the first chapter.

How to do it...

Writing your first component will be a snap. You will build a lightbulb!

Here's the relevant code:

```
Vue.component('light-bulb', {
  template: `
  <div class='light-bulb'>
    <p> Eureka!</p>
  </div>
  `
})
```

The little quote sign just after template--` --is in reality a back tick. It doesn't exist in all the keyboards; if you don't find it in yours, you will have to copy and paste it. It's part of ES6 syntax, and it tells the browser (or transpiler) that the string may span more than one line.

To use our component, we need our usual Vue instance:

```
new Vue({
    el: '#app'
})
```

Also, we need some HTML to actually place it in the page:

```
<div id="app">
  <light-bulb></light-bulb>
  <light-bulb></light-bulb>
  <light-bulb></light-bulb>
</div>
```

If you run the application now, you will see three lightbulbs. What a great idea!:

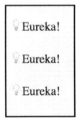

How it works...

A component is extremely similar to a Vue instance. Here, I am quoting from the official documentation:

In Vue, a component is essentially a Vue instance with predefined options.

As a matter of fact, even the anatomy of declaring a Vue instance is quite similar to declaring a Vue component. Let's put them side by side and identify the similarities and differences:

```Vue.component('light-bulb', { template: `   <div class='light-bulb'>     <p>Eureka!</p>   </div>    ` })```	```new Vue({ el: '#app' })```

The first thing you should note is the option objects present in both. While it contains only the template option in the lightbulb components, it contains only the `el` option in the Vue instance.

These two options are related but different. The `template` option talks about the shape of the component, and the `el` option tells us about the position of the component.

So, while talking about the lightbulb, we know what shape it has just by looking at the preceding code but we don't know where it is in the web page. On the other hand, looking at the code for the Vue instance, we know where it will be mounted, but we don't know how it will look. Where is the `el` for the light bulb, and where is the `template` for the Vue instance?

Well, it's express in the HTML code:

```
<div id="app">
  <light-bulb></light-bulb>
  <light-bulb></light-bulb>
  <light-bulb></light-bulb>
</div>
```

We know that the Vue instance will look like the insides of the `<div>` app, and we know that the light bulb will be mounted whenever the `<light-bulb>` tag is encountered. Why this tag you ask? It's because that's the name we gave to our component. The general syntax is as follows:

```
Vue.component('name-of-component', { ... options ... })
```

> If you specify the name in CamelCase, you have to remember that Vue will convert it to kebab-case. This is because HTML is case insensitive. So, an equivalent name for our light bulb will be `Vue.component('lightBulb', { ...options... })`.

Scope of components

In this recipe, we declared our component just above the Vue instance that will use it. This is okay because the component is in the same scope as the Vue root instance; the component is automatically registered by the instance.

In bigger applications, or when importing components, this might be a little more involved.

Inside Vue instances, there is an option called `components` that is equivalent to a registry of all the components that can be rendered inside its template. If a tag is encountered that is not standard (built-in in the browser) and not in this registry, Vue will log the following error:

```
vue.js:2643 [Vue warn]: Unknown custom element: <light-bulb> - did you
register the component correctly? For recursive components, make sure to
provide the "name" option.
(found in root instance)
```

What we have done in our recipe is to register the component in the global space; this is picked up by our Vue instance that adds the component to the registry.

Let's try another route and register the component manually:

```
var lightBulb = {
  template: `
  <div class='light-bulb'>
    <p> Eureka!</p>
  </div>
  `
}
new Vue({
  el: '#app',
  components: {
    'light-bulb': lightBulb
  }
})
```

This is called local registration. If we had a second Vue instance, it would not automatically have access to the light bulb component. This kind of registration allows you to have the light bulb defined in a separate file. You will then import the file and use the component having a neat separation of concerns. You can find more on this in the *Having recursive components* recipe.

The render function

In Vue 2, there is an alternative way to write how components are rendered. You can always use the template option, but you can also use the `render` function. Delete the light bulb options and write them again like this:

```
Vue.component('light-bulb', {
functional: true, render (createElement) {
    return createElement(
      'div',
      { class: 'light-bulb' },
      [
createElement('p', ' Eureka!')
      ]
    )
  }
})
```

The component we have written is perfectly equivalent to the previous one. We already saw an application of this style of writing components in Chapter 2, *Basic Vue.js Features*, recipe *Output raw HTML*.

The first line marks the component as functional, which means that the component is not allowed to have any internal state (no data option). It acts more like a mathematical function--it takes some input (in our case, we don't though) and renders some output, which is the light bulb emoji and the 'Eureka!' text.

The `createElement` function is oftentimes abbreviated with the letter h, so you can encounter something like this:

```
Vue.component('light-bulb', {
functional: true, render (h) {
    return h(
      'div',
      { class: 'light-bulb' },
      [
  h('p', ' Eureka!')
      ]
    )
  }
})
```

The `render` function is called when the component has to be drawn on screen and receives the `createElement` function as an argument. The `createElement` function has the following syntax:

```
createElement(
  // {String | Object | Function}
  'div', // in this case a string
  {
    'class': ...
    style: ...
    attrs: ...
    props: ...
    domProps: ...
    on: {
      click: ...
      input: ...
      ...
    },
    nativeOn: {
      input: ...
      ...
    },
    directives: ...
    slot: ...
    key: ...
    ref: ...
  },
  [ ... an array of children ... ]
)
```

While the `template` method is preferred and mostly used for displaying data in our components, the `render` function is used when we want more programming control on what we display.

Passing data to your components with props

Simple components behave a little like stamps. You can save yourself from creating the same element many times using components. While it's fine to have the exact same copy of the same component throughout the page, we must have some means of telling the component what to do. This way, we can have the same components thrice, each of which does a slightly different function.

Since everything is reactive in Vue, with props we have a direct line of communication with our components, and you will learn how to use this line in this recipe.

Getting ready

You don't need any particular knowledge to complete this recipe, just ensure that you know how to define and register basic components. Look back one recipe if you forgot how to do it.

How to do it...

We will build an icon that represents the sound volume. Adjusting the sound level will change the icon. The icon itself will be a component, like the following:

```
Vue.component('sound-icon', {
  template: "<span>{{soundEmojis[level]}}</span>",
  props: ['level'],
  data () {
    return {
      soundEmojis: ['🔇', '🔈', '🔉', '🔊']
    }
  }
})
```

Note how the `data` option is not an object but a function.

The following Vue instance will save the current sound level:

```
new Vue({
  el: '#app',
  data: {
    soundLevel: 0
  }
})
```

This sound level will be passed down as a prop to the component by an input box. The following HTML displays how:

```
<div id="app">
  <label>Sound level</label>
  <input type="number" v-model.number="soundLevel">
  <sound-icon :level="soundLevel"></sound-icon>
</div>
```

If you launch your application now, you will see how the icon changes when the volume changes.

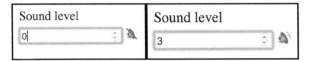

How it works...

We have put an array with only one element--the string level--in the `props` option. This is the property that our component will hold in its internal state.

You have to keep two things in mind when declaring props in your components:

- Props are one-way only communication
- They can be **fixed** or **dynamic**

Props are specifically for communicating parent to child. In our example, the Vue instance told the sound icon what the sound level was. There was no way for the sound icon to reply to the instance.

Note the colon in front of our prop in the line:

```
<sound-icon :level="soundLevel"></sound-icon>
```

Had we written `level="soundLevel"` without the initial colon, the meaning would have been different. No colon means "use this string for the value of the prop and never change it", so the value of level would have been fixed to `soundLevel` when it should, in fact, be a dynamic number.

In our child component, we didn't use the usual syntax to declare the data. In child components, the `data` option is a function. We have only one instance of a Vue, so an object will do the job. We can have multiple instances of children objects; so if we use an object, the same object will be shared among them. We want a different object for each child component, and the right way to achieve this is by calling a function at every instantiation-- the `data` function. If you try to assign an object, Vue will issue the following warning:

```
[Vue warn]: The "data" option should be a function that returns a per-
instance value in component definitions.
```

Kebab case and camel case

Kebab case is written like works are put in a shish-kebab--`like-this-for-example`. Camel case uses capitalization instead of spaces--`capitalizationLooksLikeThis`. Since HTML is case insensitive, it cannot use camel case. However, JavaScript is all about camel case; how do we make the two work together?

What Vue does is that it converts all the camel case into kebab case once it has to go in HTML. This is relevant to props because they are used in HTML.

Suppose, for a second, that our level variable is now called `soundLevel`:

```
props: ['soundLevel']
```

Consider that you try to use it as is in the HTML:

```
<sound-icon :soundLevel="soundLevel"></sound-icon>
```

It won't work because the variable is now called `sound-level` in the HTML:

```
<sound-icon :sound-level="soundLevel"></sound-icon>
```

Always remember to refer to your variable by kebab case in your HTML if you used camel case in your JavaScript.

There is an exception to this rule though. If you are writing a template of a component and are using a string (like the one we used in the `sound-icon` component), you can actually use camel case in your HTML. This is because it will be picked up by Vue for interpretation rather than the browser. This also applies to components written with the `render` function since that is not even HTML.

There's more

There's a little more to learn about `props`. It's not really recommended to use the syntax we used in a production environment:

```
props: ['level']
```

What we are doing here is declaring an array of `props` and listing the name of the `props`.

There is a richer syntax we can use, and we should use it to our advantage to specify stricter requirements for our `props`.

The first thing we can do is specify the type; this will be checked at runtime if we are in the development mode (it won't be checked, for example, if you use the minified version of Vue.js):

```
props: {
  level: Number
}
```

If this check doesn't pass, we will receive a message like the following:

```
[Vue warn]: Invalid prop: type check failed for prop "level". Expected
Number, got String.
(found in component <sound-icon>)
```

In our recipe, we specified that the variable in our input box should be casted to a number; so we won't have this problem (unless we clear the input box).

We can allow more than one type with the array syntax:

```
props: {
  level: [Number, String]
}
```

Alternatively, we can use an expanded syntax:

```
props: {
  level: {
    type: Number
  }
}
```

The available types are as follows:

- String
- Number
- Boolean
- Function
- Object
- Array

The preceding types are special. Vue will use `instanceof` under the cover to decide whether the type passed is right; so you can pass your constructors to check against the type of the passed props, like in the following code:

```
props: {
  level: {
    type: MyObject
  }
}
```

There are also three other options: one is for setting a default value, another is for having a custom validator if type checking doesn't cut it, and the last is when we require the prop to be specified, giving us more control over our `props` and what we choose to allow:

```
props: {
  level: {
    required: true,
    default: 0,
    validator (value) {
      return value >= 0 && value <= 3
    }
  }
}
```

When specifying a default value for a `prop` of type array or object, we have to specify a function, otherwise Vue will use the very same object instead of generating a new one for every component--`default () {` `return { greetings: 'hello' } }`.

Making components talk to each other

In the *Passing data to your components with props* recipe, we saw how parent components can talk to children components; this recipe is more general. How can two components exchange data in the more general case? You will learn how in the next few minutes.

Getting ready

You only need to know what a component is to proceed with this recipe. If I were you, though, I would take a look at the preceding recipe to have a sense of context of what we are talking about.

How to do it...

Our application will consist of two blabber components that talk to each other. Here's the HTML:

```
<div id="app">
  <blabber></blabber>
  <blabber></blabber>
</div>
```

Each blabber component will contain a script to recite as a dialogue. Since we want to keep it simple, the dialogue will be circular and will go on forever:

```
dialogue: [
  'hello',
  'how are you?',
  'fine thanks',
  'let's go drink!',
  'alright, where?',
  'to hello's bar',
  'hello?'
]
```

This, along with the variable that will mark the current line to say, will stay inside the component's data:

```
data () {
  return {
    currentLine: 0,
    dialogue: [
      'hello',
      'how are you?',
      'fine thanks',
      'let's go drink!',
      'alright, where?',
      'to hello's bar',
      'hello?'
    ]
  }
}
```

The template of the component will only be the current line:

```
template: "<p>{{dialogue[currentLine]}}</p>"
```

Each blabber will wait two seconds, update its current line, and increment the line for the next blabber. This behavior will start after the component is mounted:

```
mounted () {
  setInterval(() => {
    this.currentLine = line % this.dialogue.length
    line += 1
  }, 2000)
}
```

If you have done everything correctly, your final code for the component should look like this:

```
Vue.component('blabber', {
  template: "<p>{{dialogue[currentLine]}}</p>",
  data () {
    return {
      currentLine: 0,
      dialogue: [
        'hello',
        'how are you?',
        'fine thanks',
        'let's go drink!',
        'alright, where?',
        'to hello's bar',
        'hello?'
      ]
    }
  },
  mounted () {
    setInterval(() => {
      this.currentLine = line % this.dialogue.length
      line += 1
    }, 2000)
  }
})
```

There is still one missing. Just before the component, we should initialize our line variable:

```
var line = 0
```

Write the Vue instance, which is just the following code:

```
new Vue({
  el: '#app'
})
```

When you run your application, you will see the dialog of the two blabbers going on forever.

How it works...

The secret sauce that makes the two components talk to each other is the `line` variable:

Each component will try to read the variable and update it. This is not exactly a good way to write code, but it demonstrates that you can use simple variables outside of regular Vue code to make your components communicate with the external world.

A more proper way to achieve the same goal would be to leverage the parent Vue instance to hold the same state and then pass it as a prop to the two children components. Now, the problem with this is that the two components are not allowed to modify the prop since the communication is one-way (from the parent to the children). The workaround is for components to send events to the parent and tell them to update the line variable.

At this point, it becomes more obvious as to what the right solution is--make the two components talk to each other with events. Let's try and re-implement our recipe with this, more involved but more extendable, solution.

Since we cannot rely on randomness to decide who starts the dialog anymore, we are in need of a variable in the blabber component to decide who starts the communication:

```
props: {
  iceBreaker: {
    type: Boolean,
    default: false
  }
}
```

We then need to update the state variables with the initialization of `currentLine`:

```
...
data () {
  return {
    currentLine: this.iceBreaker ? 0 : -1,
    dialogue: [
      ...
```

This is to be done so that our HTML becomes as follows:

```
<div id="app">
  <blabber :ice-breaker="true"></blabber>
  <blabber></blabber>
</div>
```

To make the two components communicate, we need a bus that will exchange the messages. We can instantiate another empty Vue instance before the component definition to hold our messages:

```
var bus = new Vue()
```

Our mounted hook becomes as shown:

```
mounted () {
  if (this.iceBreaker) {
    bus.$emit('line', 0)
  }
}
```

We need to pair this with a created hook:

```
created () {
  bus.$on('line', line => {
    // is not the line I just sent
    if (line !== this.currentLine) {
      setTimeout(() => {
        this.currentLine = (line + 1) % this.dialogue.length
        bus.$emit('line', this.currentLine)
      }, 2000)
    }
  })
}
```

This means that when a line message is received after 2 seconds (in which, presumably, the blabber is thinking for a comeback), the line of the dialog is incremented by one and a line message is sent to the other blabbers connected to the bus. The blabber itself will receive its own message; that's why we need to check whether the line we receive is our own before setting a timeout. What was a number variable earlier is now a full-fledged Vue instance:

Making components talk with Vuex

Making components communicate in Vue can be done in several ways. In this recipe, you will build two components that communicate through a shared state in a structured manner, using Vuex.

Getting ready

Vuex is state management for Vue. We will talk about it more extensively in Chapter 10, *Large Application Patters with Vuex*. For now, we will try it out as an indirect means of communication between components. There are no particular skills you should have to carry out this recipe, but you should have at least an understanding of what the Flux pattern is, since Vuex is is inspired by Flux, Redux, and The Elm Architecture. You can find more information at https://facebook.github.io/flux/docs/overview.html.

We will use words such as *Mutations* and assume that you know what we are talking about. If you don't know and want a briefer nonetheless, you can take a look at Chapter 10, *Large Application Patterns with Vuex*.

How to do it...

We will centralize the state of our whole application in a Vuex store. To install Vuex, you can add it as a dependency (more instructions at `https://vuex.vuejs.org/en/installation.html`); for now, I will assume that you are working on JSFiddle or a single web page, in which you can add `https://unpkg.com/vuex` as a dependency.

We declare a new store for our state, as follows:

```
const store = new Vuex.Store({})
```

We then add properties to the empty object inside the parenthesis, just like we would do with a Vue instance.

First, we will tell Vuex to help us debug by noticing us every time we modify the state outside of a mutation:

```
strict: true
```

Then, we will declare the state that we will use to characterize the whole system:

```
state: {
  currentActor: -1,
  currentLine: -1,
  actors: [],
  dialogue: [
    'Where are you going?',
    'To the cinema',
    'What's on at the cinema?',
    ''Quo vadis?'',
    'Oh, what does it mean?'
  ]
}
```

We will fill in the actor array with objects that will represent the actors themselves. Moreover, we will access the `actor` and `dialogue` arrays in a circular manner.

The next things you have to write inside the Vuex store object are the mutations. Define one mutation that will add one actor to the scene and one mutation that will advance the current line by one:

```
mutations: {
  entersScene (state, uuid) {
    state.currentLine =
      (state.currentLine + 1) % state.dialogue.length
    state.actors.push({
      uuid,
      line: state.dialogue[state.currentLine]
    })
    state.currentActor =
      (state.currentActor + 1) % state.actors.length
  },
  nextLine (state) {
    state.currentActor =
      (state.currentActor + 1) % state.actors.length
    state.currentLine =
      (state.currentLine + 1) % state.dialogue.length
    state.actors[state.currentActor].line =
      state.dialogue[state.currentLine]
  }
}
```

You successfully completed the store. Now you need to define the component that will act in this comedy:

```
Vue.component('blabber', {
  template: '<div class="blabber">{{currentLine}}</div>',
  data () {
    return {
      uuid: Math.random()
    }
  },
  computed: {
    currentLine () {
      return store.state.actors.find(actor =>
        actor.uuid === this.uuid).line
    }
  },
  created () {
    store.commit('entersScene', this.uuid)
  }
})
```

The blabber component has a simple template (it just says its line). It retrieves its line from the store with a computed property and, at creation time, signals its entrance to the store.

You can put two blabbers in the HTML:

```
<div id="app">
  <blabber></blabber>
  <blabber></blabber>
</div>
```

Maybe add some style to frame your blabbers with some border through CSS:

```
.blabber {
  width: 200px;
  height: 40px;
  background-color: gainsboro;
  border: 1px solid grey;
}
```

The last thing you have to do to make all this machinery work is to commit the `nextLine` mutation to the store every 2 seconds so that the show goes on. You can do it in the Vue instance by installing a `setInterval`:

```
new Vue({
  el: '#app',
  mounted () {
    setInterval(() => {
      store.commit('nextLine')
    }, 2000)
  }
})
```

When you launch the application now, you will see the two blabbers talking in circle for hours.

How it works...

The blabbers always know their line because they communicate indirectly through the store.

If you look closely, the blabbers themselves have no state. Yeah they have a **UUID** (**Universally Unique Identifier**), but that is just to give them an identity, and it never really changes.

Their state is centralized in the store, and the actor array will look like this during execution:

```
[{
  uuid:0.9775738039368538,
  line:"'Quo vadis?'"
},
{
  uuid:0.7398549831424475,
  line:"Oh, what does it mean?"
}]
```

Thanks to Vue reactivity, the component is just a mirror of this state.

The communication, while indirectly, is done in the store. Every 2 seconds, a nextLine mutation is issued:

```
nextLine (state) {
    state.currentActor =
      (state.currentActor + 1) % state.actors.length
    state.currentLine =
      (state.currentLine + 1) % state.dialogue.length
    state.actors[state.currentActor].line =
      state.dialogue[state.currentLine]
  }
```

This advances the currentActor and the currentLine indexes by one step; after that, the actor at the currentActor index says the line at the currentLine index. The actors don't communicate directly to each other, instead they just watch the result (line) of a shared counter (the currentLine) that advances at every step.

More than components talking to each other, we created an orchestra director that will tell the components what to do.

There's more

If you open Vue Devtools, you will be able to see the `mutators` committed in the Vuex section:

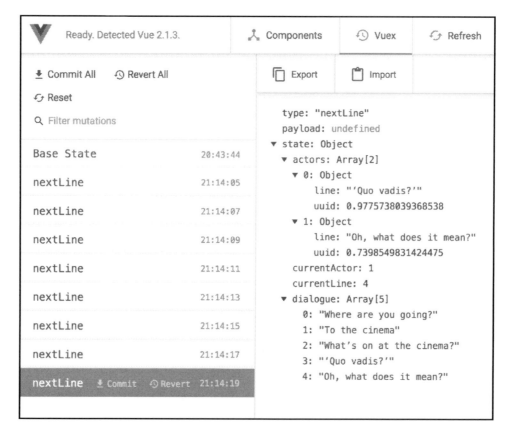

Every 2 seconds, there should be a new `nextLine` mutator. I suggest that you also expand the `actors` array and see what's inside. You can even take a peek at the `currentActor` and the `currentLine` and watch them go in circles.

If you feel adventurous, you can even add a third blabber:

```
<div id="app">
  <blabber></blabber>
  <blabber></blabber>
  <blabber></blabber>
</div>
```

You will discover whether the blabbers reorganize themselves in a sensible fashion, or whether the system we put in place for two blabbers won't work for three.

Reading a child's state

As we saw in some recipes in this chapter, communication between parent and child is unidirectional with props (top-down) and passes through a hub with events. In this recipe, we will leverage some tricks to read a child's state directly. This technique can be useful when two components are tightly coupled by design or when some debugging is needed.

Getting ready

This recipe is not for beginners, so ensure that you understand a little about components and how events and props work before moving ahead.

How to do it...

We have a child who really ate a cookie but won't admit he did. We won't let him get away with it by checking internal state and discover the truth.

Write the HTML structure of our application, which is the following:

```
<div id="app">
  <child ref="junior"></child>
  <p>Truth: {{childStomach}}</p>
</div>
```

The `ref` attribute gives the component a mark that we can later retrieve from code.

Copy the child component, like the following:

```
Vue.component('child', {
  template: "<p>{{mouth}}</p>",
  data () {
    return {
      mouth: 'I didn't eat that cookie',
      stomach: 'Yummy that cookie was delicious.'
    }
  }
})
```

This component will display only the string inside the variable mouth.

You can write the Vue instance, as illustrated:

```
new Vue({
  el: '#app',
  data: {
    childStomach: 'unknown'
  },
  mounted () {
    this.childStomach = this.$refs.junior.stomach
  }
})
```

We have a mounted hook that will assign the content of the stomach of the child inside a variable in the parent.

Now, run the application to know the truth:

I didn't eat that cookie

Truth: Yummy that cookie was delicious.

How it works...

The `ref` we used on the `child` tag is a special attribute that we can put it on components or on elements in the page to get a reference that we can use later on in the code.

The use of `ref` is not reactive, for this reason you cannot bind it to a variable. Furthermore, the `$refs` option takes some time to be populated; we had to wait for the mounted hook to be triggered before being able to use it.

This code, for example, doesn't work:

```
<div id="app">
  <child ref="junior"></child>
  <p>Truth: {{$refs.junior.stomach}}</p>
</div>
```

The reason is that since the mustaches are evaluated in the render of the template (in this case, the HTML) and the $refs variable is populated after the said render, junior is undefined at this point and nothing will be printed because the initial render of the template failed.

Using ref with v-for

If we have many components with the same ref, the handle that results will be of the array type.

We can rewrite our example for multiple children. Here's a slight modification for the child component:

```
Vue.component('child', {
  template: "<p>Child {{num}}: {{mouth}}</p>",
  props: ['num'],
  data () {
    return {
      mouth: 'I didn't eat that cookie',
      stomach: `Yummy that cookie was ${this.num} times more delicious.`
    }
  }
})
```

We want 10 children in our HTML, and we are interested in the stomach of the fourth child:

```
<div id="app">
  <child v-for="i in 10" ref="junior" :num="i" :key="i"></child>
  <p>Truth for child 4: {{child4Stomach}}</p>
</div>
```

The child4Stomach variable is initialized in the Vue instance, as follows:

```
new Vue({
  el: '#app',
  data: {
    child4Stomach: 'unknown'
  },
  mounted () {
    this.child4Stomach = this.$refs.junior[3].stomach
  }
})
```

The number 3 is there because arrays are 0-based, so it's actually the fourth element of the array of children:

Here's the result you should get:

```
Child 1: I didn't eat that cookie

Child 2: I didn't eat that cookie

Child 3: I didn't eat that cookie

Child 4: I didn't eat that cookie

Child 5: I didn't eat that cookie

Child 6: I didn't eat that cookie

Child 7: I didn't eat that cookie

Child 8: I didn't eat that cookie

Child 9: I didn't eat that cookie

Child 10: I didn't eat that cookie

Truth for child 4: Yummy that cookie was 4 times more delicious.
```

Using components in your own components

We are talking about composition. Composition is a basic principle in software engineering that allows you to build big and complex systems out of small and self-contained pieces. The working is not exoteric but is similar to playing with Legos.

Getting ready

Before venturing in composition, you should be able to create components in the first place. Go to the *Creating and registering a component* recipe if you need a refresher. Since this recipe uses props, you should also complete the *Passing data to your components with props* recipe to be on track.

How to do it...

We will build a menu for a restaurant. We will have a component for the complete course, and it will contain a smaller component for the individual dishes.

We will first go bottom-up by writing the component for every dish:

```
Vue.component('dish', {
  template: `
    <p class="dish">
      {{ham}} &lt;- Delicious!
    </p>
  `,
  props: ['ham']
})
```

The `&lt;` part is an HTML entity and means "less than"; it will be displayed as the < symbol.

The course component will have the dish component inside it, and we will add some validation for the prop, just to ensure that all the menus have a similar layout:

```
Vue.component('course', {
  template: `
    <section class="course">
      <dish v-for="ham in menu" :ham="ham" :key="ham"></dish>
    </section>
  `,
  props: {
    menu: {
      type: Array,
      required: true,
      validator (foodArray) {
        return foodArray.every(food =>
          typeof food === 'string') &&
          foodArray.length === 4
      }
    }
  }
})
```

Our validator checks whether the type of `food` is a string and whether the length of the array is equal to 4.

Normally, you will query a service or an API to retrieve the menu; but we will, instead, store two of them directly in the Vue instance for the purpose of this recipe:

```
new Vue({
  el: '#app',
  data: {
    menu1: ['🍎','🍎','🌶','🍅'],
    menu2: ['🍪','🍩','🍗','🍖']
  }
})
```

In our HTML, place two courses with the menu you just wrote:

```
<div id="app">
  <course :menu="menu1"></course>
  <course :menu="menu2"></course>
</div>
```

To visually separate the two menus, we will add a style to the CSS:

```
.course {
  border: 1px solid black;
  margin: 10px;
  padding: 10px;
}
```

It's not a high-end restaurant menu, but I hope the customers will appreciate a good composition over inheritance in Vue:

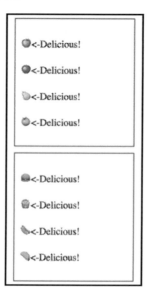

How it works...

When using composition, there's a simple rule of thumb from the official docs that you have to keep in mind.

> Everything in the parent template is compiled in parent scope; everything in the child template is compiled in child scope.

This means that you have to pay some attention to the variables you use in your templates, especially props.

Let's examine our course component more closely. We declared a prop called menu of the Array type, and we used it like this:

```
<div id="app">
  <course :menu="menu1"></course>
  <course :menu="menu2"></course>
</div>
```

In this context, we are writing the template of the Vue root instance. As a matter of fact, menu1 and menu2 are declared exactly there and we are able to use them without any problem.

Let's suppose that we have the following component:

```
Vue.component('advertising', {
  template: '<div>Buy our stuff!!!</div>',
  data () {
    return {
      show: false
    }
  }
}
```

We want it to display only when the show variable is true. We can think of writing something like this in our Vue instance template:

```
<advertising v-if="show"></advertising>
```

No! This won't work because show is not in the scope of the Vue instance but in the scope of the advertising component.

In our recipe, we have the following hierarchy:

1. The Vue instance, which contains the `menu1` and `menu2` variables
2. The Course component, which uses the `menu prop` variable
3. The Dish component, which receives a single ham from the menu as prop

So, the real data is only in one place--in the Vue instance. In general, it can also be external to the Vue instance; for example, it can be retrieved by an API. This is good because we can supply new data easily by acting only in one place. We passed the data through props, which makes where reactive variables are compiled clear.

Using mixins in your components

In Vue and in JavaScript in general, there is no general way to have inheritance as intended in programming. Vue nonetheless has some means of recycling the same features for more components. In this recipe, you will give superpowers to your components, but you will write the powers only once.

Getting ready

This recipe is fairly advanced; it uses some nasty tricks that are very useful to understand how Vue works and may be helpful as a workaround in some situations. Anyway, it is not recommended if you don't already have some experience with Vue.

How to do it...

First, we will create two regular elements: the first will represent a man--you can use the man emoji:

```
Vue.component('man', {
  template: '<p>man</p>'
})
```

Well, that was simple. Next, we will create a cat component:

```
Vue.component('cat', {
  template: '<p>cat</p>'
})
```

After those, you can instantiate Vue like this:

```
new Vue({
  el: '#app'
})
```

In your HTML, you compose all the three with the following code:

```
<div id="app">
  <man></man>
  <cat></cat>
</div>
```

Run the page and you will see the two emojis:

We will give superpowers to those two components, but we don't want to edit them both. You have to define a super powerful mixin; put the following code at the top, before the component creation and the Vue instantiation so that it's defined for them:

```
var superPowersMixin = {
  data () {
    return {
      superPowers: false
    }
  },
  methods: {
    superMe () {
      this.$el.classList.add("super")
      this.superPowers = true
    }
  },
  created () {
    this.$options.template =
    `<div><h3 v-show="superPowers">super</h3>` +
    this.$options.template +
    `<button @click="superMe" v-if="!superPowers">
      Super!
    </button></div>`
  }
}
```

The super class is a rule to your CSS:

```
.super {
  filter: hue-rotate(120deg);
}
```

Now, add the `mixin` to the two components:

```
Vue.component('man', {
  template: '<p>man</p>',
  mixins: [superPowersMixin]
})
Vue.component('cat', {
  template: '<p>cat</p>',
  mixins: [superPowersMixin]
})
```

Run the application and click on the buttons to give superpowers to your components!:

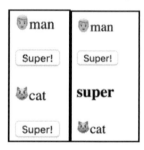

How it works...

Mixins add a lot of flexibility to our components, and it is a way to reuse a piece of functionality in different components.

The basic mechanism is that you define an object that mimics the options of a component. You then put the object in an array inside the `mixins` option inside the real component. Vue will look for mixins when it's time to create the component and will mix the options of the components with the one you defined.

What will happen in our recipe is that the created hook will encapsulate the component in a `<div>` by modifying the template. It will add a button to the creation hook; it will then add a `superMe` method that turns on the `superPowers` mixed state variable and add the CSS `super` class.

Mixin order

Vue will use different strategies for mixing different options.

As a general rule, options that contain objects are merged into one big object. For example, if you have a component that contains three methods and your mixin adds one, the final component will contain all of them. When you have two methods with the same name (or computed properties, components, directives, and so on), the mixin's keys will be discarded.

Hook functions don't get merged, but both the mixin's and the component's are launched, with the ones from the mixin taking precedence.

There's more

I want to close this recipe by telling you about **component subclassing**. To my knowledge, component subclassing is not officially supported; this doesn't mean it's impossible, of course.

I won't go in great detail, but I will give you a general direction to go in.

Write your base component, which will be a simple greeter:

```
var Greeter = {
  template: `
  <p>
    {{message}}
    <button @click="greet">greet</button>
  </p>`,
  data () {
    return {
      message: '...'
    }
  },
  methods: {
    greet () {
      this.message = 'hello'
    }
  }
}
```

It's just a simple string that will become `hello` when you press the **greet** button.

Have we really written the base component, or did we just write a mixin?

The subclassing is all in this ambivalence; we can use `Greeter` as a component and mixin because they are mostly made of the same things.

Put it in a subcomponent as a mixin:

```
var SuperGreeter = {
  mixins: [Greeter],
  template: `
  <p>
    {{message}}
    <button @click="superGreet">supergreet</button>
  </p>`,
  methods: {
    superGreet () {
      this.message = 'SUPER HELLO!'
    }
  }
}
```

Put it in the main Vue instance as a component:

```
new Vue({
  el: '#app',
  components: { Greeter, SuperGreeter }
})
```

Finally, you can add them both to the HTML:

```
<div id="app">
  <greeter></greeter>
  <super-greeter></super-greeter>
</div>
```

Now you have a component and a subcomponent in which you overwrote the template and added a method.

Note that the greet method is present in the subclass also, it is just not used. Maybe you can figure out a way to have polymorphism? It's an open problem even for me.

Content distribution with slots

Sometimes you want to build a component that can be used to put other elements or components inside it. You may want to build a generic modal dialog component but give the user of your component the ability to write the text of the modal dialog. Alternatively, maybe you want to use a general layout in a component and fill it with other elements. Slots are a way to have a fixed structure in one component and delegate the contents of certain parts of it to the father.

Getting ready

I suggest you to go on and complete the *Using components in your own components* recipe as it explains the important concept of scope. We will cover that here also, but "repetita iuvant".

How to do it...

The Russian cat mafia, in order to improve the morale of cats, decides to put up a web page with the best employee of the month and decides to write a Vue component for that.

They hire you as the principal developer to help them you write the following component:

```
Vue.component('framed', {
  template: `<div class="frame">
              <h3>Russian cat mafia
                  employee of the month</h3>
              <slot>Nothing framed.</slot>
            </div>`
})
```

The slot tag represents a placeholder in which you will put more content in the parent template. Of course, you add some CSS to embellish the component:

```
.frame {
  border: 5px dashed dodgerblue;
  width: 300px;
}
h3 {
  font-family: sans-serif;
  text-align: center;
  padding: 2px 0;
  width: 100%;
}
```

[163]

This is how the HTML looks:

```
<div id="app">
  <framed>
    <cat :name="catName"></cat>
  </framed>
</div>
```

Note how we put another component inside the framed component. The cat component that will be framed is this:

```
Vue.component('cat', {
  template: `<div>
              <figure>
                <img src="http://lorempixel.com/220/220/cats/"/>
                <figcaption>{{name}}</figcaption>
              </figure>
            </div>`,
  props: ['name']
})
```

This means that it will load a random cat image every time the page is requested, and the image will be 220px in width and 220px in height.

We can also add figcaption in the h3 rule of the CSS:

```
h3, figcaption {
  font-family: sans-serif;
  text-align: center;
  padding: 2px 0;
  width: 100%;
}
```

The Vue instance will look like the following:

```
new Vue({
  el: '#app',
  data: {
    names: ['Murzik', 'Pushok', 'Barsik', 'Vaska', 'Matroskin']
  },
  computed: {
    catName () {
      return this.names[Math.floor(Math.random() *
        this.names.length)]
    }
  }
})
```

We are just generating a random (Russian) cat name and passing it to the cat component in the template.

Launch your app now; you will discover who is the new Russian cat mafia employee of the month:

How it works...

Normally, after creating a component, it is inserted in the `template` as a simple tag. In some cases, you put some props or other attributes, but you don't put anything inside. With slots, you are expected to put stuff inside your component in their parent's template. We usually write the following:

```
<div id="app">
  <framed></framed>
</div>
```

However, since the `framed` component has a slot inside his template and we put some HTML inside it, it is as follows:

```
<div id="app">
  <framed>
<cat :name="catName"></cat>
  </framed>
</div>
```

The final render will contain the `framed` component with the `cat` component instead of the `slot`.

Actually, if we don't put anything inside, the default content will appear. The default content is defined inside the component, in the `slot` tag:

```
<div class="frame">
  <h3>Russian cat mafia
      employee of the month</h3>
  <slot>Nothing framed.</slot>
</div>
```

This is what we see when we try not to put anything inside the `framed` component:

It's also worth noting that while the cat component is a child of the framed component, it can use a variable for its prop from the main Vue instance. This is why it's in the scope of the Vue instance, since it's declared in the template of the Vue instance. It doesn't matter that it's not its direct child.

There's more

In actuality, there are two more interesting modes for `slots` to be used: named slots, when you have more than one slot and want to further customize how content should be distributed, and scoped slots, when you want to reference a child's variable in the parent.

Named slots

When you want to have more than one `slot`, you can give a name to each one of them.

To make our point, we will build an organization chart for "Scratchy co".

The main component has two `slots`:

```
Vue.component('organogram', {
  template: `<div class="organogram">
              <h3>Scratchy co.</h3>
              <div class="boss">
```

```
                        <h3>Boss</h3>
                        <slot name="boss">No boss</slot>
                      </div>
                      <div class="employee">
                        <h3>Employee</h3>
                        <slot name="employee">No employee</slot>
                      </div>
                    </div>`
    })
```

You can see that we named the first `slot` boss and the second `slot` employee.

To decorate our organization chart, we will use the following CSS:

```
.organogram {
  border: 5px dashed dodgerblue;
  width: 300px;
}
.boss {
  border: 5px double mediumvioletred;
}
.employee {
  border: 2px outset lightgrey;
}
figcaption, h3 {
  font-family: sans-serif;
  text-align: center;
  padding: 2px 0;
  width: 100%;
}
```

The composition with different `slots` is all in the HTML:

```
<div id="app">
  <organogram>
    <div slot="boss">
      <figure>
        <img src="http://lorempixel.com/210/210/cats/1"/>
        <figcaption>Sylvester</figcaption>
      </figure>
    </div>
    <cat slot="employee" :name="catName"></cat>
  </organogram>
</div>
```

The cat component has not changed, so we can use the one we built in the recipe; the only modification is that we have to add the slot attribute. This attribute is also applied at the boss <div>.

Run the page to see organogram:

Scoped slots

In Vue 2.1, a new feature was added that lets you pass data between the content of the slot and its parent component.

This is very useful when we have many slots and many of them need different styling or even when we don't know the number of slots to fill in advance.

First of all, since we plan to use the `cat` component multiple times, let's make a small modification that will get a different cat image at every instantiation:

```
Vue.component('cat', {
  template: `
    <div>
      <figure>
<img :src="'http://lorempixel.com/220/220/cats/?' + name"/>
        <figcaption>{{name}}</figcaption>
      </figure>
    </div>
    `,
  props: ['name']
})
```

We added the name of the cat at the end of the link; this way, since we pick a random cat every time, the image will also be picked at random. If we don't do this, the browser will see that the links are the same and use the same image taken from the cache.

Also, modify the organization chart to include the two top-ranked cats:

```
Vue.component('organogram', {
  template: `
    <div class="organogram">
      <h3>Scratchy co.</h3>
      <div class="boss">
      <h3>Boss</h3>
      <slot type="boss">No boss</slot>
    </div>
    <div class="employee" v-for="rank in 2">
      <h3>Employee</h3>
      <slot
        type="employee"
        :rank="rank"
      >
        No employee
      </slot>
    </div>
  </div>`
})
```

We are passing the rank variable to the `slot`. It will be picked up by the new HTML template of the Vue instance:

```
<div id="app">
  <organogram>
    <template scope="props">
      <div v-if="props.type === 'boss'">
        <figure>
          <img src="http://lorempixel.com/210/210/cats/1"/>
          <figcaption>Sylvester</figcaption>
        </figure>
      </div>
      <div v-else-if="props.type === 'employee'"
           :class="'r' + props.rank">
        <cat :name="catName()"></cat>
      </div>
    </template>
  </organogram>
</div>
```

Inside the `organogram` component, we are wrapping everything inside the `template` tag. The `scope` attribute in this tag will give a name to an object that collects all the variables we passed from the `slots` in the child component.

This way, we use `props.type` to reference the type of slot. We are using the `type` variable much like we used the `name` attribute for the named `slot` in the preceding paragraph.

If the type is employee, we are also interested in the rank. We then concatenate the rank, which is a number, with the letter `r` and add it as a class.

To give it meaning, let's add the `r1` and `r2` classes to our CSS:

```
.r1 {
  font-size: 1.5em;
  color: red;
}
.r2 {
  font-size: 1.2em;
  color: blue;
}
```

Launching the app now, we should see something like this:

Single file components with Webpack

Vue was a game changer mostly because it changed the way to partition responsibilities. It wasn't the first to do that, but it certainly extended on that. Earlier, we used one file for HTML, one for CSS, and one for JavaScript. Little did we know that the three files were all about the same thing--components. Yet, they split several components vertically instead of horizontally. In Vue, we keep components well isolated in a single file with the help of tools such as **Webpack**. In this recipe, you will learn how.

Getting ready

This recipe assumes that you already know how to register a component (the *Creating and register a component* recipe). We will also use npm and vue-cli (the *Choosing a development environment* recipe).

How do do it...

We're assuming that you already have `vue-cli` installed in your terminal type:

```
    mkdir my-component
cd my-component
vue init webpack-simple
```

You will then be asked some questions; you can answer with whatever you like; at the end, you should be presented with something like this:

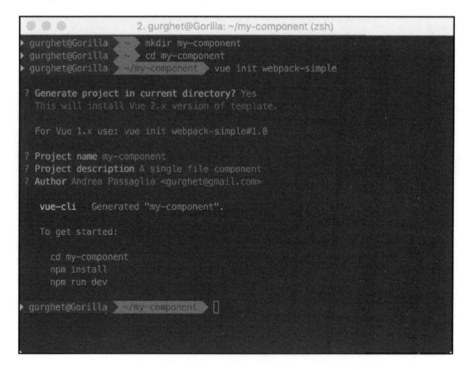

Install the dependencies and run the development server with the following commands:

```
npm install
npm run dev
```

A browser should automatically open with a welcome page, such as the following screenshot:

Now any change you make in the source file will be picked up by the browser in real time.

Open the file in `my-component/src/App.vue` with your favorite text editor and delete everything inside the outermost `<div>` tag inside the template section.

Save the file; you should see the browser page go blank instantly.

Also, delete everything inside the export default object and all the styles. The file will look like this:

```
<template>
  <div id="app">
  </div>
</template>

<script>
export default {}
</script>

<style>
</style>
```

This is our empty canvas to build our component in one file. Thanks to hot reloading, we can see the result of what we are doing in the browser.

Just to test it out, let's write our sample component. In the template, write the following script:

```
<div id="app">
  <p>I have a secret message:</p>
  <p v-if="show" class="secret">{{message}}</p>
  <button v-else @click="show = true">Show Message</button>
</div>
```

Inside the script, write as follows:

```
export default {
  data () {
    return {
      show: false,
      message: 'much secret. many reactive. wow!'
    }
  }
}
```

Let's add a style just for fun:

```
.secret {
  background-color: thistle;
}
```

While you write the code, you can save and see the changes in real time. If you don't see anything, keep an eye on the console because if there is some error, you will need to reload the page.

The final touch is to rename the file from `App.vue` to `MyComponent.vue`. After this, though, you will not be able to see the component in the browser anymore. That's because the `main.js` makes reference to the App component.

Open `main.js` and change all the occurrences of `App` with `MyComponent`. The file will look like this:

```
import Vue from 'vue'
import MyComponent from './MyComponent.vue'

new Vue({
  el: '#app',
  render: h => h(MyComponent)
})
```

This is the root Vue instance by the way. If we want two components instead of one, we can change the render function to this:

```
render: h => h('div', {}, [h(MyComponent), h(MyComponent)])
```

How it works...

If you managed to follow along but some points were not so clear, that's probably because you are not too familiar with tools such as Webpack or NPM; in this case, not everything you do with them seems obvious. I refer you to Chapter 8, *Organize + Automate + Deploy = Webpack*, for a close view of Webpack in particular.

It's probably useful to break down how the flow of data starts from the component we just wrote and goes down to `index.html`.

We have already seen how the `main.js` calls the component. The `index.html` looks like this:

```
<!DOCTYPE html>
<html lang="en">
  <head>
    <meta charset="utf-8">
    <title>my-component</title>
  </head>
  <body>
    <div id="app"></div>
    <script src="/dist/build.js"></script>
  </body>
</html>
```

So, there is a reference to a `build.js` and not `main.js`. How does it work then? The `build.js` file is not found in the source code.

To find out, you have to open `webpack.config.js` and note that we are setting `build.js` as a path in the output property. This means that when we launch Webpack (with npm run dev), we are building that file from `main.js`, which is the entry point of Webpack.

There's more

You have built a single page component. However, this is only half of the trip. You should also package the component so that you can use it on other projects. In `Chapter 8`, *Organize + Automate + Deploy = Webpack,* the *Releasing your components to the public* recipe, you do exactly that.

Loading your components asynchronously

Sometimes you need to load components while the app is already running. This can be because you have so many components that it will be too cumbersome to load all of them or maybe the shape of some component is not known in advance. With Vue, you can load components only when they have to actually render. Next time the component will need to be rendered, it will be retrieved from cache.

Getting ready

You want to load your component asynchronously only when you already know how to make AJAX requests with Vue. In this recipe, though, we will skip those, so you can follow along right away.

How to do it...

Let's suppose that we have a big vase e-commerce. We have one component for every vase, but we can't give them all to the user at once. It will be too much data. We will load the component from the Internet.

As only modification, we will simulate the AJAX call with a simple `setTimeout`. Let's go back to our favorite online editor, JSFiddle:

```
Vue.component('XuandePeriodVase', (resolve, reject) => {
  setTimeout(() => {
    if ((new Date()).getDay() !== 6) {
      resolve({
        template: '<div>Buy for only 4000000</div>',
        mounted () {
          this.$parent.$emit('loaded')
        }
      })
    } else {
      reject("Today is Sunday, Internet is closed!")
    }
  }, 1000)
})
```

Our Vue instance will hold only one variable to display the (simulated) loading of the component:

```
new Vue({
  el: '#app',
  data: {
    loading: true
  },
  created () {
    this.$on('loaded', () => {
      this.loading = false
    })
  }
})
```

Put a little `loading` message along with the vase component and you're done:

```
<div id="app">
  <span v-if="loading">loading...</span>
  <xuande-period-vase></xuande-period-vase>
</div>
```

When you load the page, you will see your component appear after 1 second, in which a real AJAX call will be happening. If it's Sunday, you will see a sorry message in the console; that will represent the case when the component can't be loaded because of network problems.

How it works...

The syntax for asynchronous component, therefore, is as follows:

```
Vue.component('comp-name', (resolve, reject) => { ... })
```

Instead of passing an object as a second argument, we are actually passing a function with two arguments. The first is a function that you will have to call once the component (more precisely, the object that contains the properties of the component) is available. The second is another function that accepts a string. When Vue is not working in production mode, the string will be displayed in the console. You can have several reasons why the component is not working, such as an actual timeout or a connection error:

```
if (response.status > 400) { reject('4XX error received') }
setTimeout(() => { reject('connection timeout') }, 5000)
```

Another feature of our code is that while our components load, even if normally the operation should take less than a few hundreds of milliseconds, we would like a courtesy message or graphics to improve user experience.

To achieve that, we are emitting a loaded message when the component is mounted:

```
mounted () {
  this.$parent.$emit('loaded')
}
```

Whoever the parent is can now receive the message and act upon it (or not). In our case, we pick up the message and turn off the loading message:

```
created () {
  this.$on('loaded', () => {
    this.loading = false
  })
}
```

Having recursive components

If you are even a little into programming, one of the first things you'll hear is iteration versus recursion. Vue has both, and if you have some tree structured graphics or menus in your application, Vue's got you covered. In this recipe, we will illustrate on this point by building a classification of animals in a recursive fashion.

Getting ready

We will use a couple of props in this recipe, so ensure that you have the *Passing data to your component with props* recipe completed before starting this one.

How to do it...

First of all, let's write an empty Vue instance that we will fill:

```
new Vue ({
  el: '#app'
})
```

You will need some material to work with; by this, I mean a whole lot of animals to classify. You can copy maybe only a part of this code in your Vue instance data, but to give you some inspiration, here it comes, the longest listing in this whole book:

```
data: {
  living: {
    animals: {
      invertebrates: {
        crab: null,
        bee: null,
        ant: null
      },
      vertebrates: {
        fish: {
          shark: null
        },
        mammals: {
          rabbit: null,
          rat: null
        }
      }
    },
    plants: {
      flowering: {
        maize: null,
        paddy: null
      },
      'non-flowering': {
        algae: {
          seaweed: null,
          spirogyra: null
        },
        fungi: {
```

```
            yeast: null,
            mushroom: null
          },
          moss: null,
          fern: null
        }
      }
    }
  }
```

We want to render all the animals and when we encounter a null, we will stop traversing the tree.

Declare a new Vue component above our Vue instance and name it `taxon`:

```
Vue.component('taxon', {})
```

Inside its option, write the following template:

```
template: `
  <li>
    <div @click="toggle">
      {{taxon}}
      <span v-if="hasChildren">[{{open ? '-' : '+'}}]</span>
    </div>
    <ul v-show="open">
      <taxon
        v-for="(child, taxon) in tree"
        :tree="child"
        :taxon="taxon"
        :key="taxon"
      >
      </taxon>
    </ul>
  </li>
  `
```

This template is a list element with a little + sign that we will click on to expand the list that is inside. The `tree` and `taxon` variables, as you can see, are passed as props. Declare them with the following code:

```
props: {
  tree: Object,
  taxon: String
}
```

The open variable is retained internally in the data of the component:

```
data () {
  return {
    open: false
  }
}
```

Write the hasChildren computed property to make your live easier in the template:

```
computed: {
  hasChildren () {
    return this.tree !== null
  }
}
```

Finally, the toggle method will switch open on and off depending on its previous state:

```
methods: {
  toggle () {
    this.open = !this.open
  }
}
```

The root of this tree is represented by the following HTML, which is the only bit you have to write:

```
<div id="app">
  <ul>
    <taxon :tree="living" taxon="living"></taxon>
  </ul>
</div>
```

You can add this CSS rule to make your mouse change to a pointer hand when hovering over the little plus sign:

```
span {
  cursor: pointer;
}
```

When you launch your app, you will have the full tree of life at your fingertips:

- living [-]
    - animals [-]
        - invertebrates [+]
        - vertebrates [-]
            - fish [+]
            - mammals [-]
                - rabbit
                - rat
    - plants [-]
        - flowering [+]
        - non-flowering [+]

How it works...

The structure of our application is recursive. We created a `taxon` component that is a `<li>` element. This element, in turn, contains another, `<ul>`, unordered list, of which the list items are taxon element themselves.

Since the first list item must be inside a list, we wrote the root of our tree manually:

```
<div id="app">
  <ul>
    <taxon :tree="living" taxon="living"></taxon>
  </ul>
</div>
```

The resulting rendered HTML, if you take a sneak peek at the browser, is like this:

```
▼<div id="app">
  ▼<ul> == $0
    ▼<li>
      ▼<div>
          "living"
          <span>[-]</span>
        </div>
      ▼<ul>
        ▼<li>
          ▼<div>
              "animals"
              <span>[-]</span>
            </div>
          ▼<ul>
            ►<li>...</li>
            ►<li>...</li>
            </ul>
          </li>
        ►<li>...</li>
        </ul>
      </li>
    </ul>
  </div>
```

In the Vue dev tools, you will find this structure:

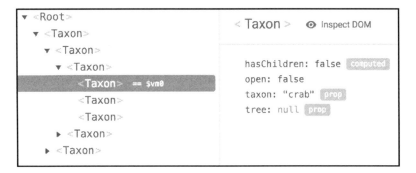

Recursive component and local registration

In our recipe, we registered the component globally. This assigns a name to the component by default. Had we registered our component locally, our application would not work. If you register your component locally, you need to manually supply a name, as in the following highlighted line of code:

```
var taxon = {
  name: 'taxon',
  template: `
  <li>
...
```

You can then register the component normally:

```
new Vue({
  el: '#app',
  components: { taxon },
...
```

If you forget to give the name to the recursive component, Vue will complain with the following error:

```
vue.js:2658 [Vue warn]: Unknown custom element: <taxon> - did you register
the component correctly? For recursive components, make sure to provide the
"name" option.
(found in component <taxon>)
```

Avoiding a stack overflows!

In our recipe, we used `v-for` to ensure that if there are no more taxa present, the taxon component will not even render. You should ensure, using `v-if` or `v-for`, that there is an end to your recursion. However, just for fun, you should make Vue explode at least once in your life.

Write the following component:

```
Vue.component('matrioska', {
  template: '<p>Hello<matrioska></matrioska></p>'
})
```

Then, put it in your Vue instance HTML:

```
<div id="app">
  <matrioska></matrioska>
</div>
```

You should receive the satisfying message from Vue:

```
vue.js:2269 Uncaught RangeError: Maximum call stack size exceeded
```

Reusable component checklist

If you are building a component for others to use, there are certain principles that apply, such as high cohesion. In this recipe, you will build a toy component that will illustrate some principles of re-usability.

Getting ready

This recipe is a wrap up of good engineering techniques for building a component. It does not require specific skills but assumes that you already know a thing or two about components.

How to do it...

You will build a generic dialog box. Write the empty component first:

```
Vue.component('dialog-box', {})
```

The template will contain a slot for the icon, another slot for the message, and an optional cancel button:

```
template: `
<div>
  <div class="icon">
    <slot name="icon"></slot>
  </div>
  <slot name="message"></slot>
  <div class="buttons">
    <button v-if="cancellable"
            @click="cancel()">
      Cancel
    </button>
    <button @click="ok()">
      OK
    </button>
  </div>
</div>`
```

This way, any user of the dialog box can customize it with the content he wants and can also decide whether the Cancel button is really necessary.

The props are then cancellable and command. The latter is a string which we'll return to the user to identify the dialog box:

```
props: {
  command: String,
  cancellable: Boolean
}
```

The cancel and ok methods don't have a fixed function but, in order for the component to be reusable, have to let the user decide what to do. We will, instead, launch generic events:

```
methods: {
  cancel () {
    this.$emit('cancel', this.command)
  },
  ok () {
    this.$emit('ok', this.command)
  }
}
```

Now for the juicy part. How is the client supposed to use this component of ours? Here's the HTML of the Vue instance that uses our component:

```
<div id="app">
  <dialog-box
    command="confirmation"
    :cancellable="true"
    @cancel="msg = 'cancelled'"
    @ok="msg = 'confirmed'">
      <span slot="icon">⚠</span>
      <span slot="message">Do you confirm?</span>
  </dialog-box>
  <p>Output: {{msg}}</p>
</div>
```

We also put an output mustache that will print the content of `msg`, a variable that we declare on the Vue instance JavaScript:

```
new Vue({
  el: '#app',
  data: {
    msg: 'undefined'
  }
})
```

Launch the application to see your dialog box take shape:

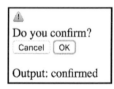

How it works...

When you build a component that you want to reuse or you want others to reuse, you will have some parts that behave in a generic way. In our box, for example, the message was customizable, so we can reuse it in other parts of a program with different messages. We used a slot so that the user has complete freedom on what to put inside (even another component). The cancel button, instead, is better controlled by props, so we do not have to pass an entire button into a slot every time, we just pass true or false.

Another concern is that our component needs to talk with the external world; in the confirmation box case, it needs to tell the main program whether the user clicked on **OK** or **Cancel**. This is best done through events. In our parent template, we specified, directly in the HTML, what should happen when the `cancel` or `ok` events are received. This way of passing data is very versatile because we can forward these events to other components or even convert them into mutations for a Vuex store.

I'll quote the documentation to summarize what we said so that you can have a proper checklist when you are in doubt:

- **Props**: They allow the external environment to pass data into the component
- **Events**: They allow the component to trigger side effects in the external environment
- **Slots**: They allow the external environment to compose the component with extra content

5
Vue Communicates with the Internet

In this chapter, the following recipes will be covered:

- Sending basic AJAX request with Axios
- Validating user data before sending it
- Creating a form and sending data to your server
- Recovering from an error during a request
- Creating a REST client (and server!)
- Implementing infinite scrolling
- Processing a request before sending it out
- Preventing XSS attacks to your app

Introduction

Web applications rarely work all by themselves. What makes them interesting is actually the fact that they enable us to communicate with the world in innovative ways that didn't exist just a few years ago.

Vue, by itself, doesn't contain any mechanism or library to make AJAX requests or open web sockets. In this chapter, we will, therefore, explore how Vue interacts with built-in mechanisms and external libraries to connect to external services.

You will start by making basic AJAX requests with the help of an external library. Then, you'll explore some common patterns with sending and getting data in forms. Finally, there are some recipes with real-world applications and how to build a RESTful client.

Sending basic AJAX requests with Axios

Axios is the recommended library for Vue for making HTTP requests. It's a very simple library, but it has some built-in features that help you in carrying out common operations. It implements a REST pattern for making requests with HTTP verbs and can also deal with concurrency (spawning multiple requests at the same time) in a function call. You can find more information at `https://github.com/mzabriskie/axios`.

Getting ready

For this recipe, you don't need any particular knowledge of Vue. We will use Axios, which itself uses **JavaScript promises**. If you have never heard of promises, you can have a primer at `https://developers.google.com/web/fundamentals/getting-started/primers/promises`.

How to do it...

You will build a simple application that gives you a wise piece of advice every time you visit the web page.

The first thing you will need is to install Axios in your application. If you are using npm, you can just issue the following command:

```
npm install axios
```

If you are working on a single page, you can import the following file from CDN, at `https://unpkg.com/axios/dist/axios.js`.

 Unfortunately, the advise slip service we will use will not work with JSFiddle because while the service runs on HTTP, JSFiddle is on HTTPS and your browser will most likely complain. You can run this recipe on a local HTML file.

Our HTML looks like this:

```
<div id="app">
  <h2>Advice of the day</h2>
  <p>{{advice}}</p>
</div>
```

Our Vue instance is as follows:

```
new Vue({
  el: '#app',
  data: {
    advice: 'loading...'
  },
  created () {
    axios.get('http://api.adviceslip.com/advice')
      .then(response => {
        this.advice = response.data.slip.advice
      })
      .catch(error => {
        this.advice = 'There was an error: ' + error.message
      })
  }
})
```

Open your app to have a refreshingly wise slip of advice:

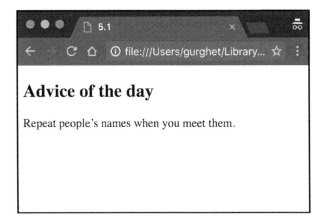

How it works...

When our application starts up, the created hook is engaged and will run the code with Axios. The first line performs a GET request to the API endpoint:

```
axios.get('http://api.adviceslip.com/advice')
```

This will return a promise. We can use the `then` method on any promise to act on the result if the promise resolves successfully:

```
.then(response => {
  this.advice = response.data.slip.advice
})
```

The response object will contain some data about the result of our request. A possible response object is the following:

```
{
  "data": {
    "slip": {
      "advice": "Repeat people's name when you meet them.",
      "slip_id": "132"
    }
  },
  "status": 200,
  "statusText": "OK",
  "headers": {
    "content-type": "text/html; charset=UTF-8",
    "cache-control": "max-age=0, no-cache"
  },
  "config": {
    "transformRequest": {},
    "transformResponse": {},
    "timeout": 0,
    "xsrfCookieName": "XSRF-TOKEN",
    "xsrfHeaderName": "X-XSRF-TOKEN",
    "maxContentLength": -1,
    "headers": {
      "Accept": "application/json, text/plain, */*"
    },
    "method": "get",
    "url": "http://api.adviceslip.com/advice"
  },
  "request": {}
}
```

We navigate to the property we want to interact with; in our case, we want `response.data.slip.advice`, which is the string. We copied the string in the variable advice in the instance state.

The last part is when something wrong happens to our request or to our code inside the first branch:

```
.catch(error => {
  this.advice = 'There was an error: ' + error.message
})
```

We will explore error handling more in depth in the *Recovering from an error during a request* recipe. For now, let's trigger an error by hand, just to see what happens.

The cheapest way to trigger an error is to run the app on JSFiddle. Since the browser detects JSFiddle on a secure connection and our API is on HTTP (which is not secure), modern browsers will complain and will block the connection. You should see the following text:

```
There was an error: Network Error
```

This is just one of the many possible errors you can experiment with. Consider that you edit the GET endpoint to some non-existent page:

```
axios.get('http://api.adviceslip.com/non-existent-page')
```

In this case, you will get a 404 error:

```
There was an error: Request failed with status code 404
```

Interestingly, you will end up in the error branch even if the request goes well but there is an error in the first branch.

Change the `then` branch to this:

```
.then(response => {
  this.advice = undefined.hello
})
```

As everybody knows, JavaScript cannot read "hello" property of an undefined object:

```
There was an error: Cannot read property 'hello' of undefined
```

It's just as I told you.

Validating user data before sending it

Generally, users hate forms. While we can't do much to change that, we can make it less frustrating for them by providing relevant instructions on how to fill them in. In this recipe, we will create a form, and we will leverage HTML standards to provide the user with a nice guidance on how to complete it.

Getting ready

This recipe does not need previous knowledge to be completed. While we will build a form (the *Sending basic AJAX requests with Axios* recipe), we will fake the AJAX call and concentrate on the validation.

How to do it...

We will build a very simple form: one field for the username and one for the user e-mail, plus one button to submit the information.

Type in this HTML:

```
<div id="app">
  <form @submit.prevent="vueSubmit">
    <div>
      <label>Name</label>
      <input type="text" required>
    </div>
    <div>
      <label>Email</label>
      <input type="email" required>
    </div>
    <div>
      <label>Submit</label>
      <button type="submit">Submit</button>
    </div>
  </form>
</div>
```

The Vue instance is trivial, as shown:

```
new Vue({
  el: '#app',
  methods: {
    vueSubmit() {
```

```
            console.info('fake AJAX request')
        }
    }
})
```

Run this app and try to submit the form with an empty field or wrong e-mail. You should see help from the browser itself:

Then, if you try to enter an invalid e-mail address, you will see the following:

How it works...

We are using a native HTML5 validation API, which internally uses pattern matching to check whether what we are typing is conformant to certain rules.

Consider the attribute required in the following line:

```
<input type="text" required>
```

This ensures that when we submit the form, the field is actually populated, while having `type="email"` in the other input element ensures that the content resembles an e-mail format.

This API is very rich and you can read more at
https://developer.mozilla.org/en-US/docs/Web/Guide/HTML/Forms/Data_form_validation.

Many a times, the problem is that to leverage this API, we need to trigger the native validation mechanism. This means that we are not allowed to prevent the default behavior of the **Submit** button:

```
<button type="submit" @click.prevent="vueSubmit">Submit</button>
```

This will not trigger the native validation and the form will always be submitted. On the other hand, if we do the following:

```
<button type="submit" @click="vueSubmit">Submit</button>
```

The form will get validated but, since we are not preventing the default behavior of the submit button, the form will be sent to another page, which will destroy the one page application experience.

The trick is to intercept the submit at form level:

```
<form @submit.prevent="vueSubmit">
```

This way, we can have form native validation and all the modern browsing experience we really like.

Creating a form and sending data to your server

HTML forms are a standard way to interact with your user. You can gather their data to register within the site, make them log in, or even carry out more advanced interactions. In this recipe, you will build your first form with Vue.

Getting ready

This recipe is very easy, but it assumes that you already know about AJAX and you want to apply your knowledge on Vue.

How to do it...

Let's pretend that we have a blog, and we want to write a new post. For that, we need a form. Here is how you lay out the HTML:

```
<div id="app">
```

```
<h3>Write a new post</h3>
<form>
  <div>
    <label>Title of your post:</label>
    <input type="text" v-model="title">
  </div>
  <div>
    <label>Write your thoughts for the day</label>
    <textarea v-model="body"></textarea>
  </div>
  <div>
    <button @click.prevent="submit">Submit</button>
  </div>
</form>
</div>
```

We have a box for the title, one for the body of our new post, and a button to send our post.

In our Vue instance, those three things along with a user ID will be part of the state of the app:

```
new Vue({
  el: '#app',
  data: {
    userId: 1,
    title: '',
    body: ''
  }
})
```

At this point, we just need to add a method to send the data to our server when we click on the **Submit** button. Since we don't have a server, we will use a very useful service by **Typicode.** It's basically a fake REST server. We will send a request and the server will respond in a realistic manner, even if nothing will really happen.

Here's our method:

```
methods: {
  submit () {
    const xhr = new XMLHttpRequest()
    xhr.open('post', 'https://jsonplaceholder.typicode.com/posts')
    xhr.setRequestHeader('Content-Type',
                         'application/json;charset=UTF-8')
    xhr.onreadystatechange = () => {
    const DONE = 4
    const CREATED = 201
    if (xhr.readyState === DONE) {
      if (xhr.status === CREATED) {
```

```
            this.response = xhr.response
        } else {
            this.response = 'Error: ' + xhr.status
        }
    }
}
xhr.send(JSON.stringify({
    title: this.title,
    body: this.body,
    userId: this.userId
}))
    }
}
```

To see the actual response of the server, we will add the response variable to our status:

```
data: {
    userId: 1,
    title: '',
    body: '',
    response: '...'
}
```

After the form in our HTML, add the following:

```
<h3>Response from the server</h3>
<pre>{{response}}</pre>
```

When you launch your page, you should be able to interact with your server. When you write a post, the server will echo the post and answer with the post ID:

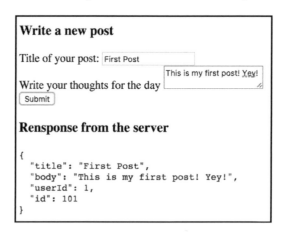

How it works...

Most of the magic happens in the `submit` method. In the first line, we are creating an `XMLHttpRequest` object, which is a native JavaScript mechanism to make AJAX requests:

```
const xhr = new XMLHttpRequest()
```

We then use the `open` and `setRequestHeader` methods to configure a new connection; we want to send a POST request, and we will send some JSON along with it:

```
xhr.open('post', 'http://jsonplaceholder.typicode.com/posts')
xhr.setRequestHeader('Content-Type', 'application/json;charset=UTF-8')
```

Since we are interacting with a RESTful interface, the POST method means that we expect our request to modify data on the server (in particular, create a new post), and that issuing the same request more than one time will get different results every time (namely we will create a new, different post ID each time).

This is different from the more common GET request that will not modify data on the server (except logs maybe) and this will always yield the same results (provided that data on the server does not change between requests).

For more details about REST, take a look at the *Creating a REST client (and server!)* recipe.

The following lines are all about the response:

```
xhr.onreadystatechange = () => {
  const DONE = 4
  const CREATED = 201
  if (xhr.readyState === DONE) {
    if (xhr.status === CREATED) {
      this.response = xhr.response
    } else {
      this.response = 'Error: ' + xhr.status
    }
  }
}
```

This will install a handler whenever we get some kind of change in our object. If the `readyState` is changed to `DONE` it means, that we have our response from the server. Next, we check the status code, which should be `201` to signal that a new resource (our new post) has been created. If that is the case, we set the variable we put in the mustaches to get a quick feedback. Otherwise, we put the error message we received in the same variable.

The last thing we need to do, after setting up the event handlers, is to actually send the request along with the data of our new post:

```
xhr.send(JSON.stringify({
  title: this.title,
  body: this.body,
  userId: this.userId
}))
```

There's more...

Another way to approach the same problem is to use Axios for sending the AJAX request. If you need to brush up on what Axios is, take a look at the *Sending basic AJAX requests with Axios* recipe.

The code for the `submit` method will become as follows (remember to add Axios as a dependency):

```
submit () {
  axios.post('http://jsonplaceholder.typicode.com/posts', {
    title: this.title,
    body: this.body,
    userId: this.userId
  }).then(response => {
    this.response = JSON.stringify(response,null,'  ')
  }).catch(error => {
    this.response = 'Error: ' + error.response.status
  })
}
```

This code is perfectly equivalent, but it's much more expressive and concise than using native browser objects.

Recovering from an error during a request

Requests to an external service take ages from the perspective of a computer. In human terms, it would be like sending a satellite to Jupiter and waiting for it to come back to Earth. You can't be 100% sure that the travel will ever be complete and how much time will the travel actually take. Networks are notoriously flacky and it's better to come prepared in case our request does not complete successfully.

Getting ready

This recipe is a little complex, but, does not use advanced concepts. You are expected, nonetheless, to be familiar with using Vue.

We will be using Axios for this recipe. You can complete the *Sending basic AJAX requests with Axios* recipe if you are unsure of what it exactly entails.

How to do it...

You will build a website for ordering pizzas on Mt. Everest. The area has notoriously poor Internet connection, so we may want to retry a couple of times before giving up on our pizza.

This is what our HTML looks like:

```
<div id="app">
  <h3>Everest pizza delivery</h3>
  <button @click="order"
          :disabled="inProgress">Order pizza!</button>
  <span class="spinner" v-show="inProgress">🍕</span>
  <h4>Pizza wanted</h4>
  <p>{{requests}}</p>
  <h4>Pizzas ordered</h4>
  <span v-for="pizza in responses">
    {{pizza.id}}:{{pizza.req}}
  </span>
</div>
```

We have a button to place orders that will be disabled while an order is in progress--a list of orders in progress (that will contain only one order for the moment) and a list of pizzas already ordered.

We can add a spinner to make the waiting a bit more pleasant. Add this CSS to make the little pizza spin:

```
@keyframes spin {
  100% {transform:rotate(360deg);}
}
.spinner {
  width: 1em;
  height: 1em;
  padding-bottom: 12px;
  display: inline-block;
  animation: spin 2s linear infinite;
```

```
}
```

Our Vue instance will keep track of a few things; write this code to start building the instance:

```
new Vue({
  el: '#app',
  data: {
    inProgress: false,
    requests: new Object(null),
    responses: new Object(null),
    counter: 0,
    impatientAxios: undefined
  }
})
```

I would like to use JavaScript sets for the requests and responses; unfortunately, sets are not reactive in Vue; the closest thing we can use is an object, which is empty for now, that is, we are initializing requests and responses to an empty object.

The `impatientAxios` variable will be filled upon creation. Normally, Axios waits as long as the browser will wait for a response. Since we are impatient, we will create an Axios that will drop the connection after 3 seconds:

```
created () {
  this.impatientAxios = axios.create({
    timeout: 3000
  })
}
```

The last thing we need to build is the order method. Since we don't have a web server to make actual requests to, we will use the `http://httpstat.us/200` endpoint that simply answers **200 OK** to all our requests:

```
methods: {
  order (event, oldRequest) {
    let request = undefined
    if (oldRequest) {
      request = oldRequest
    } else {
      request = { req: '🍕', id: this.counter++}
    }
    this.inProgress = true
    this.requests[request.id] = request
    this.impatientAxios.get('http://httpstat.us/200')
      .then(response => {
        this.inProgress = false
```

```
      this.responses[request.id] = this.requests[request.id]
      delete this.requests[request.id]
    })
    .catch(e => {
      this.inProgress = false
      console.error(e.message)
      console.error(this.requests.s)
      setTimeout(this.order(event, request), 1000)
    })
}
```

To run this program as intended, open it in Chrome and open the **Developer Tools** with
Cmd + Opt + I (*F12* on Windows):

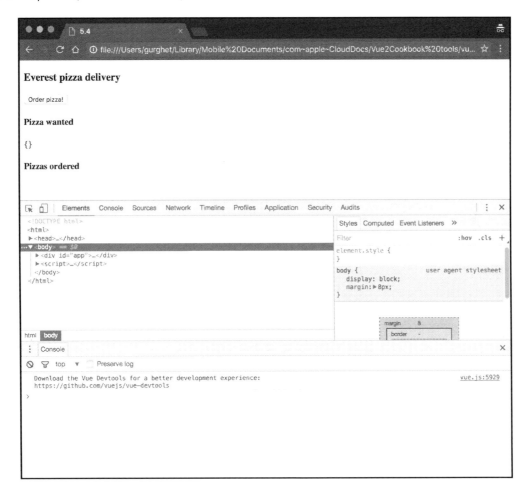

Switch the tab to **Network** and open the dropdown where you see **No Throttling**:

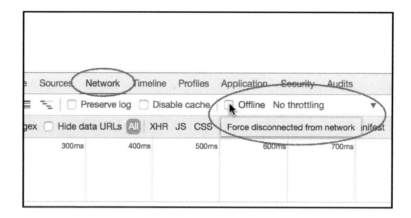

Click on it to display the drop-down menu:

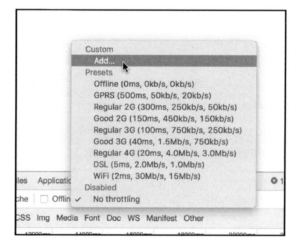

Add a new custom throttling called `Everest` with `1kb/s` for download and upload and a latency of `1,000` milliseconds, as in the following screenshot:

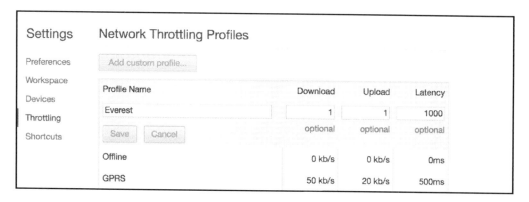

You can then select that type of throttling and try to order some pizzas. If you are lucky, you should eventually be able to order some, thanks to the persistency of Axios.

If you are not getting success or if all your pizzas are ordered correctly, try to adjust the parameters; much of this process is actually random and highly dependent on the machine.

How it works...

There are many ways to deal with flacky connections and there are many libraries out there that integrate with Axios and have more advanced retry and reattempt strategies. Here, we have seen only one basic strategy, but libraries such as **Patience JS** have more advanced ones and they are not difficult to use.

Creating a REST client (and server!)

In this recipe, we will learn about REST and how to build a REST client. To build a REST client, we will need a server that exposes a REST interface; we will build that also. Wait a minute! A whole REST server is a side note in a recipe in a book about Vue? Just follow along and you won't be disappointed.

Getting ready

This recipe is fairly advanced in the sense that you will need to be comfortable with the architecture of client and server and at least have heard or read about REST interfaces. You will also need to be familiar with the command line and have npm installed. You can read all about it in the *Choosing a development environment* recipe.

Axios will also need to be installed; read more about this in the first recipe of this chapter.

How to do it...

I remember when some years ago, building a REST server could take days or weeks. You can use `Feather.js`, and it will be quick and (hopefully painless). Open a command line and install it through npm with the following command:

```
npm install -g feathers-cli
```

After that, create a directory where you will run the server, go inside it, and launch Feathers:

```
mkdir my-server
cd my-server
feathers generate app
```

Answer all the questions with default values. When the process finishes, type in the following command to create a new resource:

```
feathers generate service
```

One of the questions is the name of the resource; call it `messages`, but other than that, use the default for all the other questions.

Exit from the feathers-cli with the `exit` command and start your new server with the following command:

```
npm start
```

After some seconds, your REST server should be started and should be listening on port `3030`. Can you honestly say it was difficult?

The preceding sequence of commands works with Feathers version 2.0.0 It's totally possible that you may be using another version but it should still be easy to get the same result with a later version; check the online install guide at `https://feathersjs.com/`.

Next, you'll build a Vue app that communicates with the server seamlessly. Now, since the server is running in your local environment through HTTP, you will not be able to use JSFiddle because it works on HTTPS and considers HTTP insecure. You can either use other methods described earlier or use services on HTTP, such as `codepen.io` or others.

You will code an app that manages sticky messages. We want to be able to view, add, edit, and delete them.

Type the following in this HTML:

```
<div id="app">
  <h3>Sticky messages</h3>
  <ol>
    <li v-for="message in messages">
      <button @click="deleteItem(message._id)">Delete</button>
      <button @click="edit(message._id, message.text)">
        edit
      </button>
      <input v-model="message.text">
    </li>
  </ol>
  <input v-model="toAdd">
  <button @click="add">add</button>
</div>
```

Our Vue instance state will consist of a list of recorded messages, plus a temporary message to be added to the list:

```
new Vue({
  el: '#app',
  data: {
    messages: [],
    toAdd: ''
  },
})
```

The first thing that we want to do is ask the server for a list of messages. Write the created hook for this:

```
created () {
  axios.get('http://localhost:3030/messages/')
    .then(response => {
      this.messages = response.data.data
    })
},
```

For creating a new message, write a method that binds to the click of the add button and send what's written in the input box to the server:

```
methods: {
  add () {
    axios.post('http://localhost:3030/messages/', {
      text: this.toAdd
    })
      .then(response => {
        if (response.status === 201) {
          this.messages.push(response.data)
          this.toAdd = ''
        }
      })
  }
}
```

Similarly, write a method for deleting a message and for editing a message:

```
deleteItem (id) {
  console.log('delete')
  axios.delete('http://localhost:3030/messages/' + id)
    .then(response => {
      if (response.status < 400) {
        this.messages.splice(
          this.messages.findIndex(e => e.id === id), 1)
      }
    })
},
edit (id, text) {
  axios.put('http://localhost:3030/messages/' + id, {
    text
  })
    .then(response => {
      if (response.status < 400) {
        console.info(response.status)
      }
    })
}
```

Launch your application and you will be able to manage your board of sticky messages:

To prove to yourself that you are really communicating with the server, you can refresh the page or close and reopen the browser and your notes will still be there.

How it works...

REST means **REpresentational State Transfer**, as in you will transfer a representation of the state of some resource. In practice, we are using a set of **verbs** to transfer the representation of the state of our messages.

Using the HTTP protocol, we have at our disposal the following verbs:

Verb	Properties	Description
GET	Idempotent, safe	Used to retrieve the representation of a resource
POST		Used to upload a new resource
PUT	Idempotent	Used to upload an existing resource (to modify it)
DELETE	Idempotent	Used to delete a resource

Idempotent means that if we use the same verb twice, nothing will happen to the resource, and safe means that nothing will happen at all.

In our application, we use the GET verb only at the beginning during creation. When we see the list changing as a result of the other actions, it is only because we are mirroring the actions on the server on the frontend.

The POST verb is used to add a new message to the list. Note how it's not idempotent, as even with the same text in the sticky message, we nonetheless create a new message that differs in ID when pressing the **add** button.

Pressing the **edit** button triggers a PUT and the **Delete** button, well, you can imagine that it uses the DELETE verb.

Axios makes this very clear by naming the methods of its API with the verbs themselves.

Implementing infinite scrolling

Infinite scrolling is a fine example of what you can do with Vue and AJAX. It is also quite popular and can improve interaction for some kind of content. You will build a random word generator that works with infinite scrolling.

Getting ready

We will use Axios. Take a look at the *Sending basic AJAX requests with Axios* recipe to know how to install it and its basic functionality. Other than that, you don't need to know much to follow along.

How to do it...

To make our app work, we will ask random words from the `http://www.setgetgo.com/ra ndomword/get.php` endpoint. Every time you point the browser at this address, you will get a random word.

The whole page will consist solely of an infinite list of words. Write the following HTML:

```
<div id="app">
  <p v-for="word in words">{{word}}</p>
</div>
```

The list of words needs to grow as we scroll down. So we need two things: understanding when the user reaches the bottom of the page, and getting new words.

To know when the user has reached the bottom of the page, we add a method in our Vue instance:

```
new Vue({
  el: '#app',
  methods: {
    bottomVisible () {
      const visibleHeight = document.documentElement.clientHeight
      const pageHeight = document.documentElement.scrollHeight
      const scrolled = window.scrollY
      const reachedBottom = visibleHeight + scrolled >= pageHeight
      return reachedBottom || pageHeight < visibleHeight
    }
  }
})
```

This will return true if either the page is scrolled until the bottom or the page itself is smaller than the browser.

Next, we need to add a mechanism to bind the result of this function to a state variable bottom and update it every time the user scrolls the page. We can do that in the created hook:

```
created () {
  window.addEventListener('scroll', () => {
    this.bottom = this.bottomVisible()
  })
}
```

The state will be composed of the bottom variable and the list of random words:

```
data: {
  bottom: false,
  words: []
}
```

We now need a method to add words to the array. Add the following method to the existing method:

```
addWord () {
  axios.get('http://www.setgetgo.com/randomword/get.php')
    .then(response => {
      this.words.push(response.data)
      if (this.bottomVisible()) {
        this.addWord()
      }
    })
}
```

The method will recursively call itself until the page has enough words to fill the whole browser view.

Since this method needs to be called every time we reach the bottom, we will watch for the bottom variable and fire the method if it's `true`. Add the following option to the Vue instance just after the data:

```
watch: {
  bottom (bottom) {
    if (bottom) {
      this.addWord()
    }
  }
}
```

We also need to call the `addWord` method in the created hook to kick-start the page:

```
created () {
  window.addEventListener('scroll', () => {
    this.bottom = this.bottomVisible()
  })
  this.addWord()
}
```

If you launch the page now, you will have an infinite stream of random words, which is useful when you need to create a new password!

How it works...

In this recipe, we used an option called `watch`, which uses the following syntax:

```
watch: {
  'name of sate variable' (newValue, oldValue) {
    ...
  }
}
```

This is the counterpart of computed properties when we are not interested in a result after some reactive variable changes. As a matter of fact, we used it to just fire another method. Had we been interested in the result of some calculations, we would have used a computed property.

Processing a request before sending it out

This recipe teaches you how to use interceptors to edit your request before it goes out to the Internet. This can be useful in some cases, such as when you need to supply an authorization token along with all the requests to your server or when you need a single point to edit how your API calls are performed.

Getting ready

This recipe uses Axios (the *Sending basic AJAX requests with Axios* recipe); apart from that, it will be useful to have completed the *How to validate user data before sending it* recipe since we will build a small form for demonstration.

How to do it...

In this recipe, you will build a filter for curse words for a hypothetical comment system. Suppose there's an article on our website that can potentially start a flame war:

```
<div id="app">
  <h3>Who's better: Socrates or Plato?</h3>
  <p>Technically, without Plato we wouldn't have<br>
  much to go on when it comes to information about<br>
  Socrates. Plato ftw!</p>
```

After that article, we place a comment box:

```
<form>
  <label>Write your comment:</label>
  <textarea v-model="message"></textarea>
  <button @click.prevent="submit">Send!</button>
</form>
<p>Server got: {{response}}</p>
</div>
```

We also added a line after the form to debug the response that we will get from the server.

In our Vue instance, we write all the support code to send the comment to our server, which, in this case, will be `http://jsonplaceholder.typicode.com/comments`, a fake REST interface that will behave like a real server.

Here's the submit method that is triggered on the press of the **Submit** button:

```
methods: {
  submit () {
    axios.post('http://jsonplaceholder.typicode.com/comments',
    {
      body: this.message
    }).then(response => {
      this.response = response.data
    })
  }
}
```

The state of the Vue instance will only be two variables:

```
data: {
  message: '',
  response: '...'
}
```

As usual, we want to mount it to the `<div>` app:

```
new Vue({
  el: '#app',
  ...
```

As soon as the instance is mounted, we want to install the word filter in Axios; for this, we tap into the `mounted` hook of Vue:

```
mounted () {
  axios.interceptors.request.use(config => {
    const body = config.data.body.replace(/punk/i, '***')
    config.data.body = body
    return config
  })
}
```

We can launch our application now and try to write our salty comment:

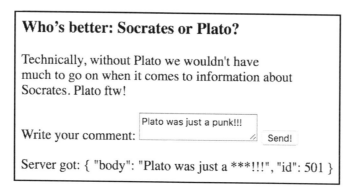

How it works...

In the `mounted` hook, we are installing a so called `interceptor`. In particular, it is a request interceptor, which means it will take our request and manipulate it before sending it out to the Internet:

```
axios.interceptors.request.use(config => {
  const body = config.data.body.replace(/punk/i, '***')
  config.data.body = body
  return config
})
```

The `config` object contains a lot of things we can edit. It contains the headers and URL parameters. It also contains Axios configuration variables. You can check out the Axios documentation for an up-to-date list.

We are taking what's inside the data part that got sent along with the POST request and sniffing if the `punk` word is found. If that is the case, it will get substituted with asterisks. The returned object will be the new config for the current request.

Preventing XSS attacks to your app

Writing applications without thinking about security will inevitably lead to vulnerabilities, especially if it has to run on a web server. **Cross site scripting** (**XSS**) is among the most popular security issues nowadays; even if you are not a security expert, you should be aware of how it works and how to prevent it in a Vue application.

Getting ready

This recipe does not need any previous knowledge except for Axios. You can find more on Axios and how to install it in the *Sending basic AJAX requests with Axios* recipe.

How to do it...

The first thing you should do is to discover how your backend is giving you the CSRF token (more on this in the next paragraph). We will suppose that the server will place a cookie in your browser with the name, XSRF-TOKEN.

You can simulate your server, setting a cookie with the `document.cookie = 'XSRF-TOKEN=abc123'` command issued in the browser console (in the developer tools).

Axios automatically reads such a cookie and transmits it in the next request.

Consider that we call an Axios `get` request in our code, as follows:

```
methods: {
  sendAllMoney () {
    axios.get('/sendTo/'+this.accountNo)
  }
}
```

Axios will pick up that cookie and add a new header to the request called **X-XSRF-TOKEN**. You can see such headers in the **Network** tab of the **Developer Tools** in Chrome by clicking on the name of the request:

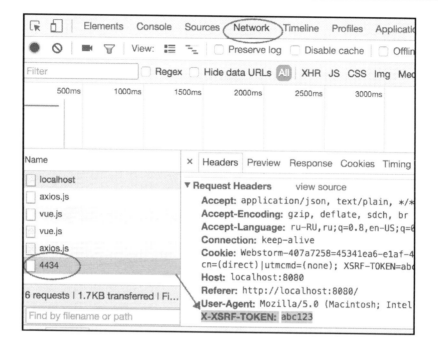

How it works...

To prevent XSS attacks, you must ensure that no user input can appear as code in your app. This means you must be very careful about using the `v-html` attribute (the *Output raw HTML* recipe).

Unfortunately, you can't control what happens outside your page. If one of your users receives a fake e-mail that contains a link that corresponds to an action in your application, clicking on the link in the e-mail will trigger the action.

Let's make a concrete example; you developed a bank app, *VueBank*, and a user of your app receives the following fake e-mail:

```
Hello user!
Click here to read the latest news.
```

As you can see, the mail is not even about our application and the `here` hyperlink is hidden in the HTML of the mail itself. In reality, it points to the `http://vuebank.com?give_all_my_money_to_account=754839534` address.

If we are logged in to VueBank, the link may work right away. It does not look good for our finances.

To prevent these kinds of attacks, we should have our backend generate a **CSRF (Cross Site Request Forgery)** token for us. We will take the token and send it along the request to prove that the request originated from the user. The preceding link will become

`http://vuebank.com?give_all_my_money_to_account=754839534&csrf=s83Rnj.`

Since the token is generated randomly every time, the link in the mail cannot be forged correctly because the attacker does not know the token that the server gave to the web page.

In Vue, we use Axios to send the token. Usually, we won't send it as part of the link, but in a header of the request; in fact, Axios does this for us and puts in the token in the next request automatically.

You can change the name of the cookie that Axios will pick up by setting the `axios.defaults.xsrfCookieName` variable, and you can edit the name of the header that will return the token acting on the `axios.defaults.xsrfHeaderName` variable.

6
Single Page Applications

In this chapter, the following recipes will be covered:

- Creating an SPA with vue-router
- Fetching data before switching route
- Using named dynamic routes
- Having more than one router-view in your page
- Composing your routes hierarchically
- Using route aliases
- Adding transitions between your routes
- Managing errors for your routes
- Adding a progress bar to load pages
- How to redirect to another route
- Saving scrolling position when hitting back

Introduction

Many modern applications are based on the **SPA** or **Single Page Application** model. From the users perspective, this means that the whole website looks similar to an application in a single page.

This is good because, if done correctly, it enhances the user experience, mainly reducing waiting times, because there are no new pages to load--the whole website is on a single page. This is how Facebook, Medium, Google, and many other websites work.

URLs don't point to HTML pages anymore, but to particular states of your application (that most often look like different pages). In practice, on a server, assuming that your application is inside the `index.html` page, this is implemented by redirecting the user that is requesting ,say, about me to `index.html`.

The latter page will take the suffix of the URL and will interpret it as a **route**, which in turn will create a page-like component with biographical information.

Creating an SPA with vue-router

Vue.js implements the SPA pattern through its core plugin, vue-router. To vue-router, every route URL corresponds to a component. This means that we will tell vue-router how to behave when the user goes to a particular URL in terms of its component. In other words, every component in this new system is a page in the old system.

Getting ready

For this recipe, you will only need to install vue-router and have some knowledge about Vue components.

To install vue-router, follow the instructions at `https://router.vuejs.org/en/installation.html`.

If you are using JSFiddle to follow along, you can add a link similar to `https://unpkg.com/vue-router/dist/vue-router.js`.

How to do it...

We are preparing a modern website for a restaurant and we will use the SPA pattern.

The website will consist of three pages: a home page, the restaurant menu, and the bar menu.

The whole HTML code will be like this:

```
<div id="app">
  <h1>Choppy's Restaurant</h1>
  <ul>
    <li>Home</li>
    <li>Menu</li>
```

```
    <li>Bar</li>
  </ul>
  <router-view></router-view>
</div>
```

The `<router-view>` component is the entry point for vue-router. It's where the components are displayed as pages.

The list elements will become the link. For now, they are only list elements; to turn them into links, we can use two different syntaxes. Wrap the first link as in the following line:

```
<li><router-link to="/">Home</router-link></li>
```

Another example is as follows:

```
<li><router-link to="/menu">Menu</router-link></li>
```

Another syntax we can use is the following (for the **Bar** link):

```
<li>
  <router-link
    tag="li" to="/bar"
      :event="['mousedown', 'touchstart']"
  >
    <a>Bar</a>
  </router-link>
</li>
```

This, more verbose but more explicit, syntax can be used to bind a custom event to a particular routing.

To instruct Vue that we want to use the vue-router plugin, write the following in the JavaScript:

```
Vue.use(VueRouter)
```

The part of three pages we listed at the beginning will be played by these three dummy components (add them to the JavaScript):

```
const Home = { template: '<div>Welcome to Choppy's</div>' }
const Menu = { template: '<div>Today we have cookies</div>' }
const Bar = { template: '<div>We serve cocktails</div>' }
```

Now, you can finally create the router. The code for it is as follows:

```
const router = new VueRouter({})
```

This router doesn't do much; we have to add routes (which correspond to URLs) and their associated components:

```
const router = new VueRouter({
  routes: [
    { path: '/', component: Home },
    { path: '/menu', component: Menu },
    { path: '/bar', component: Bar }
  ]
})
```

Now our application is almost complete; we only need to declare a simple Vue instance:

```
new Vue({
  router,
  el: '#app'
})
```

Our application will now work; before launching it, add this CSS rule to have slightly better feedback:

```
a.router-link-active, li.router-link-active>a {
  background-color: gainsboro;
}
```

When you open your app and click on the **Bar** link, you should see something similar to the following screenshot:

How it works...

The first thing your program does is to register vue-router as a plugin. The vue-router, in turn, registers the routes (which are parts of URLs) and connects components to each of them.

When we visit the application for the first time, the URL on the browser (you won't be able to see it changing inside JSFiddle because it is inside an iframe) will end with `index.html/#/`. Everything after the hash symbol is a route for the vue-router. In this case, it is only a slash (/) and so it matches the first home route.

When we click on the links, the content of the `<router-view>` changes according to the component we associated with that route.

There's more...

The astute reader will certainly find what can be interpreted as a bug--we added a couple of CSS styles before running the application. The `.router-link-active` class is automatically injected in the `<router-link>` component whenever the page corresponds to the link actually pointed to.

When we click on **Menu** and **Bar**, the background color changes but it seems that it remains stuck to be selected for the **Home** link. This is because the matching performed by the `<router-link>` component is not **exact**. In other words, `/bar` and `/menu` contain the `/` string and, for this reason, `/` is always matched.

A quick fix for this is to add the attribute exactly the same as the first `<router-link>`:

```
<li><router-link to="/" exact>Home</router-link></li>
```

Now, the `Home` link is highlighted only when the route exactly matches the home page link.

Another thing to note is the rule itself:

```
a.router-link-active, li.router-link-active>a {
  background-color: gainsboro;
}
```

Why do we match two different things? It depends on how you wrote the router link.

```
<li><router-link to="/" exact>Home</router-link></li>
```

The preceding code will be translated in the following DOM portion:

```
<li><a href="#/" class="router-link-active">Home</a></li>
```

While:

```
<router-link tag="li" to="/" exact>Home</router-link>
```

Becomes:

```
<li class="router-link-active">Home</li>
```

Note how in the first case, the class is applied to the child anchor element; in the second case, it is applied to the parent element.

Fetching data before switching route

In the previous version of Vue, we had a dedicated method to fetch data from the Internet before changing the route. With Vue 2, we have a more general method that will take care of this and possibly other things before switching route.

Getting ready

To complete this recipe, you are expected to already know the basics of vue-router and how to make AJAX requests (more on this in the last chapter).

How to do it...

We will write a simple web portfolio composed of two pages: a home page and an about me page.

For this recipe, we will need to add Axios as a dependency.

The basic layout is clear from the following HTML code:

```
<div id="app">
  <h1>My Portfolio</h1>
  <ul>
```

```
    <li><router-link to="/" exact>Home</router-link></li>
    <li><router-link to="/aboutme">About Me</router-link></li>
  </ul>
  <router-view></router-view>
</div>
```

In the JavaScript, you can start building your `AboutMe` component:

```
const AboutMe = {
  template: `<div>Name:{{name}}<br>Phone:{{phone}}</div>`
}
```

It will display only a name and a telephone number. Let's declare the two variables in the `data` option of the component, as follows:

```
data () {
  return {
    name: undefined,
    phone: undefined
  }
}
```

The vue-router, before actually loading the component onto the scene, will look for an option in our object, called `beforeRouteEnter`; we will use this to load the name and phone from a server. The server we are using will provide fake data just for the purpose of displaying something, which is as follows:

```
beforeRouteEnter (to, from, next) {
  axios.post('https://schematic-ipsum.herokuapp.com/', {
    "type": "object",
    "properties": {
      "name": {
        "type": "string",
        "ipsum": "name"
      },
      "phone": {
        type": "string",
        "format": "phone"
      }
    }
  }).then(response => {
    next(vm => {
      vm.name = response.data.name
      vm.phone = response.data.phone
    })
  })
}
```

For the other component, the home page, we will just write a small component as a placeholder:

```
const Home = { template: '<div>This is my home page</div>' }
```

Next thing is that you have to register the `router` and its `paths`:

```
Vue.use(VueRouter)
const router = new VueRouter({
  routes: [
    { path: '/', component: Home },
    { path: '/aboutme', component: AboutMe },
  ]
})
```

Also, of course, you have to register a `Vue` root instance, which is as follows:

```
new Vue({
  router,
  el: '#app'
})
```

When you launch your application and click on the **About Me** link, you should see something similar to this:

My Portfolio

- Home
- About Me

Name:Jacob Aall
Pone:(177) 314 5361

You will note that there is no page reload when you click on the link, but it still takes quite some time to display the bio. This is because it is fetching the data from the Internet.

How it works...

The `beforeRouteEnter` hook takes three parameters:

- `to`: This is a `Route` object that represents the route requested by the user.
- from: This is also a Route object that represents the current route. This is the route the user will be kept at in case of errors.

- `next`: This is a function we can use when we are ready to go on with the switching of the route. Calling this function with false will prevent the route from being changed, and it is useful in case of errors.

When the preceding functions are called, we made a call with Axios to a web service that provided a string for a name and a string for a phone number.

When we are inside this hook, it's important to remember that we don't have access to this. It's because this hook runs before the component is actually instantiated, so there is no `this` to refer to.

When the server responds, we are inside the `then` function and want to assign the name and phone returned from the server but, as said, we don't have access to this. The next function receives a reference to our component as an argument. We use this to set the variables to the received value:

```
...
}).then(response => {
  next(vm => {
    vm.name = response.data.name
    vm.phone = response.data.phone
  })
})
```

Using named dynamic routes

Registering all the routes by hand can be time consuming and, when the routes are not known in advance, it is impossible. vue-router lets you register routes with an argument so that you can have links for all the objects in a database and cover other use-cases where the user chooses a route, following some pattern that will result in too many routes to be registered by hand.

Getting ready

Except for the basics on vue-router (refer to the *Creating an SPA with vue-router* recipe), you won't need any additional information to complete this recipe.

How to do it...

We will open an online restaurant with ten different dishes. We will create a route for every dish.

The HTML layout of our website is the following:

```
<div id="app">
  <h1>Online Restaurant</h1>
  <ul>
    <li>
      <router-link :to="{ name: 'home' }" exact>
        Home
      </router-link>
    </li>
    <li v-for="i in 10">
      <router-link :to="{ name: 'menu', params: { id: i } }">
        Menu {{i}}
      </router-link>
    </li>
    </ul>
  <router-view class="view"></router-view>
</div>
```

This will create 11 links, one for the home page and ten for the dishes.

After registering the VueRouter in the JavaScript part, the code is as follows:

```
Vue.use(VueRouter)
```

Create two components; one will be a placeholder for the home page:

```
const Home = { template: `
  <div>
    Welcome to Online Restaurant
  </div>
` }
```

The other routes will be connected to a Menu component:

```
const Menu = { template: `
  <div>
    You just ordered
    <img :src="'http://lorempixel.com/200/200/food/' + $route.params.id">
  </div>
` }
```

In the preceding component, we refer to the global router object with $route, and we take the id parameter from the URL. Lorempixel.com is a website that provides sample images. We are connecting a different image for every id.

Finally, create the router itself using the following code:

```
const router = new VueRouter({
  routes: [
    { path: '/', name:'home', component: Home },
    { path: '/menu/:id', name: 'menu', component: Menu },
  ]
})
```

You can see that the path for the menu contains /:id, which is a placeholder for the id parameter that will appear in the URL.

At last, write a root Vue instance:

```
new Vue({
  router,
  el: '#app'
})
```

You can launch the application now and should be able to see all the menu items. Clicking on any one of them should order a different dish:

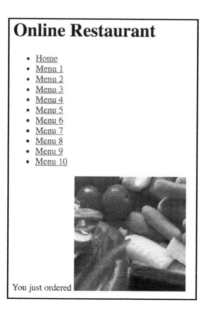

How it works...

There are two main parts of the code that contribute to creating the routes for the different dishes.

First, we registered a generic route using the colon syntax and assigned a name to it, which is as follows code:

```
{ path: '/menu/:id', name: 'menu', component: Menu }
```

This means that we can have a URL that ends in /menu/82, and the Menu component will be displayed with the $route.params.id variable set to 82. So, the following line should be changed as per the following:

```
<img :src="'http://lorempixel.com/200/200/food/' + $route.params.id">
```

The preceding line will be replaced by the following line in the rendered DOM:

```
<img src="'http://lorempixel.com/200/200/food/82">
```

Never mind the fact that there is no such image in real life.

Note that we also gave a name to this route. This is not strictly necessary, but it enabled us to write the second main part of the code, as shown:

```
<router-link :to="{ name: 'menu', params: { id: i } }">
  Menu {{i}}
</router-link>
```

Instead of writing a string, we can pass an object to the to prop and specify the params. In our case, the param is given by the v-for wrapping. This means that, for example, at the fourth cycle of the v-for:

```
<router-link :to="{ name: 'menu', params: { id: 4} }">
  Menu 4
</router-link>
```

This will result in the DOM as follows:

```
<a href="#/menu/4" class="">Menu 4</a>
```

Having more than one router-view in your page

Having multiple `<router-view>` enables you to have pages that can be organized with more complex layouts. For example, you can have a sidebar and the main view. This recipe is all about that.

Getting ready

This recipe doesn't use any advanced concept. You are advised to familiarize yourself with the vue-router and learn how to install it, though. Go to the first recipe in the chapter to find out more.

How to do it...

This recipe will use a lot of code to drive the point home. Don't be discouraged though, the mechanism is really simple.

We will build a second-hand hardware store. We will have a main view and a sidebar; these will be our router-views. The sidebar will contain our shopping list so that we always know what we are shopping for and will have no distractions.

The whole HTML code is quite short because it only contains a title and the two `router-view` components:

```
<div id="app">
  <h1>Second-Hand Hardware</h1>
    <router-view name="list"></router-view>
    <router-view></router-view>
</div>
```

In this case, the list is named `router-view`. The second one does not have a name; thus, it gets named as `Vue` by default.

Register the `vue-router` in the JavaScript:

```
Vue.use(VueRouter)
```

After that, register the routes:

```
const router = new VueRouter({
  routes: [
    { path: '/',
      components: {
        default: Parts,
        list: List
      }
    },
    { path: '/computer',
      components: {
        default: ComputerDetail,
        list: List
      }
    }
  ]
})
```

Components is not a single object anymore; it's become an object with two components inside it: one for the list and the other for the default router-view.

Write the list component, as illustrated, before the router code:

```
const List = { template: `
  <div>
    <h2>Shopping List</h2>
      <ul>
        <li>Computer</li>
      </ul>
  </div>
  ` }
```

This will display just the computer as an item we ought to remember to buy.

The parts component is the following; write it before the router code:

```
const Parts = { template: `
  <div>
    <h2>Computer Parts</h2>
    <ul>
      <li><router-link to="/computer">Computer</router-link></li>
      <li>CD-ROM</li>
    </ul>
  </div>
  ` }
```

This contains a link to see more about the computer on sale; the next component is bound to that page, so write it before the `router` code:

```
const ComputerDetail = { template: `
  <div>
    <h2>Computer Detail</h2>
    <p>Pentium 120Mhz, CDs sold separately</p>
  </div>
  ` }
```

Of course, don't forget to add the `Vue` instance:

```
new Vue({
  router,
  el: '#app'
})
```

When you launch the app, you should see the two router views one above the other. If you want them side by side, you can add some CSS styles:

Second Hand Hardware

Shopping List

- Computer

Computer Parts

- Computer
- CD-ROM

How it works...

When adding the `<router-view>` components to the page, you just have to remember to add a name to refer to it later during route registration:

```
<router-view name="view1"></router-view>
<router-view name="view2"></router-view>
<router-view></router-view>
```

If you don't specify a name, the route will be referred to as default:

```
routes: [
  { path: '/',
    components: {
      default: DefaultComponent,
      view1: Component1,
      view2: Component2
    }
  }
]
```

This way, the components will be displayed in their respective router-view elements.

> If you don't specify one or more components for a named view, the router-view associated with that name will be empty.

Compose your routes hierarchically

In many cases, the organization tree of your website may be complex. In some cases, there is a clear hierarchical organization that you can follow and with nested routes, vue-routes helps you keep everything orderly. The best situation is if there is an exact correspondence with how URLs are organized and how components are nested.

Getting ready

In this recipe, you will use components and other basic features of Vue. You will also use dynamic routes. Go to the *Using named dynamic routes* recipe to find out more about them.

How to do it...

In this recipe, you will build an online accounting website for an imaginary world. We will have two users--Stark and Lannister--and we will be able to see how much gold and how many soldier these two have.

The HTML layout of our website is as follows:

```
<div id="app">
  <h1>Kindoms Encyclopedia</h1>
  <router-link to="/user/Stark/">Stark</router-link>
  <router-link to="/user/Lannister/">Lannister</router-link>
  <router-view></router-view>
</div>
```

We have a title and two links--one for `Stark` and one for `Lannister`--and, finally, the `router-view` element.

We add the `VueRouter` to the plugins:

```
Vue.use(VueRouter)
```

Then, we register the `routes`:

```
const router = new VueRouter({
  routes: [
    { path: '/user/:id', component: User,
      children: [
        {
          path: 'soldiers',
          component: Soldiers
        },
        {
          path: 'gold',
          component: Gold
        }
      ]
    }
  ]
})
```

What we've said is to register a dynamic route, `/user/:id`, and inside the `User` component, there will be another router-view that will have the nested paths for gold and soldiers.

The three components just mentioned are written as shown; add them before the routing code:

```
const User = { template: `
  <div class="user">
    <h1>Kindoms Encyclopedia</h1>
    User {{$route.params.id}}
    <router-link to="gold">Gold</router-link>
    <router-link to="soldiers">Soldiers</router-link>
```

```
    <router-view></router-view>
  </div>
`}
```

As anticipated, there is another router-view entry point inside the User component that will contain the nested routes components.

Then, write the Soldiers and Gold components, always before the routing code:

```
const Soldiers = { template: `
  <div class="soldiers">
    <span v-for="soldier in $root[$route.params.id].soldiers">
🗡
    </span>
  </div>
`}
const Gold = { template: `
  div class="gold">
    <span v-for="coin in $root[$route.params.id].gold">
💰
    </span>
  </div>
`}
```

These components will just display as many emojis as the gold or soldiers variable inside the Vue root instance data option.

This is what the Vue root instance looks like:

```
new Vue({
  router,
  el: '#app',
  data: {
    Stark: {
      soldiers: 100,
      gold: 50
    },
    Lannister: {
      soldiers: 50,
      gold: 100
    }
  }
})
```

Launching the application will enable you to have a visual representation of the gold and the number of soldiers of the two users:

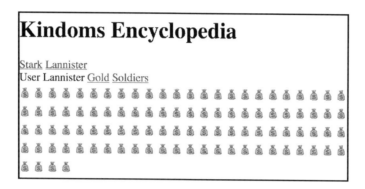

How it works...

To understand how nested routes work better, it's useful to take a look at the following diagram:

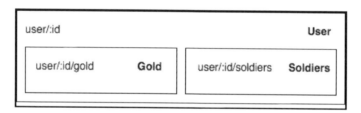

There are only two levels in our recipe. The first level, which is the top level, is represented by the the big wrapping rectangle that corresponds to the /user/:id route, meaning that every potential matching ID will be on the same level.

The inner rectangle instead is a nested route and a nested component. It corresponds to the route gold and to the Gold component.

When nested routes correspond to nested components, this is the right choice. There are two other cases to consider.

When we have nested components but don't have nested routes, we can just prefix the nested route with a slash, /. This will make it behave like a top-level route.

For example, consider that we change our code to the following:

```
const router = new VueRouter({
  routes: [
    { path: '/user/:id', component: User,
      children: [
        {
          path: 'soldiers',
          component: Soldiers
        },
        {
          path: '/gold',
          component: Gold
        }
      ]
    }
  ]
})
```

Prefixing the /gold route will make the Gold component appear when we point the browser to the /gold URL instead of /user/Lannister/gold (which will result in an error and an empty page in this case because the user is not specified).

The other, opposite, case is when having nested routes but no components on the same level. In this case, just use the regular syntax to register routes.

Using route aliases

Sometimes it's necessary to have multiple URLs that point to the same page. This may be because the page has changed name or because the page is referred to differently in different parts of the site.

In particular, when a page changes its name, it is very important to also leave the former name in many settings. Links may break and the page may become unreachable from some parts of the website. In this recipe, you will prevent exactly that.

Getting ready

For this recipe, you are only required to have some knowledge of the vue-router component (how to install it and basic operations). More information about vue-router will start from the *Creating a SPA with vue-router* recipe.

How to do it...

Let's imagine that we have a fashion website and Lisa, the employee responsible for giving titles to dresses, creates two new links for two pieces of clothing:

```
<router-link to="/green-dress-01/">Valentino</router-link>
<router-link to="/green-purse-A2/">Prada</router-link>
```

The developers create the corresponding routes in the vue-router:

```
const router = new VueRouter({
  routes: [
    {
      path: '/green-dress-01',
      component: Valentino01
    },
    {
      path: '/green-purse-A2',
      component: PradaA2
    }
  ]
})
```

Later, it is discovered that the two items are not green but red. Lisa is not to blame since she is color-blind.

You are now in charge of changing all the links to reflect the true color of the listing. The first thing you do is change the links themselves. Here's what the HTML layout looks like after you edit it:

```
<div id="app">
  <h1>Clothes Shop</h1>
  <router-link to="/red-dress-01/">Valentino</router-link>
  <router-link to="/red-purse-A2/">Prada</router-link>
  <router-view></router-view>
</div>
```

You add the VueRouter plugin to Vue:

```
Vue.use(VueRouter)
```

Then, register the new routes as well as aliases for the old ones:

```
const router = new VueRouter({
  routes: [
    {
      path: '/red-dress-01',
      component: Valentino01,
```

```
      alias: '/green-dress-01'
    },
    {
      path: '/red-purse-A2',
      component: PradaA2,
      alias: '/green-purse-A2'
    }
  ]
})
```

Here's what the mentioned components look like:

```
const Valentino01 = { template: '<div class="emoji">👗</div>' }
const PradaA2 = { template: '<div class="emoji">👜</div>' }
```

Before launching the app, remember to instantiate a `Vue` instance:

```
new Vue({
  router,
  el: '#app'
})
```

You can add a CSS rule to make the emojis look like images, as shown in the following screenshot:

```
.emoji {
  font-size: 3em;
}
```

How it works...

Even if we changed all of our links, we cannot control how other entities are linked to our page. For search engines, such as Google, there is no way to tell them to remove their link to the old page and use the new one. This means that if we weren't to use aliases, we may have a lot of bad publicity in the form of broken links and 404 pages; in some cases, even from advertisers we are paying to link to a non-existent page.

Adding transitions between your routes

We explored transitions in detail in `Chapter 3`, *Transitions and Animations.* Here, we will use them when changing routes instead of changing elements or components. The same observations apply here as well.

Getting ready

Before trying this recipe, I highly suggest that you complete some recipes in `Chapter 3`, *Transitions and Animations,* as well as this one. This recipe is a mixture of concepts learned up to now.

How to do it...

In this recipe, we will build a website for a restaurant for ghosts. It won't be much different from the website of a regular restaurant, except for the requirements that the pages must fade instead of appearing instantly.

Let's put down some HTML layout, shall we:

```
<div id="app">
  <h1>Ghost's Restaurant</h1>
  <ul>
    <li><router-link to="/">Home</router-link></li>
    <li><router-link to="/menu">Menu</router-link></li>
  </ul>
  <transition mode="out-in">
  <router-view></router-view>
  </transition>
</div>
```

Note how we wrapped the main router display port with a `transition` tag. The mode `out-in` is set because we want the animation for the disappearing component to finish before the other component appears. If we hadn't we set that, the two fading components would be stacked for a brief time. For a more detailed discussion, you can refer to the *Letting an element leave before the enter phase in a transition* recipe.

Let's create the two pages/components:

```
const Home = { template: '<div>Welcome to Ghost's</div>' }
const Menu = { template: '<div>Today: invisible cookies</div>' }
```

Now, let's register `routes`:

```
Vue.use(VueRouter)
const router = new VueRouter({
  routes: [
     { path: '/', component: Home },
     { path: '/menu', component: Menu }
  ]
})
```

Before launching the application, instantiate a `Vue` object:

```
new Vue({
  router,
  el: '#app'
})
```

For the transition to work, you have to add a few CSS rules:

```
.v-enter-active, .v-leave-active {
  transition: opacity .5s;
}
.v-enter, .v-leave-active {
  opacity: 0
}
```

Launch your application now. You successfully added a fade transition between page changes.

How it works...

Wrapping the whole `<router-view>` inside a transition tag will perform the same transition for all the components.

If we want a different transition for every component, we have an alternate option: we have to wrap the individual components inside transitions themselves.

Let's say, for example, that we have two transitions: spooky and delicious. We want to apply the first when the `Home` component appears, and the second when the `Menu` component appears.

We need to modify our components, as follows:

```
const Home = { template: `
  <transition name="spooky">
    <div>Welcome to Ghost's</div>
  </transition>
` }
const Menu = { template: `
  <transition name="delicious">
    <div>Today: insisible cookies!</div>
  </transition>
` }
```

Managing errors for your routes

It does not make much sense to go to a link if the page we go to is not found or is not working. Traditionally, we are presented with an error page when this happens. In an SPA, we are more powerful and we can prevent the user from going there altogether, displaying a little courtesy message stating that the page is not available. This greatly enhances the UX since the user can immediately take another action without the need to go back.

Getting ready

In order to follow along, you should complete the *Fetching data before switching route* recipe.

This recipe will build up on top of it and I'll assume that you already have all the relevant code in place.

How to do it...

As said, we will edit the resulting code from the *Fetching data before switching route* recipe to manage errors. Just so you remember, when going to the /aboutme page, we were loading information from the Internet. We want to avoid going to that page in case the information is not available.

For this recipe, add Axios as a dependency, as done in the previous recipes.

First, enrich the HTML layout with the highlighted code:

```
<div id="app">
  <h1>My Portfolio</h1>
  <ul>
    <li><router-link to="/" exact>Home</router-link></li>
    <li><router-link to="/aboutme">About Me</router-link></li>
  </ul>
  <router-view></router-view>
  <div class="toast" v-show="showError">
    There was an error
  </div>
</div>
```

This is a toast message that will appear on the screen whenever there is an error. Add some style to it with this CSS rule:

```
div.toast {
    width: 15em;
    height: 1em;
    position: fixed;
    bottom: 1em;
    background-color: red;
    color: white;
    padding: 1em;
    text-align: center;
}
```

The next thing you want to do is have a global mechanism to set `showError` to `true`. At the top of the JavaScript code, declare the `vm` variable:

```
let vm
```

Then, assign our Vue root instance to it:

```
vm = new Vue({
  router,
  el: '#app',
  data: {
    showError: false
  }
})
```

We also added the showError variable to the data option.

The last thing to do is actually manage the error on the retrieval of our data, before displaying the bio information.

Add the highlighted code to the beforeRouteEnter hook:

```
beforeRouteEnter (to, from, next) {
  axios.post('http://example.com/', {
    "type": "object",
    "properties": {
      "name": {
        "type": "string",
        "ipsum": "name"
      },
      "phone": {
        "type": "string",
        "format": "phone"
      }
    }
  }).then(response => {
  next(vm => {
    vm.name = response.data.name
    vm.phone = response.data.phone
  })
}).catch(error => {
  vm.showError = true
  next(false)
})
}
```

The next (false) command will make the user stay where they are, and we also edited the endpoint to `example.com`, which will return an error code on a POST request:

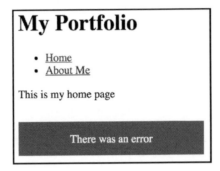

How it works...

Axios will receive an error from `example.com` and this will trigger a rejection of the promise created when we called post. The rejection of a promise will, in turn, trigger the function passed inside the catch.

It's worth noting that at this point in the code, vm is referring to the root Vue instance; this is because the code is always executed after the Vue instance is initialized and assigned to vm.

Adding a progress bar to load pages

It's true that with an SPA the user does not have to wait for a new page to load, but he still has to wait for the data to load. In the *Fetching data before switching route* recipe, we had to wait a while longer after we clicked on the button to the /aboutme page. There was nothing to suggest that the data was loading, and then suddenly the page appeared. Wouldn't it be great if the user had at least some feedback that the page is loading?

Getting ready

In order to follow along, you should complete the *Fetching data before switching route* recipe.

This recipe will build up on top of it and I'll assume that you have all the relevant code in place already.

How to do it...

As stated earlier, I will assume that you have all the code resulting from the *Fetching data before switching route* recipe in place and working.

For this recipe, we will use an additional dependency--NProgress, a small utility to display a loading bar on top of the screen.

Add the following two lines inside the head of your page or the list of dependencies in JSFiddle (there is also a package for npm):

```
<link rel="stylesheet"
href="https://cdn.bootcss.com/nprogress/X/nprogress.css">
<script src="https://cdn.bootcss.com/nprogress/X/nprogress.js"></script>
```

Here, X is the version of NProgress. At writing time it was 0.2.0, but you can look it up online.

After we've done this, the next step is to define the behavior we want from the progress bar.

First, we'd like the progress bar to appear as soon as we click on the link. For this, we can add an event listener to the click event, but it will be a poor design if we had, say, a hundred links. A much more sustainable and clean way to do it is by creating a new hook for the router and connecting the appearance of the progress bar with the switching of the route. This will also have the advantage of offering a consistent experience throughout the application:

```
router.beforeEach((to, from, next) => {
  NProgress.start()
  next()
})
```

In a similar fashion, we want the bar to disappear when loading is completed successfully. This means that we want to do it inside the callback:

```
beforeRouteEnter (to, from, next) {
  axios.post('http://schematic-ipsum.herokuapp.com/', {
    "type": "object",
    "properties": {
      "name": {
        "type": "string",
        "ipsum": "name"
      },
      "phone": {
        "type": "string",
        "format": "phone"
```

```
        }
      }
    }).then(response => {
       NProgress.done()
       next(vm => {
          vm.name = response.data.name
          vm.phone = response.data.phone
       })
    })
  }
```

You can now launch the application and your progress bar should already work:

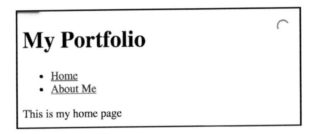

How it works...

This recipe also demonstrates that it is not at all difficult to leverage external libraries, provided they are easy to install.

Since the NProgress component is so simple and useful, I report its API as a reference here:

- NProgress.start(): Shows the progress bar
- NProgress.set(0.4): Sets a percentage of the progress bar
- NProgress.inc(): Increments the progress bar by a little
- NProgress.done(): Completes the progress

We have used two of the preceding functions.

As a precaution, I would also suggest not relying on the done() function being called by the individual components. We are calling it in the then function, but what if the next developer forgets? After all, we are starting the progress bar before *any* switch in route.

It would be better to add a new hook to the `router`:

```
router.afterEach((to, from) => {
  NProgress.done()
})
```

Since the `done` function is idempotent, we can call it as many times as we want. This will, therefore, not modify the behavior of our application and will ensure that even if future developers forget to close the progress bar, it will disappear by itself once the route has changed.

How to redirect to another route

There are infinite reasons you may wish to redirect the user. You may want the user to log in before accessing a page, or maybe a page has moved and you want your user to take note of the new link. In this recipe, you will redirect the user to a new home page as a way to quickly modify the website.

Getting ready

This recipe will only use basic knowledge about vue-router. If you have completed the *Creating a SPA with vue-router* recipe, you are good to go.

How to do it...

Suppose that we have an online clothing shop.

This will be the HTML layout of the site:

```
<div id="app">
  <h1>Clothes for Humans</h1>
  <ul>
    <li><router-link to="/">Home</router-link></li>
    <li><router-link to="/clothes">Clothes</router-link></li>
  </ul>
  <router-view></router-view>
</div>
```

It's just a page with a link to a clothes listing.

Let's register the `VueRouter`:

```
Vue.use(VueRouter)
```

We have three pages in our website, represented by the following components:

```
const Home = { template: '<div>Welcome to Clothes for Humans</div>' }
const Clothes = { template: '<div>Today we have shoes</div>' }
const Sales = { template: '<div>Up to 50% discounts! Buy!</div>' }
```

They represent the home page, the clothes listing, and a page we used last year with some discounts.

Let's register some `routes`:

```
const router = new VueRouter({
  routes: [
    { path: '/', component: Home }
    { path: '/clothes', component: Clothes },
    { path: '/last-year-sales', component: Sales }
  ]
})
```

Finally, we add a root `Vue` instance:

```
new Vue({
  router,
  el: '#app'
})
```

You can launch the application, and it should work without any problems.

Black Friday is tomorrow and we forgot that it's the biggest event in fashion around the world. We don't have time to rewrite the home page, but there's that page from last year's sales that can do the trick. What we will do is redirect users who visit our home page to that page.

To implement this, we need to modify how we registered our `routes`:

```
const router = new VueRouter({
  routes: [
    { path: '/', component: Home, redirect: '/last-year-sales' },
    { path: '/clothes', component: Clothes },
    { path: '/last-year-sales', component: Sales }
  ]
})
```

Only by adding that redirect we did save the day. Now, you will be presented with the sales page whenever you visit the home page.

How it works...

When the root route is matched, the `Home` component won't be loaded. The path of `/last-year-sales` will be matched instead. We can also omit the component altogether since it will never be loaded:

```
{ path: '/', redirect: '/last-year-sales' }
```

There's more...

Redirecting in vue-router is more powerful than what we just saw. Here, I will try to enrich the application we just created with more functionality from redirecting.

Redirecting to 404s

Redirecting not found pages is done by adding a catch-all as the last route. It will match everything that is not matched by the other routes:

```
...
{ path: '/404', component: NotFound },
{ path: '*', redirect: '/404' }
```

Named redirecting

Redirection can be combined with named routes (refer to the *Using named dynamic routes* recipe). We can specify the destination by name:

```
...
{ path: '/clothes', name: 'listing', component: Clothes },
{ path: '/shoes', redirect: { name: 'listing' }}
```

Redirecting with parameters

You can also retain the parameters while redirecting:

```
...
{ path: '/de/Schuh/:size', redirect: '/en/shoe/:size' },
{ path: '/en/shoe/:size', component: Shoe }
```

Dynamic redirecting

This is the ultimate redirect. You can access the route the user is trying to access and decide where you want to redirect him (you can't cancel the redirection though):

```
...
{ path: '/air', component: Air },
{ path: '/bags', name: 'bags', component: Bags },
{ path: '/super-shirt/:size', component: SuperShirt },
{ path: '/shirt/:size?', component: Shirt},
{ path: '/shirts/:size?',
  redirect: to => {
    const { hash, params, query } = to
    if (query.colour === 'transparent') {
      return { path: '/air', query: null }
    }
    if (hash === '#prada') {
      return { name: 'bags', hash: '' }
    }
    if (params.size > 10) {
      return '/super-shirt/:size'
    } else {
      return '/shirt/:size?'
    }
  }
}
```

Saving scrolling position when hitting back

In vue-router, there are two modes of navigation: hash and history. The default mode and the one used in the previous recipes is previouslye. Traditionally, when you visit a website, scroll down a bit and click on a link to another page; the new page displays from the top. When you click on the browser's back button, the page displays from the previous scrolled height and the link you just clicked on is visible.

This is not true when you are in an SPA, or at least is not automatic. The vue-router history mode lets you simulate this or, even better, have fine-grained control of what happens to your scrolling.

Getting ready

To complete this recipe, we will need to switch to history mode. History mode only works when the app is running on a properly configured server. How to configure a server for SPA is out of the scope of this book (but the principle is that every route gets redirected from the server side to `index.html`).

We will use an npm program to launch a small server; you are expected to have npm installed (you can take a look at the *Choosing a development environment* recipe to find out more about npm).

How to do it...

First, you'll install a compact server for SPAs so that history mode will work.

In your favorite command line, go inside the directory that will contain your application. Then, type the following commands:

```
npm install -g history-server
history-server .
```

After the server is run, you will have to point your browser to `http://localhost:8080` and if you have a file called `index.html` in your directory, it will be shown; otherwise you won't see much.

Create a file called `index.html` and fill in some boilerplate, like in the *Choosing a development environment* recipe. We want an empty page with only `Vue` and `vue-router` as dependencies. Our empty canvas should look like this:

```html
<!DOCTYPE html>
<html>
<head>
  <script src="https://unpkg.com/vue/dist/vue.js"></script>
  <script src="https://unpkg.com/vue-router/dist/vue-router.js"></script>
</head>
<body>
  <div id="app">
  </div>
```

```
    <script>
      new Vue({
        router,
        el: '#app'
      })
    </script>
  </body>
</html>
```

As HTML layout, put this in the body:

```
<div id="app">
  <h1>News Portal</h1>
    <ul>
      <li><router-link to="/">Home</router-link></li>
      <li><router-link to="/sports">Sports</router-link></li>
      <li><router-link to="/fashion">Fashion</router-link></li>
    </ul>
  <router-view></router-view>
</div>
```

We have a heading with three links and a router-view entry point. We will create two long pages for the sports and fashion pages:

```
const Sports = { template: `
  <div>
    <p v-for="i in 30">
      Sample text about sports {{i}}.
    </p>
    <router-link to="/fashion">Go to Fashion</router-link>
    <p v-for="i in 30">
      Sample text about sports {{i + 30}}.
    </p>
  </div>
  ` }
const Fashion = { template: `
  <div>
    <p v-for="i in 30">
      Sample text about fashion {{i}}.
    </p>
    <router-link to="/sports">Go to Sports</router-link>
    <p v-for="i in 30">
      Sample text about fashion {{i + 30}}.
    </p>
  </div>
  ` }
```

We only need a stub for the home page component:

```
const Home = { template: '<div>Welcome to BBCCN</div>' }
```

Write a reasonable router for this news website:

```
Vue.use(VueRouter)
const router = new VueRouter({
  routes: [
    { path: '/', component: Home },
    { path: '/sports', component: Sports },
    { path: '/fashion', component: Fashion }
  ]
})
```

If you go with your browser now to the address specified earlier, you should see the site live.

Go to the sports page, scroll down until you see the link, and click on it.

Note how the page you are visiting is not displayed from the beginning. This will not happen with a traditional website and is not desirable.

Click on the back button and note how we are where we last left the page; we want to retain this behavior.

Lastly, note how the URL of the page does not look natural but has the hash symbol inside; we would like the URL to look better:

To accomplish this, let's modify our router code to the following:

```
const router = new VueRouter({
  mode: 'history',
  routes: [
    { path: '/', component: Home },
    { path: '/sports', component: Sports },
    { path: '/fashion', component: Fashion }
  ],
  scrollBehavior (to, from, savedPosition) {
    if (savedPosition) {
      return savedPosition
    } else {
      return { x: 0, y: 0 }
    }
  }
})
```

We added a line that specifies the new mode to be history (no hash in the link) and we defined the `scrollBehavior` function to go back to the last position if present; if it's a new page, it should scroll to the top-left corner.

You can try this by refreshing the browser and going back to the home page.

Open the sports page and click on the link in the middle of the page. The new page now displays from the beginning.

Click on back and the `savedPosition` gets restored.

Note how the URL looks much nicer now:

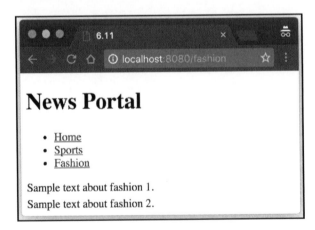

How it works...

When you use a URL that contains the hash symbol in the browser, the browser will send a request for the URL without the suffix after the hash, that is, when you have an event inside a page that goes to the same page but with a different hash suffix:

```
http://example.com#/page1 on  http://example.com#/page2
```

The browser will not reload the page; this is why vue-router can modify the content of the page when the user clicks on a link that only modifies the hash, without the page being reloaded.

When you change the mode from `hash` to `history`, vue-router will drop the hash notation and will leverage the `history.pushState()` function.

This function adds another virtual page and changes the URL to something else:

```
http://example.com/page1 =pushState=> http://example.com/page2
```

The browser will not send a `GET` request to look for `page2` though; in fact, it won't do anything.

When you press the back button, the browser reverts the URL and vue-router receives an event. It will then read the URL (which is now `page1`) and match the associated route.

The role of our compact history server is to redirect every GET request to the `index.html` page. This is why when we try to go to `http://localhost:8080/fashion` directly, we don't get a *404* error.

7
Unit Testing and End-to-End Testing

In this chapter, the following recipes will be covered:

- Using Jasmine for testing Vue
- Adding some Karma to your workflow
- Testing your application state and methods
- Testing the DOM
- Testing DOM asynchronous updates
- End-to-end testing with nightwatch
- Simulating a double-click in nightwatch
- Different styles of unit testing
- Stubbing external API calls with Sinon.JS
- Measuring the coverage of your code

Introduction

Testing is what really differentiates professional software from amateur software. From industry experience and studies, it has been discovered that much of the cost of software lies in correcting bugs while the software is in production. Testing software reduces bugs in production and makes correcting those bugs much less expensive.

In this chapter, you will learn how to set up your test harness and how to write unit tests and integration tests that will help speed up your app development and help it grow in complexity without leaving bugs behind.

You will gain familiarity with the most popular testing framework and slang; after completing the recipes, you will be able to confidently ship software that works just as expected.

Using Jasmine for testing Vue

Jasmine is a library for testing, it's very easy to use and it's capable of displaying the results of the tests directly in the browser. In this recipe, you will build a simple Vue application and you will test it with Jasmine.

Getting ready

I hope you don't start learning Vue with this recipe because I'm going to assume, as I will with the rest of the chapter, that you already know the basics of building simple applications in Vue.

You should also be able to find four files on the Internet. I will write the link as I found them at writing time but, of course, they may change:

- `https://cdnjs.cloudflare.com/ajax/libs/jasmine/2.5.2/jasmine.css`
- `https://cdnjs.cloudflare.com/ajax/libs/jasmine/2.5.2/jasmine.js`
- `https://cdnjs.cloudflare.com/ajax/libs/jasmine/2.5.2/jasmine-html.js`
- `https://cdnjs.cloudflare.com/ajax/libs/jasmine/2.5.2/boot.js`

You can conveniently copy-paste all the links from the `https://cdnjs.com/libraries/jasmine` page.

The files are dependent on each other, so the order in which you add them matters! In particular, `boot.js` is dependent on `jasmine-html.js`, which is dependent on `jasmine.js`.

How to do it...

Jasmine is a library composed of various modules. To make it work, you need to install a few dependencies related to Jasmine. I will assume that you are using JSFiddle to follow along. If you are using npm or other methods instead, you should be able to derive what you need to change as the code will be simple in principle.

To install Jasmine in your app, you will need four different dependencies, of which one is just for CSS styling.

The four files are (*in order of dependence*):

- jasmine.css
- jasmine.js
- jasmine-html.js (which depends on the preceding js)
- boot.js (which depends on the preceding js)

You should be able to find all these files on CDNJS or other CDNs. Install them in the order shown, or they won't work properly.

When you have all the files in place, write the following HTML code:

```
<div id="app">
  <p>{{greeting}}</p>
</div>
```

Then, add the following script as the JavaScript part:

```
new Vue({
  el: '#app',
  data: {
    greeting: 'Hello World!'
  }
})
```

You can launch the application now and, as expected, the Hello World message should appear on the screen.

We would like to be 100% sure that our application always displays this message when we make modifications to it and add new features.

Jasmine will help us in this regard. Just after the Vue instance, we write the following JavaScript:

```
describe('my app', () => {
  it('should say Hello World', () => {
    expect(document.querySelector('p').innerText)
      .toContain('Hello World')
  })
})
```

In order for this to work in JSFiddle, **Load Type** needs to be set to **No wrap - in <body>**. If you keep the default **Load Type onLoad**, it will load Jasmine before Vue has a chance to start.

Now try and launch the application. You will see a detailed report by Jasmine at the end of the page that tells you weather there is something wrong with your app.

If everything goes as expected, you should see a happy green bar, like the following:

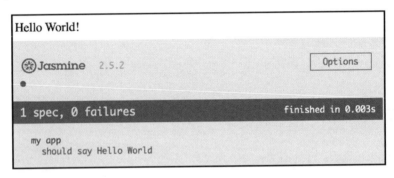

How it works...

You wrote your very first unit test for a Vue application. If you write unit tests already, everything should be quite clear since we have not used any feature unique to Vue to write the test.

In any case, let's spend a little time analyzing the code we have written; after that, I'll provide some considerations about when you should write similar tests when writing a real application.

The test we wrote displays `my app should say Hello World` when you read it as a sentence on the web page.

This is a fairly generic message; however, let's look at the code closely:

```
expect(document.querySelector('p').innerText)
  .toContain('Hello World')
```

Read it as an English phrase--we expect the <p> element inside the document to contain the text `Hello World`.

The `document.querySelector('p')` code selects the first p element inside the page, to be precise. `innerText` looks inside the HTML element and returns the readable text that's inside. We then verify that this text contains `Hello World`.

In a real application, you wouldn't write the tests just under your web pages. Tests are of great importance to a developer to check whether everything is working correctly without manually verifying every single feature after every code change. On the other hand, you don't want your users to see the results of your tests.

In general, you will have a dedicated page, accessible only by developers, that runs all the tests for you.

There's more...

There is a widespread practice in software called **TDD** or **Test-Driven Development**. It encourages you to think about the features of your software as tests. This, in turn, enables you to ensure that the features in your software work because the tests themselves work.

In this bit, we will add a feature to our recipe using TDD. We want the page to have a header that says `Welcome`.

First, we will write a (failing) test for the feature inside the `describe` function after the hello world test:

```
it('should have an header that says `Welcome`', () => {
  expect(document.querySelector('h1').innerText)
    .toContain('Welcome')
})
```

When we launch the test, we should see it fail:

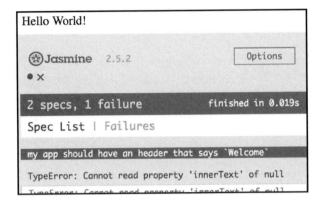

Now, don't pay too much attention to the stack trace. The important thing you should note is that we have the name of the test that is failing (the other test is still working.)

It's important to write the test and see that it fails before implementing the feature itself. To understand why, try to imagine that we write the test before implementing the feature, then we launch it, and then it succeeds. It would mean that the test is not really working because we never implemented the feature in the first place.

If you think this is just strange and impossible, think again. In practice, it often happens that a test that seems perfectly okay is not testing anything in reality and will always succeed, even if the feature is broken.

At this point, we are ready to actually implement the feature. We edit the HTML layout, like this:

```html
<div id="app">
  <h1>Welcome</h1>
  <p>{{greeting}}</p>
</div>
```

When we launch the page, the result should be similar to this:

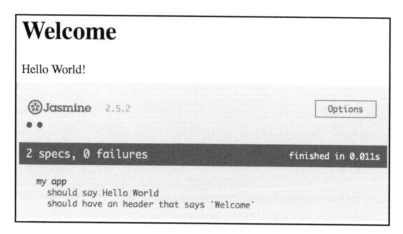

Adding some Karma to your workflow

Karma is a JavaScript test runner. This means that it will run your tests for you. Software often grows quickly and Karma gives you a way to run all your unit tests at once. It also gives you the power to add tools that monitor for test coverage and code quality.

Karma is used traditionally in Vue projects and is present in the official Vue templates as a tool. Learning Karma is a great addition for your JavaScript toolbelt even if you are not working with Vue.

Getting ready

I would consider having completed the *Using Jasmine for testing Vue* recipe a prerequisite. Since Karma is a test runner, you should first be able to write a test.

We will use npm in this recipe, so you should first read the basics on how to use it in the *Choosing a development environment* recipe.

How to do it...

For this recipe, we will need the command line and npm, so be sure to have it installed before moving ahead.

In a new folder, create a file named `package.json` and write the following inside it:

```
{
  "name": "my-vue-project",
  "version": "1.0.0"
}
```

Just having this file in your folder creates a new npm project. We will edit this file later.

In your command line, go to the directory where your project is and type the following command inside it to install the necessary dependencies:

```
npm install --save-dev vue karma jasmine karma-jasmine karma-chrome-
launcher
```

This will install Vue along with Karma, Jasmine, and a couple of plugins of Karma as dependencies of our project.

If you take a look at the `package.json` now, you will see that it has changed accordingly.

The next command will create a file named `karma.conf.js` that will contain the configuration for Karma:

```
./node_modules/karma/bin/karma init
```

This will ask you some questions, just leave the default for all the questions except when it asks you the location of your source and test files. For that question, just write `*.js`. After this, you should be able to see the `karma.conf.js` file in your directory. Open it and take a quick look at all the settings you just set by answering the questions.
Since Karma doesn't know about Vue natively, you'll need to perform a small modification to add Vue as a dependency to Karma. There are a couple of ways to do this; the quickest is probably to add a line to the list of the files you want to load. In the `karma.conf.js` file, add the following line in the `files` array:

```
...
    // list of files / patterns to load in the browser
    files: [
      'node_modules/vue/dist/vue.js',
      '*.js'
    ],
...
```

Note that when you answered the question, you could have also added the line directly.

The next step is to write the application we want to test.

In your folder, create a file named `myApp.js`; inside it, write the following:

```
const myApp = {
  template: `
    <div>
      <p>{{greetings}}</p>
    </div>
  `,
  data: {
    greetings: 'Hello World'
  }
}
```

The object we are assigning to `myApp` is just a simple Vue instance.

Next, we will create a test for it. Specifically, we will check weather the `Hello World` text is contained somewhere in the component.

Create a file named `test.js` and write the following inside it:

```
describe('my app', () => {
  beforeEach(() => {
    document.body.innerHTML = `
      <div id="app"></div>
    `
    new Vue(myApp)
      .$mount('#app')
  })
  it('should say Hello World', () => {
    expect(document.querySelector('p').innerText)
      .toContain('Hello World')
  })
})
```

The `beforeEach` block will run before each test (now we have only one), resetting the state of our Vue app before checking additional features.

We are now in a position to run our test. Write the following command in your terminal:

```
./node_modules/karma/bin/karma start
```

You should see Chrome starting and if you go back to your command line, you should receive a message similar to this:

```
./node_modules/karma/bin/karma start
29 01 2017 22:13:54.939:WARN [karma]: No captured browser, open http://localhost:9876/
29 01 2017 22:13:54.951:INFO [karma]: Karma v1.4.0 server started at http://0.0.0.0:9876/
29 01 2017 22:13:54.952:INFO [launcher]: Launching browser Chrome with unlimited concurrer
29 01 2017 22:13:54.975:INFO [launcher]: Starting browser Chrome
29 01 2017 22:13:55.968:INFO [Chrome 55.0.2883 (Mac OS X 10.12.2)]: Connected on socket ra
Chrome 55.0.2883 (Mac OS X 10.12.2) INFO: 'You are running Vue in development mode.
Make sure to turn on production mode when deploying for production.
See more tips at https://vuejs.org/guide/deployment.html'

Chrome 55.0.2883 (Mac OS X 10.12.2): Executed 1 of 1 SUCCESS (0.011 secs / 0.018 secs)
```

This means that your tests worked successfully.

How it works...

After your recipe is complete, you should note the general structure of your application. You have the application itself in `myApp.js`, and then you have your tests in `test.js`. You have some configuration files, such as `karma.conf.js` and `package.json`, and you have your libraries inside the `node_modules` directory. All these files work together to make your application testable.

In a real application, you will probably have more files for the source code and for the test, while the configuration files usually grow much slower.

In this whole setup, you may be wondering how you launch the application itself. After all, there is no HTML and the only thing we launched are tests; we've never seen this `Hello World` program.

Actually, you are right; there is no program to launch here. As a matter of fact, we had to write a fixture for the HTML layout inside the `beforeEach` of the tests:

```
beforeEach(() => {
  document.body.innerHTML = `
    <div id="app"></div>
  `
  new Vue(window.myApp)
    .$mount('#app')
})
```

In the preceding code, we are injecting the HTML, which consists only of a `<div>` element (the rest of the layout is inside `myApp.js`) in the page.

We then create a new Vue instance, passing the option object contained in the `myApp` variable that was defined in `myApp.js`; we then use the `$mount('#app')` Vue API that effectively materializes the application in the `<div>` element we just injected.

There's more...

Calling Karma from inside the `node_modules` directory every time can be annoying. There are two ways to make this more pleasant: we can install Karma globally or we can add Karma to our npm scripts; we'll do both.

First, let's add Karma to our npm scripts. Go inside the `package.json` file and add the following block:

```
...
"version": "1.0.0",
  "scripts": {
    "test": "./node_modules/karma/bin/karma start"
  },
"devDependencies": {
...
```

Now, you can type `npm run test` and Karma will automatically launch. The next thing we can do is install Karma globally with the following line:

```
npm install -g karma
```

Now we can write commands such as `karma init` and `karma start`, and they will be recognized. We can also edit our `package.json`, like this:

```
...
"version": "1.0.0",
  "scripts": {
    "test": "karma start"
  },
"devDependencies": {
...
```

Testing your application state and methods

In this recipe, we will write a unit test to touch and check the state of our Vue instance directly. The advantage of testing the state of our components instead of looking for something in our web page is that we don't have to wait for the DOM to be updated and that, even if something changes in the HTML layout, the state changes much more slowly, reducing the amount of maintenance required for our tests.

Getting ready

Before trying this recipe, you should complete *Adding some Karma to your workflow* as we will describe how to write the test but we won't mention much about the setup of the testing environment.

How to do it...

Let's suppose that we have an application that greets you with `Hello World!`, but it also has a button to translate the greeting to Italian, as `Ciao Mondo!`.
For this, you need to create a new npm project in a new folder. There, you can install the dependencies required for this recipe with the following command:

```
npm install --save-dev vue karma jasmine karma-jasmine karma-chrome-
    launcher
```

To set up Karma like in the previous recipe, run the following command:

```
./node_modules/karma/bin/karma init
```

Leave the default answers, except for the question `What is the location of your source and test files ?`; for that, you should answer with the following two lines:

- `node_modules/vue/dist/vue.js`
- `*.js`

Create a file called `test.js` and write a `beforeEach` that will bring the application back to it's starting state inside it so that it can be tested independently of other tests:

```
describe('my app', () => {
  let vm
  beforeEach(() => {
    vm = new Vue({
      template: `
```

```
      <div>
        <p>{{greetings}}</p>
        <button @click="toItalian">
          Translate to Italian
        </button>
      </div>
      `,
      data: {
        greetings: 'Hello World!'
      },
      methods: {
        toItalian () {
          this.greetings = 'Ciao Mondo!'
        }
      }
    }).$mount()
  })
})
```

Note how you are declaring the vm variable at the beginning to reference our Vue instance.

Just after the `beforeEach` (but inside the `describe`), add the following (empty for now) test:

```
it(`should greet in Italian after
  toItalian is called`, () => {
})
```

In the first part of the test, you will bring the component to the desired state (after `toItalian` is called):

```
it(`should greet in Italian after
    toItalian is called`, () => {
  vm.toItalian()
})
```

Now, we want to check whether the greeting has changed:

```
it(`should greet in Italian after
    toItalian is called`, () => {
  vm.toItalian()
  expect(vm.greetings).toContain('Ciao Mondo')
})
```

Now, to prove to yourself that the state is reset before each test, add the following:

```
it('should greet in English', () => {
  expect(vm.greetings).toContain('Hello World')
})
```

If the state is really reset, it should contain the English greeting, and if you launch the tests (with the `./node_modules/karma/bin/karma start` command), you'll find that (if there are no errors) indeed it does.

How it works...

Since we have the reference to the Vue instance itself, we can access methods and status variables directly in our tests.

I would like you to spend some time appreciating the name of the tests. The first is titled `should greet in Italian after toItalian is called`. It doesn't make any reference to the page or the graphics, and it doesn't make any assumption on preconditions. Note that the button is never clicked on and, as a matter of fact, the button is not mentioned in the test title.

Had we titled the test `should display 'Ciao Mondo' when Translate button is clicked on`, we would have lied because we never check whether the greeting is actually displayed and we never click on the button in our test.

Naming the test the right way is very important in real applications because when you have thousands of tests and one breaks, the first thing you read about it is the title or what the test should check. If the title is misleading, you are in for a lot of time spent chasing after a red herring.

Testing the DOM

In this recipe, you will learn a technique to quickly test weather the DOM or the web page itself is what it is supposed to be, even when the Vue component is not present in the page.

Getting ready

For this recipe, you should have a test setup already up and working; complete the *Using Jasmine for testing Vue* recipe if you don't know what that means.

I will assume that you have Jasmine installed and you can perform tests.
Basically, all you need is a web page (JSFiddle is okay) and these four dependencies installed:

- `jasmine.css`
- `jasmine.js`
- `jasmine-html.js`
- `boot.js`

If you are using JSFiddle or adding them manually, remember to add them in the specified order.
Find the link to these files in the *Using Jasmine for testing Vue* recipe.

How to do it...

Let's suppose that you are writing a component that displays the `Hello World!` greeting; you want to test that the greeting is actually displayed, but the web page you are testing is already complex enough and you want to test your component in isolation.

Turns out you don't have to actually display the component to prove that it works. You can display and test your component outside the document.

Write the following setup for your greeting in your test file or test part of your page:

```
describe('my app', () => {
  let vm
  beforeEach(() => {
    vm = new Vue({
      template: '<div>{{greetings}}</div>',
      data: {
        greetings: 'Hello World'
      }
    })
  })
})
```

To materialize our Vue instance as an off-document element, we just need to add the `$mount()` API call:

```
beforeEach(() => {
    vm = new Vue({
        template: '<div>{{greetings}}</div>',
        data: {
```

```
        greetings: 'Hello World'
      }
    }).$mount()
  })
```

Since we have the reference to vm, we can now test our component to access the element rendered off-document:

```
it('should say Hello World', () => {
  expect(vm.$el.innerText).toContain('Hello World')
})
```

The vm.$el element represents our component, but it's not reachable from the normal DOM.

How it works...

On initialization, the Vue instance checks whether there is an el option. In our recipes, we usually include an el option, but this time we have a template instead:

```
vm = new Vue({
  template: '<div>{{greetings}}</div>',
  data: {
    greetings: 'Hello World'
  }
}).$mount()
```

When the Vue instance has the el option, it automatically mounts to that element (if found); in our case, the Vue instances waits for the $mount call instead. We don't provide any arguments to the function and so the component gets rendered off-document.

At this point, the only way to retrieve it in the DOM is through the $el property. The $el property is always present once the component is mounted, irrespective of whether the component was mounted manually or automatically.

From there, we can access it as we would access any normal component and test whether everything is as we expect.

Testing DOM asynchronous updates

In Vue, when the status of your component changes, the DOM is changed accordingly; that's why we call the status reactive. The only gotcha here is that the update is not synchronous; it happens that we have to wait additional time for the changes to actually propagate.

Getting ready

For this recipe, I will assume that you have already completed the *Using Jasmine for testing Vue* recipe, and you know how to write a basic test.

How to do it...

The test we will write is an illustration of how Vue's update mechanism works. From there, you will then be able to write asynchronous tests on your own.

In the `beforeEach` function of our test suite, write the following Vue instance:

```
describe('my app', () => {
  let vm
  beforeEach(() => {
    vm = new Vue({
      template: `
        <div>
          <input id="name" v-model="name">
          <p>Hello from
            <span id="output">{{name}}</span>
          </p>
        </div>
      `,
      data: {
        name: undefined
      }
    }).$mount()
  })
})
```

This will create a component with a text box and a span element that will contain the `Hello from` ... phrase and whatever is written in the text box.

What we will do to test this component is write `Herman` in the text box (programmatically, not manually), and then wait for the DOM to update. When the DOM has updated, we check whether the `Hello from Herman` phrase appears.

Let's start with an empty test just after the `beforeEach` function:

```
it('should display Hello from Herman after Herman is typed in the text-
box', done => {
  done()
})
```

The preceding test passes already. Note that we are taking the done argument and then we are calling it as a function. The test will not pass until `done()` is called.

Assign the `<span>` element to a variable for convenience and then insert the text `Herman` in to the text box:

```
it('should display Hello from Herman after Herman is typed in the text-
box', done => {
  const outputEl = vm.$el.querySelector('#output')
  vm.$el.querySelector('#name').value = 'Herman'
  done()
})
```

While we have to wait for the DOM to update when we modify the state, the opposite is not true; when we have modified the DOM, we can already check whether the `name` variable has changed:

```
it('should display Hello from Herman after Herman is typed in the text-
box', done => {
  const outputEl = vm.$el.querySelector('#output')
  vm.$el.querySelector('#name').value = 'Herman'
  expect(vm.name = 'Herman')
  done()
})
```

Launch the test while you edit it to check whether it works.

Next, we will install a listener for the next update cycle of the `Vue` component, called a tick:

```
it('should display Hello from Herman after Herman is typed in the text-
box', done => {
  const outputEl = vm.$el.querySelector('#output')
  vm.$el.querySelector('#name').value = 'Herman'
  expect(vm.name = 'Herman')
  vm.$nextTick(() => {
    done()
```

```
    })
  })
```

Everything inside the `$nextTick` block is run only after the DOM is updated. We will check that the content of the `<span>` element has changed:

```
it('should display Hello from Herman after Herman is typed in the text-
box', done => {
  const outputEl = vm.$el.querySelector('#output')
  vm.$el.querySelector('#name').value = 'Herman'
  expect(outputEl.textContent).not.toContain('Herman')
  expect(vm.name = 'Herman')
  vm.$nextTick(() => {
    expect(outputEl.textContent).toContain('Herman')
    done()
  })
})
```

Note how we also verify that the DOM is unchanged before the tick.

How it works...

The official documentation states the following:

Vue performs DOM updates **asynchronously**. *Whenever a data change is observed, it will open a queue and buffer all the data changes that happen in the same event loop.*

For this reason, many tests require the `$nextTick` helper. There is, however, an ongoing effort to create better tools to deal with testing and synchronicity so, while this recipe illustrates the problem, it might not be the most up-to-date method to deal with the test.

End-to-end testing with nightwatch

Sometimes unit tests just don't cut it. We may need to integrate two features developed independently and, while each works and is unit tested, there is no easy way to test them along with a unit test. Also, it defeats the purpose of unit tests--testing atomic units of the software. Integration testing and e2e (end-to-end) testing can be performed in these cases. Nightwatch is software that basically mimics a user clicking and typing around in a website. This is probably what we want as an ultimate verification that the whole system works.

Getting ready

Before beginning your journey in this somewhat advanced recipe, you should already be familiar with the command line and npm. Check the *Choosing a development environment* recipe if you are not familiar with them.

How to do it...

Create a new folder for this recipe and create a new file inside it, named `index.html`.

This file will contain our Vue application and it is what we will test. Write the following in this file:

```
<!DOCTYPE html>
<html>
<head>
  <title>Nightwatch tests</title>
  <script src="https://unpkg.com/vue/dist/vue.js"></script>
</head>
<body>
  <div id="app">
  </div>
  <script>
  </script>
</body>
</html>
```

As you can see, this is just the usual boilerplate for a small Vue application. Inside the `<div>`, put a header and a button; when we click on the button, the text `Hello Nightwatch!` will be displayed:

```
<div id="app">
  <h2>Welcome to my test page</h2>
  <button @click="show = true">Show</button>
  <p v-show="show">Hello Nightwatch!</p>
</div>
```

Inside the script tag, write the following JavaScript to make it work:

```
<script>
  const vm = new Vue({
    el: '#app',
    data: {
      show: false
    }
```

```
    })
  </script>
```

Our application is complete; now we move into the test part of the recipe.

Launch these commands to install what would be your dependencies:

```
npm install -g selenium-standalone http-server nightwatch
```

This will install the Selenium server, which is necessary to automate browser actions, and it is what really makes nightwatch work. The `http-server` command will be useful to serve our working website without having to memorize a long file path. Finally, it will install nightwatch itself which, for the most part, is a wrapper and JavaScript API for Selenium.

When npm finishes installing all these tools, create a new file, named `nightwatch.json`, that will contain the nightwatch configuration and write this inside it:

```
{
  "src_folders" : ["tests"],
  "test_settings" : {
    "default" : {
      "desiredCapabilities": {
        "browserName": "chrome"
      }
    }
  }
}
```

The first setting says that you will write all your tests inside a folder called tests (which we will create); the second setting just sets Chrome as our default browser to run tests into.

Now, create, `test` directory and a `test.js` file inside it. In the file, we will test the app. We will verify that when the app launches, the <p> tag is not visible and that when we click on the button it should appear.

An empty test will look like this:

```
module.exports = {
  'Happy scenario' :client => {}
}
```

Here, the client is the browser (Chrome in this case).

We will serve our application at the `http://localhost:8080` address, so first we want the browser to go to this address. For this we would write the following code:

```
module.exports = {
  'Happy scenario' :client => {
client
     .url('http://localhost:8080')
  }
}
```

Next, we wait for the page to load; we do this indirectly by waiting for the `<div>` with `id="app"` to appear:

```
module.exports = {
  'Happy scenario' :client => {
    client
      .url('http://localhost:8080')
      .waitForElementVisible('#app', 1000)
  }
}
```

The second argument is the number of milliseconds we are willing to wait before considering the test failed.

Next, we want to ensure that the header is also displayed correctly and there is no `<p>` element visible:

```
module.exports = {
  'Happy scenario' :client => {
    client
      .url('http://localhost:8080')
      .waitForElementVisible('#app', 1000)
.assert.containsText('h2', 'Welcome to')
      .assert.hidden('p')
  }
}
```

We then click on the button and assert that the `<p>` element is visible and contains the word `Nightwatch`:

```
module.exports = {
  'Happy scenario' :client => {
    client
      .url('http://localhost:8080')
      .waitForElementVisible('#app', 1000)
      .assert.containsText('h2', 'Welcome to')
      .assert.hidden('p')
```

```
.click('button')
    .waitForElementVisible('p', 1000)
    .assert.containsText('p', 'Nightwatch')
    .end();
  }
}
```

The `end()` function will mark the test as having succeeded, as there are no more things to check for.

To actually launch this test, you will need to launch the following command:

```
selenium-standalone install
```

This will install Selenium, then open three different command lines. In the first, launch the Selenium server with the following command:

```
selenium-standalone start
```

In the second command line, go to the root of your recipe folder, where `index.html` is, and launch `http-server`:

```
http-server .
```

This will tell you after it's launched that your website is served at `http://localhost:8080`. This is just like the address we wrote in our test. You can navigate to it right now to see the application running:

Lastly, in the third command line, again go inside your recipe folder and type the following command:

```
nightwatch
```

If everything goes well, you will see the browser flashing before your eyes and displaying the application for a fraction of a second (depending on the speed of your computer), and in the console, you should see something like this:

```
sting and e2e testing/7.6    7.6 •   nightwatch

[Test] Test Suite

Running:  Happy scenario
  ✓ Element <#app> was visible after 51 milliseconds.
  ✓ Testing if element <h2> contains text: "Welcome to".
  ✓ Testing if element <p> is hidden.
  ✓ Element <p> was visible after 24 milliseconds.
  ✓ Testing if element <p> contains text: "Nightwatch".

OK. 5 assertions passed. (1.777s)
```

How it works...

If this recipe looked like a lot of effort, don't despair, Vue templates already have this setup all sorted out inside them. You know how all this machinery works but when, in the later recipes, we use Webpack, you will only need one command to run e2e tests because everything is already set up.

Note how the title of the end-to-end test is rather generic, and it refers to a particular action flow rather than detailing the context and what is expected. This is common for e2e tests as you are usually better off building user stories and then branching them and naming each branch after a particular scenario. So, just to give an example, if we were expecting a response from the server and it didn't come back, we could test a scenario in which we give an error and call the test *Server error scenario*.

Simulating a double-click in nightwatch

This recipe is candy for all those who have struggled to simulate a double-click in nightwatch. Being one of them in the first place, I'm sympathetic. As it turns out, there is a `doubleClick` function in nightwatch but, at least in the opinion of the author, it doesn't work as expected.

Getting ready

This recipe is for developers who are starting out in nightwatch and struggle with this particular problem. You want to learn how to simulate a double-click for testing and you don't know nightwatch? Go back one recipe.

I will assume that your setup with nightwatch is working and you can launch tests. I will also assume that you have all the commands installed from the preceding recipe.

How it works...

Let's assume that you have the following Vue application in an `index.html` file:

```
<!DOCTYPE html>
<html>
<head>
  <title>7.6</title>
  <script src="https://unpkg.com/vue/dist/vue.js"></script>
</head>
<body>
  <div id="app">
    <h2>Welcome to my test page</h2>
    <button id="showBtn" @dblclick="show = true">
      Show
    </button>
    <p v-show="show">Hello Nightwatch!</p>
  </div>
</body>
</html>
```

Just after the `<div>` element, add this script:

```
<script>
  const vm = new Vue({
    el: '#app',
    data: {
      show: false
    }
  })
</script>
```

You can serve your app with `http-server`. Go to `http://localhost:8080` with your browser, and you can try double-clicking on the button to make the text appear.

Now, if we want to test that, we look at nightwatch's API and discover that it has a function call named `doubleClick()`.

We can then write a test similar to the one in the preceding recipe:

```
'Happy scenario' : function (client) {
  client
    .url('http://localhost:8080')
    .waitForElementVisible('#app', 1000)
    .assert.containsText('h2', 'Welcome to')
    .assert.hidden('p')
.doubleClick('button') // not working
    .waitForElementVisible('p', 1000)
    .assert.containsText('p', 'Nightwatch')
    .end();
}
```

Except that this won't work as expected. The right way to do it is the following:

```
'Happy scenario' : function (client) {
  client
    .url('http://localhost:8080')
    .waitForElementVisible('#app', 1000)
    .assert.containsText('h2', 'Welcome to')
    .assert.hidden('p')
    .moveToElement('tag name', 'button', 0, 0)
    .doubleClick()
    .waitForElementVisible('p', 1000)
    .assert.containsText('p', 'Nightwatch')
    .end();
}
```

Double-click only works if you first *move* to the element you want to double-click on; only then you can call `doubleClick` without any argument.

How it works...

The arguments for the `moveToElement` function are the following:

- `selector`: We used `tag name` as a selector
- `tag/selector`: We looked for the `button` tag; had we used another selector here, we would have put a different format

- `xoffset`: This is where the virtual mouse will be positioned in x coordinates; for us, 0 was okay as, even on the edge of a button, clicking is valid
- `yoffset`: This is similar to the preceding argument, but on the y-axis

There is a range of commands that, after having been brought to the right position, can release events. We used `doubleClick`, but there are others as well.

Different styles of unit testing

We've discovered and used Jasmine in the previous recipes. In this recipe, we will explore and compare different styles of unit testing. This is particularly relevant because Vue templates come with Mocha and Chai preinstalled. Chai enables you to write your tests in three different styles.

Getting ready

This recipe doesn't require any particular previous knowledge, but I highly suggest that you complete the *Using Jasmine for testing Vue* recipe.

How to do it...

For this recipe to work, you will need two dependencies: Mocha and Chai. You will find them in no time with Google; just remember that Mocha comes in two different files: `mocha.js` and `mocha.css`. You will have to add them both if you want it to display nicely.

If you are using JSFiddle, continue as usual; otherwise, just make sure to have Vue as well in the dependencies.

Our HTML layout will look like this:

```
<div id="app">
  <p>{{greeting}}</p>
</div>
<div id="mocha">
</div>
```

The mocha bit is where all the results will be presented.

In the JavaScript part, write the simplest `Vue` application and assign it to a variable:

```
const vm = new Vue({
  el: '#app',
  data: {
    greeting: 'Hello World!'
  }
})
```

We will write a test to see whether the `Hello world` text really gets displayed.

Just after the `Vue` application is finished, write the following:

```
mocha.setup('bdd')
chai.should()
describe('my app', () => {
  it('should say Hello World', () => {
    vm.$el.innerText.should.contain('Hello World')
  })
})
mocha.run()
```

The preceding code is preparing `mocha` and `chai` (by installing the `describe`, `it` and `should` functions) and then asserting that the inner text of our component should contain `Hello World`. Pretty readable, don't you think?

You can launch your application and you will see this:

There are two other ways `chai` lets us write the very same test. The first one is as follows:

```
vm.$el.innerText.should.contain('Hello World')
```

To use the second one, you have to add `const expect = chai.expect` before it:

```
expect(vm.$el.innerText).to.contain('Hello World')
```

Finally, add the `const assert = chai.assert` line before:

```
assert.include(vm.$el.innerText,
    'Hello World',
    'Component innerText include Hello World')
```

It's idiomatic for the assert style to add a message as an additional argument to make a test more verbose when something goes wrong.

How it works...

Chai is a simple library that implements some functions and throws exceptions when some conditions are not satisfied. Mocha, on the other hand, runs certain bits of code, collects the exceptions, and tries to display them to the user in a nice way.

While it's largely a matter of taste as to what style to use, there are some subtle differences between the three styles.

- `Should` has the added value of being more eloquent and readable. Unfortunately, it extends `Object`, adding the `should` function to everything. You shouldn't mind if you don't know how to react to the last phrase, but the correct way to behave is run and scream in pain; never extend `Object`.
- `Assert` means writing a detailed description of every assertion, and this is usually good if you write multiple assertions for each test. Personally, I consider it a good practice to write at most one assertion per test and concentrate on the title for description.
- `Expect` does not extend `Object` and is very readable with a good balance, and normally I prefer to use it over the other alternatives.

Stubbing external API calls with Sinon.JS

Normally, when you do end-to-end testing and integration testing, you will have the backend server running and ready to respond to you. I think there are many situations in which this is not desirable. As a frontend developer, you take every opportunity to blame the backend guys.

Getting ready

No particular skills are required to complete this recipe, but you should install Jasmine as a dependency; this is explained in detail in the *Using Jasmine for testing Vue* recipe.

How to do it...

First of all, let's install some dependencies. For this recipe, we will use Jasmine to run the whole thing; you can find detailed instructions in the *Using Jasmine for testing Vue* recipe (the four files you'll need are `jasmine.css`, `jasmine.js`, `jasmine-html.js`, and `boot.js`, in this order)

Also, install Sinon.JS and Axios before continuing; you just need to add the `js` files relative to them.

We will build an application that retrieves a post at the click of a button. In the HTML part, write the following:

```
<div id="app">
  <button @click="retrieve">Retrieve Post</button>
  <p v-if="post">{{post}}</p>
</div>
```

Instead, the JavaScript part will look like the following:

```
const vm = new Vue({
  el: '#app',
  data: {
    post: undefined
  },
  methods: {
  retrieve () {
    axios
      .get('https://jsonplaceholder.typicode.com/posts/1')
      .then(response => {
        console.log('setting post')
        this.post = response.data.body
      })
    }
  }
})
```

If you launch your application now, you should be able to see it working:

```
Retrieve Post

quia et suscipit suscipit recusandae consequuntur expedita et cum
reprehenderit molestiae ut ut quas totam nostrum rerum est autem sunt
rem eveniet architecto
```

Now we want to test the application, but we don't want to connect to the real server. This will take additional time and it will not be reliable; instead, we will take a sample correct response from the server and use that instead.

Sinon.JS has the concept of a sandbox. It means that whenever a test starts, some dependencies, such as Axios are overwritten. After each test, we can discard the sandbox and everything returns to normal.

An empty test with Sinon.JS looks like the following (add it after the Vue instance):

```
describe('my app', () => {
  let sandbox
  beforeEach(() => sandbox = sinon.sandbox.create())
  afterEach(() => sandbox.restore())
})
```

We want to stub the call to the get function for axios:

```
describe('my app', () => {
  let sandbox
  beforeEach(() => sandbox = sinon.sandbox.create())
  afterEach(() => sandbox.restore())
it('should save the returned post body', done => {
const promise = new Promise(resolve =>
      resolve({ data: { body: 'Hello World' } })
    )
    sandbox.stub(axios, 'get').returns(promise)
    ...
    done()
  })
})
```

We are overwriting axios here. We are saying that now the get method should return the resolved promise:

```
describe('my app', () => {
  let sandbox
  beforeEach(() => sandbox = sinon.sandbox.create())
```

```
    afterEach(() => sandbox.restore())
    it('should save the returned post body', done => {
      const promise = new Promise(resolve =>
        resolve({ data: { body: 'Hello World' } })
      )
      sandbox.stub(axios, 'get').returns(promise)
      vm.retrieve()
      promise.then(() => {
        expect(vm.post).toEqual('Hello World')
        done()
      })
    })
  })
})
```

Since we are returning a promise (and we need to return a promise because the `retrieve` method is calling `then` on it), we need to wait until it resolves.

We can launch the page and see whether it works:

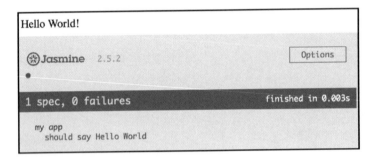

If you are using JSFiddle, remember to set **Load Type** to **No wrap - in** <body> or Vue won't get a chance to start.

How it works...

In our case, we used the sandbox to stub a method of one of our dependencies. This way, the `get` method of axios never gets fired and we receive an object that is similar to what the backend will give us.

Stubbing the API responses will get you isolated from the backend and its quirks. If something goes wrong, you won't mind and, moreover, you can run your test without relying on the backend running correctly.

There are many libraries and techniques to stub API calls in general, not only related to HTTP. Hopefully, this recipe has given you a head start.

Measuring the coverage of your code

Code coverage is one of the most used and understandable metrics to evaluate the quality of a piece of software. If a test exercises a particular portion of code, the code is said to be covered. This suggests that that particular portion of code is working correctly and has less chance of containing bugs.

Getting ready

Before measuring your code coverage, ensure that you complete the *Adding some Karma to your workflow* recipe as we will be using Karma to help us.

How to do it...

Create a new directory and place a file named `package.json` in it. Inside it, write the following:

```
{
  "name": "learning-code-coverage",
  "version": "1.0.0"
}
```

This creates an npm project. In the same directory, run the following command to install our dependencies:

```
npm install vue karma karma jasmine karma-jasmine karma-coverage karma-chrome-launcher --save-dev
```

The `package.json` file changes accordingly.

The `karma-coverage` plugin uses the underlying software, Istanbul, to measure and display the coverage of our tests.

To make the next step a little easier, we will install Karma globally (if you have not already done it). Run the following command:

```
npm install -g karma
```

When Karma is installed, run the following command in your directory; it will create a Karma configuration file:

```
karma init
```

Answer the default value for all questions except when it asks you the files to load; in that case, write the following two lines:

- node_modules/vue/dist/vue.js
- *.js

Leave a blank line after that to confirm.
This will load Vue and all the files that end with the js extension in the root of the directory.

Open the file that Karma created; it should be called karma.conf.js and it should be in your directory along with the other files.

There should be a part like the following:

```
preprocessors: {
},
```

Inside the preprocessors object, insert coverage, as follows:

```
preprocessors: {
'myApp.js': ['coverage']
},
```

This means that we want to preprocess the myApp.js file with the coverage preprocessor. The myApp.js file will contain our application to test.

Just after that, in the reporters array, add coverage:

```
reporters: ['progress', 'coverage'],
```

This will make the coverage reporter print a web page with the coverage measurements. In order for the setup to work properly, you need to set another property, called `plugins`, between `frameworks` and `files`:

```
plugins: [
  'karma-jasmine',
  'karma-coverage',
  'karma-chrome-launcher'
],
```

Next, we will write a simple Vue application that we want to test.

Create a file named `myApp.js`; we will create a number guessing game.

Write the following inside the file:

```
const myApp = {
  template: `
    <div>
      <p>
        I am thinking of a number between 1 and 20.
      </p>
      <input v-model="guess">
      <p v-if="guess">{{output}}</p>
    </div>
  `
}
```

The user will input a number and the output will display a hint or a text to celebrate victory if the number is right. Add the following status to the `myApp` object:

```
data: {
  number: getRandomInt(1, 20),
  guess: undefined
}
```

At the top of the file, you can add a `getRandomInt` function, as illustrated:

```
function getRandomInt(min, max) {
  return Math.floor(Math.random() * (max - min)) + min;
}
```

We also need a computed property to display the hints:

```
computed: {
  output () {
    if (this.guess < this.number) {
      return 'Higher...'
```

```
        }
        if (this.guess > this.number) {
            return 'Lower...'
        }
        return 'That's right!'
    }
}
```

Our application is complete. Let's test weather it works as expected.

Create a file named `test.js` at the root of the directory and write the following test:

```
describe('my app', () => {
  let vm
  beforeEach(() => {
    vm = new Vue(myApp).$mount()
    vm.number = 5
  })
  it('should output That's right! if guess is 5', () => {
    vm.guess = 5
    expect(vm.output).toBe('That's right!')
  })
})
```

To run the tests, use the following command:

karma start

If the preceding command fails to ask for the `karma-coverage` plugin to be installed when it's already installed, you can either install the plugin globally or use the locally installed Karma to run the tests from `./node-modules/karma/bin/karma start`.

If your browser opens, go back to the console and, when the test finishes, hit *Ctrl + C* to stop Karma.

If everything went well, you should have a new folder named coverage with a directory named Chrome inside it. You should also find a file named `index.html` inside it. Open it, and you will see a page like this:

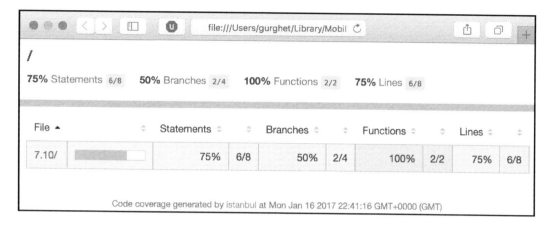

Right from the start, we can see that yellow indicates that something is wrong. We tested 100% of the functions but only 50% of the if branches.

If you navigate through and open the details of the `myApp.js` file, you will see that we are not testing two branches of the `if` statement:

```
18        },
19        computed: {
20          output () {
21 1x           if (this.guess < this.number) {
22                 return 'Higher...'
23             }
24 1x           if (this.guess > this.number) {
25                 return 'Lower...'
26             }
27 1x           return 'That's right!'
28           }
29        }
30
```

We can have errors inside those branches and we may not even know it!

Try adding these two tests inside the test file:

```
it('should output Lower... if guess is 6', () => {
  vm.guess = 6
  expect(vm.output).toBe('Lower...')
})
it('should output Higher... if guess is 4', () => {
  vm.guess = 4
  expect(vm.output).toBe('Higher...')
})
```

Now if you run the test and open the report, it looks much greener:

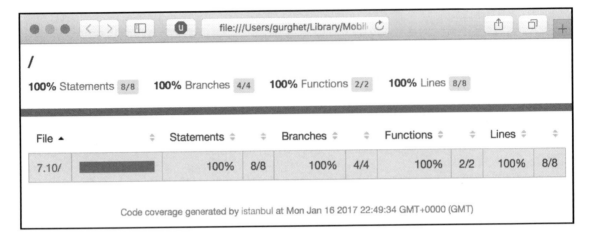

How it works...

We never even opened the application, but we are already pretty sure that it works correctly, thanks to our tests.

Furthermore, we have a report that shows us that we covered 100% of the code. Although we have only tested the guessing game for three numbers, we covered all the possible branches.

We will never be sure that our software is free of bugs, but these kinds of tool help us developers a great deal in adding features to our software without having nightmares that we might have broken something.

8
Organize + Automate + Deploy = Webpack

In this chapter, we will talk about the following topics:

- Extracting logic from your components to keep the code tidy
- Bundling your component with Webpack`Preview`
- Organizing your dependencies with Webpack
- Using external components in your Webpack project
- Developing with continuous feedback with hot reloading
- Using Babel to compile from ES6
- Running a code linter while developing
- Using only one command to build both a minified and a development .js file
- Releasing your components to the public

Introduction

Webpack coupled with npm is a very powerful tool. In essence, it's just a bundler that takes some files along with their dependencies and bundles everything into one or more consumable files. It's now in its second version and represents much more than before, especially for Vue developers.

Webpack will enable you to write components conveniently isolated in single files and shippable on command. It will enable you to use different JavaScript standards, such as ES6, but also other languages altogether, all thanks to **loaders**, a concept that will recur in the following recipes.

Extracting logic from your components to keep the code tidy

Vue components can become very complex sometimes. In these cases, it's better to split them up and try to hide some complexity with abstraction. The best place to put such complexity is external JavaScript files. This way you have the added benefit that, if necessary, it's easier to share the extracted logic with additional components.

Getting ready

This recipe is of intermediate level. Before coming here, you should have completed the *Choosing a development environment* recipe in `Chapter 1`, *Getting Started with Vue.js*, and should know how to set up a project with npm.

Also, ensure that you have the `vue-cli` package installed globally with the following command:

```
npm install -g vue-cli
```

How to do it...

We will build a calculator for compound interest; you will discover how much money you will have after an initial investment.

Creating a clean Webpack project

Create a new directory and a new `Vue` project inside it with the following command:

```
vue init webpack
```

You can choose the default values for the questions asked.

Run `npm install` to install all the required dependencies.

Then, navigate to `src/App.vue` in the directory structure and delete pretty much everything inside the file.

The final result should be as follows:

```
<template>
  <div id="app">
  </div>
</template>

<script>
export default {
  name: 'app'
}
</script>

<style>
</style>
```

> I've already done this for you, and, you can use another template with the following command instead:
> `vue init gurghet/webpack`

Building the compound interest calculator

To build the compound interest calculator, you need three fields: the initial capital or principal, the yearly interest rate, and the investment length. You will then add an output field to display the final result. Here's the corresponding HTML code:

```
<div id="app">
  <div>
    <label>principal capital</label>
    <input v-model.number="principal">
  </div>
  <div>
    <label>Yearly interestRate</label>
    <input v-model.number="interestRate">
  </div>
  <div>
    <label>Investment length (timeYears)</label>
    <input v-model.number="timeYears">
  </div>
  <div>
    You will gain:
    <output>{{final}}</output>
```

```
    </div>
  </div>
```

We put the `.number` modifier, or otherwise the numbers we put inside will be converted to strings by JavaScript.

In the JavaScript part, declare the three model variables by writing the following code:

```
export default {
  name: 'app',
  data () {
    return {
      principal: 0,
      interestRate: 0,
      timeYears: 0
    }
  }
}
```

To calculate the compound interest, we take the math formula for it:

$$FinalCapital = (1 + YearlyInterestRate)^{Years}$$

In JavaScript, it can be written as follows:

```
P * Math.pow((1 + r), t)
```

You have to add this to the `Vue` component as a computed property, as shown:

```
computed: {
  final () {
    const P = this.principal
    const r = this.interestRate
    const t = this.timeYears
    return P * Math.pow((1 + r), t)
  }
}
```

You can run your application with the following command (launched from your directory):

```
npm run dev
```

Now that our application works, you can see how much we will gain by putting 0.93 dollars into a bank account with 2.25 percent interest and hibernating for 1,000 years (4.3 billion dollars!):

principal capital	0.93
Yearly interestRate	0.0225
Investment length (timeYears)	1000
You will gain: 4283508449.711061	

The formula inside the code is not much of a bother right now. Still, what if we had another component that also does the same calculation? We would also like to make it more explicit that we are computing the compound interest and we don't actually care what the formula does in this scope.

Create a new file, named `compoundInterest.js`, inside the `src` folder; write the following code inside it:

```
export default function (Principal, yearlyRate, years) {
  const P = Principal
  const r = yearlyRate
  const t = years
  return P * Math.pow((1 + r), t)
}
```

We then modify the code in `App.vue` accordingly:

```
computed: {
  final () {
    return compoundInterest(
        this.principal,
        this.interestRate,
        this.timeYears
    )
  }
}
```

Also, remember to import the file we just created at the top of the JavaScript part:

```
<script>
  import compoundInterest from './compoundInterest'
  export default {
  ...
```

How it works...

When working in a component or when programming in general, it's much better to reduce the scope of the code to only one layer of abstraction. When we write a computed function that returns the final capital value, we should only worry about calling the right function-- the one that does the right calculation for our purpose. The internals of the formula are on a lower layer of abstraction and we don't want to deal with that.

What we have done is that we brought all the nitty gritty of the calculations in a separate file. We then exported the function from the file with the following line:

```
export default function (Principal, yearlyRate, years) {
...
```

This makes the function available by default when we import the file from our `Vue` component:

```
import compoundInterest from './compoundInterest'
...
```

So, now `compoundInterest` is the function we defined in the other file. Furthermore, this separation of concerns allow us to use this function to compute compound interest everywhere in our code, even in other files (potentially other projects too).

Bundling your component with Webpack

Webpack lets you package your project in minified JavaScript files. You can then distribute these files or use them yourself. When you use the inbuilt templates that come with `vue-cli`, Webpack is configured to build an entire working application with it. Sometimes we want to build a library to publish or use in another project. In this recipe, you will tweak the default configuration of the Webpack template to release a component instead.

Getting ready

This recipe will make sense to you only after you have installed npm (refer to the *Choosing a development environment* recipe in `Chapter 1`, *Getting Started with Vue.js*) and got familiar with `vue-cli` and the Webpack template.

How to do it...

For this recipe, you will build a reusable component that shakes whatever you put into it; for this, we will use the excellent CSShake library.

Create a new clean project based on the Webpack template. You can take a look at the previous recipe to see how to do that, or you can use the prebuilt template I made. You can use my template by creating a new directory and running this command:

```
vue init gurghet/webpack
```

Choose the default answers if you don't know what they mean. Remember to run npm install to bring in the dependencies.

Let's first rename a couple of things: rename the App.vue file to Shaker.vue.

Inside it, write the following as the HTML template:

```
<template>
  <span id="shaker" class="shake">
    <link rel="stylesheet" type="text/css"
href="https://csshake.surge.sh/csshake.min.css">
    <slot></slot>
  </span>
</template>
```

Note how we changed the <div> into a <span> with respect to the original template. That's because we want our shaker to be an inline component.

The component is complete as it is; we just need a minor cosmetic edit in the JavaScript part:

```
<script>
  export default {
    name: 'shaker'
  }
</script>
```

To manually test our application, we can modify the main.js file in the following way (the highlighted text is the modified code):

```
// The Vue build version to load with the `import` command
// (runtime-only or standalone) has been set in webpack.base.conf with an
alias.
import Vue from 'vue'
import Shaker from './Shaker'
```

```
/* eslint-disable no-new */
new Vue({
  el: '#app',
  template: `
    <div>
       This is a <Shaker>test</Shaker>
    </div>
    `
  ,
  components: { Shaker }
})
```

This will create a sample page as shown in the following screenshot, in which we can prototype our component with hot-reloading. Launch it by running the following command:

npm run dev

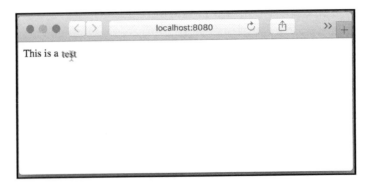

Placing the cursor over the word test should make it shake.

Now, we would like to package this component in a single JavaScript file that can be reused in the future.

There is no configuration present for this in the default template, but it's easy enough to add one.

First of all, you have to do some hammering in the webpack.prod.js file inside the build folder.

Let's get rid of some plugins that we don't need for releasing a library; find the `plugins` array inside the file. It's an array containing plugins in the form of the following code:

```
plugins: [
  new Plugin1(...),
  new Plugin2(...),
  ...
  new PluginN(...)
]
```

We only need the following plugins:

- `webpack.DefinePlugin`
- `webpack.optimize.UglifyJsPlugin`
- `webpack.optimize.OccurrenceOrderPlugin`

Get rid of all the other plugins as we don't need them; the final array should look like this:

```
plugins: [
  new webpack.DefinePlugin({
    'process.env': env
  }),
  new webpack.optimize.UglifyJsPlugin({
    compress: {
      warnings: false
    }
  }),
  new webpack.optimize.OccurrenceOrderPlugin()
]
```

The first one allows you to add some more configuration, the second plugin minifies the file, and the third one will optimize the size of the resulting file.

Another property we need to edit is `output`, as we want to simplify the output path.

The original property looks like this:

```
output: {
  path: config.build.assetsRoot,
  filename: utils.assetsPath('js/[name].[chunkhash].js'),
  chunkFilename: utils.assetsPath('js/[id].[chunkhash].js')
}
```

What it does originally is create a series of output files inside a `js` directory. There are variables in square parentheses; we won't need them because you only have one self-contained module for our application, which we'll call *shaker*. We need to obtain the following code:

```
output: {
  path: config.build.assetsRoot,
  filename: utils.assetsPath('shaker.js')
}
```

Since, as just said, you want the component to be self-contained, we need some more modifications, which will also depend on your needs.

If you want the component to have any CSS styling built-in (we have none in our case as we are using an external CSS library), you should disable the `ExtractTextPlugin`; we already deleted the plugin from the list but some other files are still using it. Find the `extract` option inside the `vue-loader.conf.js` file (the `vue` section of the same file in some versions) and replace it with the following code:

```
... {
  loaders: utils.cssLoaders({
    ...
    extract: false
  })
}
```

Our component will normally contain the Vue library inside; if you want to use the component in a Vue project, you don't need this, as it would be duplicated code. You can tell Webpack to just search for dependencies externally and not include them. Add the following property in the `webpack.prod.js` file you just modified before `plugins`:

```
externals: {
  'vue': 'Vue'
}
```

This will tell Webpack not to write the Vue library into the bundle but to just take a global, named `Vue`, and use it wherever the `vue` dependency is imported in our code. The Webpack configuration is almost done; we just need to add another property before the `module` property:

```
var webpackConfig = merge(baseWebpackConfig, {
  entry: {
    app: './src/dist.js'
  },
  module: {
    ...
```

This will start the compilation reading code from the `dist.js` file. Wait a minute, this file doesn't exist yet. Let's create it and add the following code inside:

```
import Vue from 'vue'
import Shaker from './Shaker'
Vue.component('shaker', Shaker)
```

In the final JavaScript minified file, the Vue dependency will be taken externally, and then we register the component globally.

As the last change, I would suggest modifying the folder in which the minified file gets saved. In the `config/index.js` file, edit the following line:

```
assetsSubDirectory: 'static',
```

Swap the preceding line with the following code:

```
assetsSubDirectory: '.',
```

Now run the command to build the minified file with npm:

```
npm run build
```

You will see an output that looks like this:

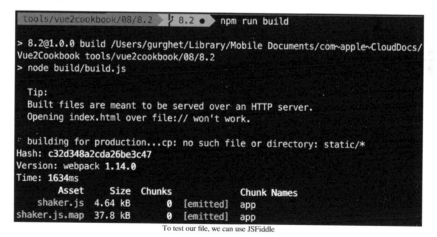

To test our file, we can use JSFiddle

Copy the content of the file you created inside dist/shaker.js, then go to https://gist. github.com/ (you may need to register) and paste the content of the file inside the text area. Name it shaker.js:

Since the text is a single line, you will not see much with the **No wrap** option on. Click on **Create public gist** and when you are presented with the next page, click on **Raw**, as shown in the following screenshot:

Copy the URL in the address bar and go to `http://rawgit.com/`, where you can paste the link:

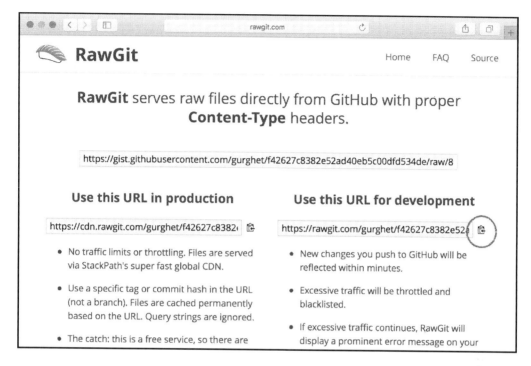

Click and copy the link you get on the right. Congratulations, you just published your component on the Web!

Now head to JSFiddle and pick **Vue** as a library. You can now add the link you copied in the left and you have your component available to use:

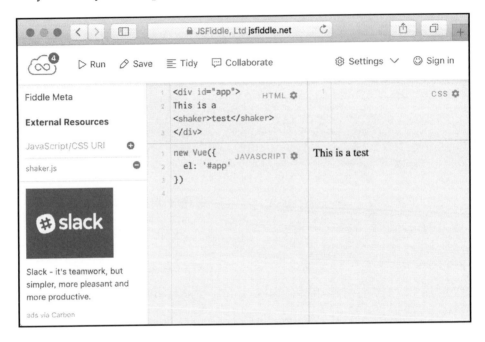

How it works...

Webpack configuration in the official templates is quite involved. On the other hand, don't try to understand everything straight away, or you will get stuck and not learn much anyway.

We created a **UMD (Universal Module Definition)** module that will try and see whether there is a Vue dependency available and install itself as a component.

You can even add CSS and styling to your component and, the way we configured Webpack, the styles will still ship with your component.

There's more...

In the *Releasing your components to the public* recipe in this chapter, you will learn how to publish your component in the npm publish registry. We'll use a different approach than this, but you'll find there the missing steps to publish it to the registry.

Organizing your dependencies with Webpack

Webpack is a tool for organizing your code and dependencies. Furthermore, it gives you a way to develop and build with JavaScript files that embed all the dependencies and modules that we pass to them. We'll use this in this recipe to build a small Vue application and bundle everything in a single file.

Getting ready

This recipe doesn't require any particular skill except the use of npm and some knowledge of the command line. You can find out more in the *Organizing your dependencies with Webpack* recipe in this chapter.

How to do it...

Create a new folder for your recipe and create a `package.json` file with the following content inside it:

```
{
  "name": "recipe",
  "version": "1.0.0"
}
```

This defines an npm project in our folder. You can, of course, use `npm init` or `yarn init` if you know what you're doing.

We will install Webpack 2 for this recipe. To add it to your project dependencies, run the following command:

```
npm install --save-dev webpack@2
```

The `--save-dev` option means that we will not ship the code for Webpack in our final product, but we will use it only for development purposes.

Create a new `app` directory and an `App.vue` file inside it.

This file will be a simple Vue component; it can be as simple as the following:

```
<template>
  <div>
    {{msg}}
  </div>
</template>
<script>
export default {
  name: 'app',
  data () {
    return {
      msg: 'Hello world'
    }
  }
}
</script>
<style>
</style>
```

We need to tell Webpack how to turn .vue files into .js files. To do that, we create a configuration file in the root folder, named webpack.config.js; this file will be automatically picked up by Webpack. Inside this file, write as follows:

```
module.exports = {
  module: {
    rules: [
      {test: /.vue$/, use: 'vue-loader'}
    ]
  }
}
```

The line inside rules says the following:

Hey Webpack, when you see a file that ends in .vue, *use the* vue-loader *to turn it into a JavaScript file.*

We need to install such a loader with npm using the following command:

```
npm install --save-dev vue-loader
```

This loader internally uses other dependencies that will not be installed automatically; we need to do it manually by running the following command:

```
npm install --save-dev vue-template-compiler css-loader
```

Let's also take this opportunity to install Vue itself:

```
npm install --save vue
```

Now our Vue component is ready. We need to write a page in which to place it and try it. Create a file called index.js inside the app folder. We will instantiate the component in a Vue instance. Inside index.js, write the following:

```
import Vue from 'vue'
import App from './App.vue'
new Vue({
  el: '#app',
  render: h => h(App)
})
```

This will mount the Vue instance inside an element with id="app", and it will contain a single component--our App.vue.

We need one more file--an HTML file. In the root directory, create index.html with this code:

```
<!DOCTYPE html>
<html>
  <head>
    <title>Webpack 2 demo</title>
  </head>
  <body>
    <div id="app"></div>
    <script src="dist/bundle.js"></script>
  </body>
</html>
```

We don't want to refer to app/index.js directly here; this is because index.js itself doesn't contain much. It has an import statement that won't be recognized by the browser. Webpack can instead easily create dist/bundle.js with index.js inside, along with all its dependencies. To do it, run this command:

```
./node_modules/webpack/bin/webpack.js app/index.js dist/bundle.js
```

This should generate an output similar to this:

```
 8.3  ● ▶ ./node_modules/webpack/bin/webpack.js app/index.js dist/bundle.js
Hash: 50e77638cffa51b001f1
Version: webpack 2.2.0
Time: 1056ms
    Asset     Size  Chunks            Chunk Names
bundle.js  183 kB      0  [emitted]  main
   [0] ./app/App.vue 1.79 kB {0} [built]
   [1] ./~/vue/dist/vue.runtime.common.js 162 kB {0} [built]
   [2] ./~/css-loader!./~/vue-loader/lib/style-rewriter.js?id=data-v-7057c7d3!./~/vue-loader/lib/selector
.js?type=styles&index=0!./app/App.vue 192 bytes {0} [built]
   [3] ./~/css-loader/lib/css-base.js 1.51 kB {0} [built]
   [4] ./~/process/browser.js 5.3 kB {0} [built]
   [5] ./~/vue-loader/lib/selector.js?type=script&index=0!./app/App.vue 113 bytes {0} [built]
   [6] ./~/vue-loader/lib/template-compiler.js?id=data-v-7057c7d3!./~/vue-loader/lib/selector.js?type=tem
plate&index=0!./app/App.vue 376 bytes {0} [built]
   [7] ./~/vue-style-loader/addStyles.js 6.24 kB {0} [built]
   [8] ./~/vue-style-loader!./~/css-loader!./~/vue-loader/lib/style-rewriter.js?id=data-v-7057c7d3!./~/vu
e-loader/lib/selector.js?type=styles&index=0!./app/App.vue 1.31 kB {0} [built]
   [9] (webpack)/buildin/global.js 509 bytes {0} [built]
  [10] ./app/index.js 99 bytes {0} [built]
```

You can now open `index.html` and you'll see the component working.

However, it's not so much fun to launch this long command every time. Webpack and npm can do better.

In `webpack.config.js`, add the following properties:

```
module.exports = {
entry: './app/index.js',
  output: {
    filename: 'bundle.js',
    path: __dirname + '/dist'
  },
  module: {
  ...
```

This will specify the entry point of Webpack and where the resulting file should be saved.

We can also add a script to `package.json`:

```
"scripts": {
  "build": "webpack"
}
```

Now, launching `npm run build` will have the same effect as the long command we used.

How it works...

In this recipe, we basically created a JavaScript file (`bundle.js`) that simultaneously contains Vue and the component we wrote. In the `index.html`, there is no trace of Vue because it's embedded in `bundle.js`.

This way of working is much better when we have a lot of dependencies. We don't need to add a lot of tags in the head or the body of the page anymore. Also, we don't have to be afraid to load a dependency that we don't need.

As an added bonus, Webpack has the power and flexibility to minify our final file and other advanced optimizations that are simply not possible by loading the dependencies manually.

Using external components in your Webpack project

Using external Vue components in your own project is usually straightforward. Sometimes though, things aren't so simple. In particular, there are some configurations in the official templates with Webpack that (weirdly) actually prevent you from using some external components. In this recipe, we will install a modal dialog component from the Bulma project.

Getting ready

In this recipe, we will tweak the Webpack configuration. It is suggested to have completed the *Organizing your dependencies with Webpack* recipe before taking up this task.

How to do it...

We will start with a fresh Webpack project. You can create a new one using the `vue-cli` and the official Webpack template. My suggestion, however, is to begin with my Webpack template, which is a clean slate. To do it, run the following command in a new directory:

```
vue init gurghet/webpack
```

We will install `vue-bulma-modal`, which is a component written in Vue with the Bulma CSS framework:

```
npm install --save vue-bulma-modal bulma
```

In the preceding command we installed `bulma` too, which contains the actual CSS styles.

To actually make the styles work, we need to turn them into JavaScript for Webpack; this means we need to install a couple of loaders:

```
npm install --save-dev node-sass sass-loader
```

The SASS loader is already configured, so there is no need to touch anything. What we will touch though, is the Webpack configuration related to the Babel loader (learn more about it in the *Developing with continuous feedback with hot reloading* recipe).

In the official template (but this may change, watch out), there is a line that prevents Webpack from compiling dependencies. Go to `build/webpack.base.conf.js` and find this block:

```
{
  test: /.js$/,
  loader: 'babel-loader',
  include: [
    path.join(projectRoot, 'src')
  ],
  exclude: /node_modules/
},
```

Depending on the version of Webpack you are using, you may need to slightly tweak the loader syntax. In older versions of Webpack, for example, you would write `babel` instead of `babel-loader`.

You have to remove the highlighted line and, instead, write the following:

```
{
  test: /.js$/,
  loader: 'babel-loader',
  include: [
    path.join(projectRoot, 'src'),
    path.join(projectRoot, 'node_modules/vue-bulma-modal')
  ]
},
```

This is telling Webpack to compile the component we just installed with `babel-loader`.

Now, write the following HTML layout in `App.vue`:

```
<template>
  <div id="app">
    <card-modal
      @ok="accept"
      ok-text="Accept"
      :visible="popup"
      @cancel="cancel"
    >
      <div class="content">
        <h1>Contract</h1>
          <p>
            I hereby declare I have learned how to
            install third party components in my
            own Vue project.
          </p>
      </div>
    </card-modal>
    <p v-if="signed">It appears you signed!</p>
  </div>
</template>
```

Then, you can write the logic, as shown, in the JavaScript:

```
<script>
import { CardModal } from 'vue-bulma-modal'
export default {
  name: 'app',
  components: { CardModal },
  data () {
    return {
      signed: false,
      popup: true
    }
  },
  methods: {
    accept () {
      this.popup = false
      this.signed = true
    },
    cancel () {
      this.popup = false
    }
  }
}
</script>
```

To actually use the Bulma styles, we need to kick in the SASS loader and import the `bulma` file. Add the following lines:

```
<style lang="sass">
@import '~bulma';
</style>
```

Note how we are specifying the language of our styles in the first line (we are writing SCSS, but in this case we write it as it is).

If you now try to run your app with the `npm run dev` command, you will see the Bulma modal dialog in all its splendor:

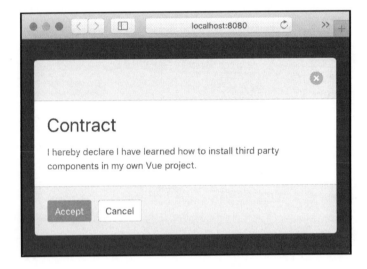

How it works...

The official Webpack template contains the configuration rule to never compile files inside the `node_modules` directory. This means that authors of web components are encouraged to distribute an already compiled file because otherwise users will import raw JavaScript files (since Webpack won't compile them) in their projects, causing all sorts of errors in browsers. Personally, I don't think this is good engineering. One problem with this setup is that since the files you are importing in your project are compiled against one version of Vue, the component might not work (this actually happened in the past) if you use a newer version of Vue.

A better approach is to import the raw files and components and let Webpack compile them in a single file. Unfortunately, the majority of components available in the wild are distributed already compiled, so while it's very quick to import them given the official template, you're more likely to encounter compatibility problems.

When importing external components, the first thing to do is to examine their `package.json` file. Let's see what the `vue-bulma-modal` package contains in this file:

```
{
  "name": "vue-bulma-modal",
  "version": "1.0.1",
  "description": "Modal component for Vue Bulma",
  "main": "src/index.js",
  "peerDependencies": {
    "bulma": ">=0.2",
    "vue": ">=2"
  },
  ...
  "author": "Fangdun Cai <cfddream@gmail.com>",
  "license": "MIT"
}
```

The file referred to by the `main` property is the file we are importing when we write the following line in JavaScript:

```
import { CardModal } from 'vue-bulma-modal'
```

The `src/index.js` file, in turn, contains the following code:

```
import Modal from './Modal'
import BaseModal from './BaseModal'
import CardModal from './CardModal'
import ImageModal from './ImageModal'

export {
  Modal,
  BaseModal,
  CardModal,
  ImageModal
}
```

This is not a compiled file; it's raw ES6 and we know it because `import` is not defined in regular JavaScript. That's why we need Webpack to compile this for us.

On the other hand, consider that we write the following:

```
<style lang="sass">
@import '~bulma';
</style>
```

With the tilde sign (~), we tell Webpack to resolve the style like it was a module and so, what we are really importing is the file referred to by the main in the `package.json` of the `bulma` package, which, if we check, looks as follows:

```
{
  "name": "bulma",
  "version": "0.3.1",
  ...
  "main": "bulma.sass",
  ...
}
```

Since we are importing a SASS with the SASS syntax, we need to specify in the Vue component that we are using `lang="sass"`.

Developing with continuous feedback with hot reloading

Hot reloading is a really useful technology that lets you develop while looking at the results in the browser, without even refreshing the page. It's a very tight loop and can really speed up your development process. In the official Webpack template, hot reloading is installed by default. In this recipe, you will learn how to install it yourself.

Getting ready

Before attempting this recipe, you should have at least a vague idea of how Webpack works; the *Organizing your dependencies with Webpack* recipe in this chapter will have you covered.

How to do it...

Create a new npm project in a new directory, either with `npm init -y` or `yarn init -y`. I personally prefer the second one because the resulting `package.json` is much more compact.

 To install Yarn, you can use the `npm install -g yarn` command. The main benefit of Yarn is that you will be able to lock your dependencies to a known version. This prevents bugs when working in teams and the application gets cloned from Git with slightly different versions that introduce incompatibilities.

You will create a digital swear jar. For every swear word you pronounce, you donate an amount of money to a swear jar for a long term objective.

Create a new file, named `SwearJar.vue`, and add the following code inside it:

```
<template>
  <div>
    Swears: {{counter}} $$
    <button @click="addSwear">+</button>
  </div>
</template>
<script>
export default {
  name: 'swear-jar',
  data () {
    return {
      counter: 0
    }
  },
  methods: {
    addSwear () {
      this.counter++
    }
  }
}
</script>
```

You will insert this component in a web page.

Create a file named `index.html` in the same directory and write the following code:

```html
<!DOCTYPE html>
<html>
  <head>
    <title>Swear Jar Page</title>
  </head>
  <body>
    <div id="app"></div>
    <script src="bundle.js"></script>
  </body>
</html>
```

The `bundle.js` file will be created (in memory) by Webpack for us.

The last app file you need is a JavaScript file that will contain our Vue root instance. Create it in the same directory and name it `index.js`; put the following content in it:

```js
import Vue from 'vue'
import SwearJar from './SwearJar.vue'
new Vue({
  el: '#app',
  render: h => h(SwearJar)
})
```

Now you need to create a file, `webpack.config.js`, to tell Webpack a couple of things. The first thing is the entry point of our application (`index.js`) and where we would like to place the compiled files:

```js
module.exports = {
  entry: './index.js',
  output: {
    path: 'dist',
    filename: 'bundle.js'
  }
}
```

Next, we will tell Webpack to turn `.vue` files into JavaScript with `vue-loader`:

```js
module.exports = {
  entry: './index.js',
  output: {
    path: 'dist',
    filename: 'bundle.js'
  },
  module: {
    rules: [
      {
```

```
        test: /.vue$/,
        use: 'vue-loader'
      }
    ]
  }
}
```

To make everything work, we still need to install the dependencies we implied in our code. We can install them with the following two commands:

```
npm install --save vue
npm install --save-dev vue-loader vue-template-compiler webpack webpack-
dev-server
```

The last one in particular--webpack-dev-server--is a development server that will help us develop with hot reloading.

Run the following command to start the server:

```
./node_modules/webpack-dev-server/bin/webpack-dev-server.js --output-path /
--inline --hot --open
```

Actually, let's put this command in an npm script.

Open package.json and add the following lines:

```
"scripts": {
  "dev": "webpack-dev-server --output-path / --inline --hot --open"
}
```

We can now run npm run dev and we'll get the same result--a browser will pop up--as illustrated in the following screenshot:

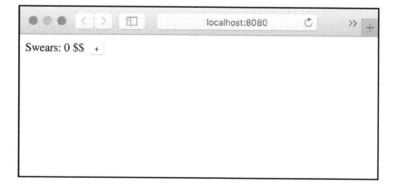

Clicking on the plus button will make the counter go up, but what about the style of this application? Let's make it more attractive.

Open your code editor and the window side by side and make the following modifications to `SwearJar.vue`:

```
<template>
  <div>
  <p>Swears: {{counter}} $$</p>
      <button @click="addSwear">Add Swear</button>
  </div>
</template>
```

Save the file, and you will see the page updating itself. Even better, the state will be retained if the counter was already set above zero, and this means that if you have a complex component you don't have to bring it manually into the same state again after each modification. Try to set the swear count to some number and edit the template. Most of the time, the counter will not get reset to zero.

How it works...

The Webpack dev server is very helpful software that lets you develop with a very tight feedback loop. We used plenty of arguments to make it run:

```
webpack-dev-server --output-path / --inline --hot --open
```

All these parameters are the same inside the `webpack.config.js`. Instead, we are putting these parameters in the command line for convenience. The `--output-path` is where the Webpack server will serve `bundle.js`; in our case, we said that we want it served at the root path, so it will effectively bind the `/bundle.js` path to the actual `bundle.js` file.

The second parameter, `--inline`, will inject some JavaScript code in our browser so that our app can communicate with the Webpack dev server.

The `--hot` parameter will activate the Hot Module Replacement plugin, which will communicate with the `vue-loader` (actually with the `vue-hot-reload-api`, which is inside it) and will either restart or rerender (preserving the state) each Vue model inside the page.

Finally, `--open` just opens the default browser for us.

Using Babel to compile from ES6

ES6 has a lot of useful features, and in this recipe you will learn how you can use it in your projects. It's worth noting that ES6 currently has very good browser support. You won't have compatibility issues with 80% of the browsers in the wild, but you may need to even reach people who're still using Internet Explorer 11, depending on your audience, or you may just want to maximize your audience. Moreover, some tools for development and Node.js still don't fully support ES6, deeming Babel necessary even for development.

Getting ready

In this recipe, we will use npm and the command line. If you completed the *Choosing a development environment* recipe in `Chapter 1`, *Getting Started with Vue.js*, you are probably good to go.

How to do it...

Create a new directory with an empty npm project. You can use the `npm init -y` command or, if you have Yarn installed, you can use `yarn init -y` inside the directory. This command will create a new `package.json` inside the directory. (Refer to the note in the *Developing with continuous feedback with hot reloading* recipe on Yarn.)

For this npm project, we will need a couple of dependencies other than Vue: Webpack, and Babel in the form of a loader for Webpack. Oh yes, we will need the `vue-loader` as well for Webpack. To install them, launch the following two commands:

```
npm install --save vue
npm install --save-dev webpack babel-core babel-loader babel-preset-es2015
vue-loader vue-template-compiler
```

In the same directory, let's write a component that uses ES6 syntax; let's call it `myComp.vue`:

```
<template>
  <div>Hello</div>
</template>
<script>
var double = n => n * 2
export default {
  beforeCreate () {
    console.log([1,2,3].map(double))
  }
}
```

```
</script>
```

This component doesn't do much except print the [2, 4, 6] array to the console, but it does it with arrow syntax at the following line:

```
var double = n => n * 2
```

This is not understood by some browsers and tools; we need to compile this component with Webpack, but we need to do it with the Babel loader.

Create a new webpack.config.js file and write the following inside it:

```
module.exports = {
  entry: 'babel-loader!vue-loader!./myComp.vue',
  output: {
    filename: 'bundle.js',
    path: 'dist'
  }
}
```

This will tell Webpack to start compiling from our myComp.vue file, but before that, it will be processed by the vue-loader to turn it into a js file and then by the babel-loader to turn the arrow function into something simpler and more compatible.

We can achieve the same thing with a different and more standard configuration:

```
module.exports = {
  entry: './myComp.vue',
  output: {
    filename: 'bundle.js'
  },
  module: {
    rules: [
      {
        test: /.vue$/,
        use: 'vue-loader'
      },
      {
        test: /.js$/,
        use: 'babel-loader'
      }
    ]
  }
}
```

This is a more general configuration and it says that whenever we encounter a file that ends with .vue, it should be parsed and processed with the vue-loader and .js files with the babel-loader.

To configure the Babel loader, there are a couple of options; we'll follow the recommended way. Create a file called .babelrc inside your project folder (note the initial point) and to specify that we want the es2015 preset applied, we write the following code:

```
{
    "presets": ["es2015"]
}
```

Lastly, I always like to add a new script to the package.json file to make launching commands easier. Add the following line at the end of the file (but before the last curly brace):

```
"scripts": {
    "build": "webpack"
}
```

Then run npm run build. This creates a file inside the dist directory, named bundle.js; open it and search for a line that contains, for example, double. You should find something like this:

```
...
var double = function double(n) {
    return n * 2;
};
...
```

This was our var double = n => n * 2, transformed from ES6 to *regular* JavaScript.

How it works...

The es2015 Babel preset is a collection of Babel plugins that aims to transform ECMAScript2015 (ES6) syntax into simpler JavaScript. For example, it contains the babel-plugin-transform-es2015-arrow-functions plugin, which as you may have guessed, transforms arrow functions:

```
var addOne = n => n + 1
```

Transform the arrow functions into simpler JavaScript as follows:

```
var addOne = function addOne(n) {
  return n + 1
}
```

To select the files and their respective loaders, we filled the test field inside `webpack.config.js` and to match the `.vue` files, we wrote the following:

```
test: /\.vue$/
```

This syntax is a regular expression and it always starts with a forward slash and ends with another forward slash. The first character it matches is the point, which is expressed as `\.` because the `.` character is already taken for other purposes. The point has to be followed by the `vue` string and the end of string character is expressed as a dollar sign. If you put them all together, it will match all the strings that end with `.vue`. A similar thing is followed for the `.js` files.

Running a code linter while developing

Linting your code drastically reduces small bugs and inefficiencies that accumulate during development, it guarantees that the coding style is consistent across a team or organization, and it makes your code more readable. Instead of running the linter once in a while, it's useful to have it constantly running. This recipe teaches you how to do it with Webpack.

Getting ready

In this recipe, we will play with Webpack once again. You will build a tight loop with `webpack-dev-server`, which is covered in the *Developing with continuous feedback with hot reloading* recipe.

How to do it...

In a new folder, create a new npm project (you can use `npm init -y` or `yarn init -y`).

Inside the folder, create a new directory named `src` and put a file inside it, called `MyComp.vue`. Let the file contain the following code:

```
<template>
  <div>
```

```
      Hello {{name}}!
    </div>
  </template>
  <script>
  export default {
    data () {
      return {
        name: 'John',
        name: 'Jane'
      }
    }
  }
  </script>
```

We can already spot a problem--the `John` name property will be overwritten by the later property, `Jane`, with the same key. Let's pretend that we didn't notice this and put the component inside a web page. For this, we need another file, named `index.js`, in the `src` directory. Write the following code inside it:

```
import Vue from 'vue'
import MyComp from './MyComp.vue'
new Vue({
  el: '#app',
  render: h => h(MyComp)
})
```

In the root directory, place an `index.html` file with the following code:

```
<!DOCTYPE html>
<html>
  <head>
    <title>Hello</title>
  </head>
  <body>
    <div id="app"></div>
      <script src="bundle.js"></script>
    </body>
</html>
```

We now need a `webpack.config.js` file to tell Webpack how to compile our files; write the following inside it:

```
module.exports = {
  entry: './src/index.js',
  module: {
    rules: [
      {
        test: /.vue$/,
```

```
            use: 'vue-loader'
        }
      ]
    }
  }
```

This just tells Webpack to start compiling from the `index.js` file and, whenever it finds a `.vue` file, to turn it into JavaScript with the `vue-loader`. Beyond this, we want to scan all our files with a linter to ensure that we didn't make silly mistakes in our code.

Add the following loader to the `rules` array:

```
{
  test: /.(vue|js)$/,
  use: 'eslint-loader',
  enforce: 'pre'
}
```

The `enforce: 'pre'` property will run this loader before the others, so it will apply to the code you wrote and not a transformation of it.

The last thing we need is to configure ESLint. Create a new file in the root directory named `.eslintrc.js`, and add the following inside it:

```
module.exports = {
  "extends": "eslint:recommended",
  "parser": "babel-eslint",
  plugins: [
    'html'
  ]
}
```

We are saying a couple of things here. First is the set of rules we want to apply to our code; in other words, our set of rules (which is empty now) is extending the recommended set of rules. Second, we are using the `babel-eslint` parser instead of the default one. Finally, we are using the HTML ESLint plugin, which will help us to deal with the `.vue` files and will extract the JavaScript code in them.

We are now ready to launch our development machinery, but first we need to install the dependencies using the following command:

```
npm install --save vue
npm install --save-dev babel-eslint eslint eslint-loader eslint-plugin-html
vue-loader vue-template-compiler webpack webpack-dev-server
```

We can launch the Webpack dev server directly, but I highly suggest adding the following code to the `package.json` file:

```
"scripts": {
  "dev": "webpack-dev-server --entry ./src/index.js --inline --hot --open"
}
```

Now, if we launch `npm run dev`, a browser should open with the component incorrectly displaying the following:

Hello Jane!

You should also be able to see the problem in the console:

```
11:7   error   Duplicate key 'name'   no-dupe-keys
```

This means that we have two keys with the same *name*. Correct the error by removing the property:

```
data () {
  return {
    name: 'John'
  }
}
```

In the console, after you save the Vue component, you should note that Webpack already performed the compilation again, this time with no errors.

How it works...

Basically, what happens here is that the linter loader processes the files before other compilation steps and writes the errors in the console. This way, you will be able to see imperfections in your code while you develop continuously.

ESLint and Webpack are available in the Vue official template. You now know that if, for some reason, you want to modify the ESLint rules, you can do it from the `.eslintrc.js` file and that if you want to use another linter altogether, you can use another loader in the Webpack configuration file.

Using only one command to build both a minified and a development .js file

While working on the release of your components, you may need a reliable process to issue your built files. A common operation is to release two versions of a library/component: one for development purposes and one to be consumed in production code, usually minified. In this recipe, you will tweak the official template to release both a minified and a development JavaScript file at the same time.

Getting ready

This recipe makes sense if you are already building and distributing your own components. If you want to learn more, I suggest you refer to the *Bundling your component with Webpack* recipe.

How to do it...

We'll start with a project with the official Webpack template. You can use your own, or you can spin up a new project with `vue init webpack` and install the dependencies with `npm isntall`.

Go inside the `build` directory. When you launch the `npm run build` command, you are effectively launching the `build.js` file in this directory.

If you examine the file, you will find something like this near the end:

```
webpack(webpackConfig, function (err, stats) {
...
})
```

This is equivalent to launching Webpack from the command line using the same configuration specified in the first argument, `webpackConfig`. To have a minified and non-minified file, we have to bring the `webpackConfig` to a common denominator, then we will specify only the differences between the development and production versions of the files.

To do this, go inside `webpack.prod.conf.js` in the same directory. Here, you can see the configuration we are passing; in particular, you will find `UglifyJsPlugin`, which is responsible for minifying the file if you look at the plugin array. Remove the plugin since it represents the main difference between the two distributions.

Now, write the following in `build.js` before the Webpack command:

```
const configs = [
  {
    plugins: [
      new webpack.optimize.UglifyJsPlugin({
        compress: {
          warnings: false
        },
        sourceMap: true
      })
    ]
  },
  {
    plugins: []
  }
]
```

You now have an array with two different configurations, one with the plugin required to minify the file and one without it. If you merge each of them with the configuration inside the `webpack.prod.conf.js`, you will obtain a different result.

To merge the two configurations, we will use the `webpack-merge` package. Add the following line to the top of the file:

```
var merge = require('webpack-merge')
```

Then, modify the first line of the Webpack command to the following:

```
configs.map(c => webpack(merge(webpackConfig, c), function (err, stats) {
...
```

This will launch as many different merged configurations as we specify in the configs array.

You can launch the `npm run build` command now, but the problem is that the files will have the same name. Cut the output property from the `webpack.prod.conf.js` and paste it in the `config` array, which should now look like this:

```
const configs = [
  {
output: {
      path: <whatever is your path>,
      filename: 'myFilename.min.js'),
      <other options you may have>
    },
    plugins: [
```

```
            new webpack.optimize.UglifyJsPlugin({
               compress: {
                 warnings: false
               }
            })
         ]
      },
      {
   output: {
         path: <whatever is your path>,
         filename: 'myFilename.js'),
         <other options you may have>
      },
      plugins: []
   }
]
```

If you build your project now, you will have both a minified and a development file. You can, of course, personalize your configurations to grow very different. For example, you can add source maps in one and leave the other as is.

How it works...

We first created an array of objects that represent differences in the Webpack configuration. We then mapped each piece of configuration into a larger, common configuration with the help of webpack-merge. When we now call the npm run build command, both the configurations run one after the other.

It's a common convention to postfix the name of the file with min to signal that the file is minified and ready to be used in production.

Releasing your components to the public

At a certain point, there comes a moment when you want to give back to the community. Maybe you built a "fart button" or maybe you built an automates stock options trader; whatever it is that you've built, the JavaScript and Vue community will be happy to welcome you. There is a big chunk of things to be done on the side of marketing and licensing, but in this recipe you will concentrate on the more technical aspects.

Getting ready

This recipe is directed at those who want to share their work in Vue with the rest of the community. In the *Bundling your component with Webpack* recipe, you will find how to tweak the official Webpack template to bundle your component correctly; this recipe can be thought of as a second part. We will not use the official template though.

How to do it...

The approach I will take for this recipe is to use the excellent `vue-share-components` template by *Guillaume Chau*. We'll build a joke button from that starting point.

In your command line, create a new directory and type the following command inside it:

```
vue init Akryum/vue-share-components
```

It will ask you some questions; you can copy the responses from the following image. The only thing to note is that you (sadly) cannot use the `joke-button` name for your project because I have already registered it while writing this recipe. However, you can come up with a similar sounding name (you may want to check whether the name is available in the `npm` registry before moving ahead):

```
▶ vue init Akryum/vue-share-components

? Generate project in current directory? Yes
? Plugin name joke-button
? Library name for browser usage JokeButton
? Plugin description A button to display jokes
? Initial version 0.0.1
? Author Andrea Passaglia <gurghet@gmail.com>
? GitHub Account gurghet
? Pick a css language css

    vue-cli · Generated "8.9".

    To get started:

        cd 8.9
        npm install
        npm run dev
```

Once the project is created, you can install the dependencies with `npm install`, just as in the console output.

Inside the project, let's create the joke button component. Inside the `component` folder, you will find a `Test.vue` component; rename it to `JokeButton.vue` and make it look like the following code:

```
<template>
  <div class="test">
    <button @click="newJoke">New Joke</button>
    <p>{{joke}}</p>
  </div>
</template>
<script>
const jokes = [
 'Chuck Norris/'s keyboard has the Any key.',
 'Chuck Norris can win at solitaire with only 18 cards.',
 'Chuck Norris/' first job was as a paperboy. There were no survivors.',
 'When Chuck Norris break the build, you can/'t fix it.',
]
export default {
  name: 'joke-button',
  data () {
    return {
      joke: '...',
    }
  },
  methods: {
    newJoke () {
      this.joke = jokes[Math.floor(Math.random() * jokes.length)]
    },
  },
}
</script>
```

Obviously, you can create the component you prefer; this is just an example.

In the `index.js` file, you will see the `Test` component imported and installed; you will need to install the `JokeButton` instead. The lines you need to change are highlighted:

```
import JokeButton from './components/JokeButton.vue'
// Install the components
export function install (Vue) {
  Vue.component('jokeButton', JokeButton)
  /* -- Add more components here -- */
}
// Expose the components
```

```
export {
JokeButton,
  /* -- Add more components here -- */
}
...
```

Our component is ready!

Now you have to go to the npm website to register for an account (if you don't have one already).

Go to npmjs.com:

Click on **sign up** and enter your details, like I did here:

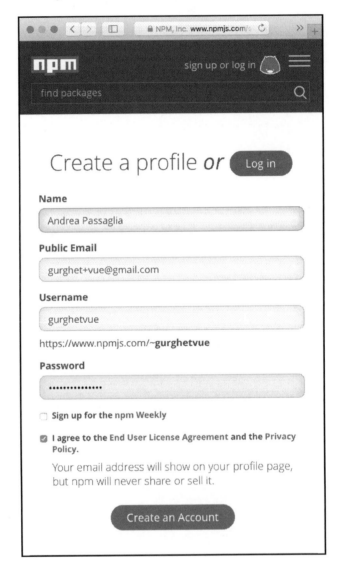

Of course, you can subscribe to the npm weekly newsletter if you like.

Once registered, you're done and can come back to the command line. You must log in to the npm registry from the terminal with the following command:

```
npm adduser
```

You will see something like this:

You will have to enter the password you just entered for the npm website.

The next command will publish your library in the public repository:

```
npm publish
```

Now you can even look up your package and, sure enough, you will find it as shown in the following screenshot:

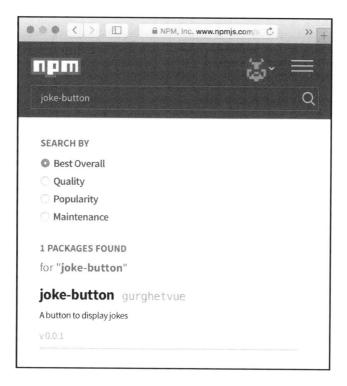

To try it, you can find the instructions in your own README, how cool is that?

How it works...

The vue-share-components is simpler than the official template, so it's a good way to learn by examining it.

The first thing we can take a look at is the package.json file. The following lines are relevant:

```
...
"main": "dist/joke-button.common.js",
"unpkg": "dist/joke-button.browser.js",
"module": "index.js",
"scripts": {
  "dev": "cross-env NODE_ENV=development webpack --config
config/webpack.config.dev.js --progress --watch",
  "build": "npm run build:browser && npm run build:common",
  "build:browser": "cross-env NODE_ENV=production webpack --config
config/webpack.config.browser.js --progress --hide-modules",
  "build:common": "cross-env NODE_ENV=production webpack --config
config/webpack.config.common.js --progress --hide-modules",
  "prepublish": "npm run build"
},
...
```

The main property is what we actually get when we write the following command in our programs:

```
import JokeButton from 'JokeButton'
```

Alternatively, we get it when we add the following code:

```
var JokeButton = require("JokeButton")
```

So, the JokeButton variable will actually contain what is exported in our joke-button.common.js.

You can edit the main property of `package.json` to point directly to a
`.vue` component. This way, you give the user the responsibility to compile
the component. While this is more work for the user, it also helps when
one wants the freedom to compile against the most recent version of Vue.
In the latter case, if you have some logic of your component exported in

`external.js` files (like in the first recipe of this chapter), always
remember to add the directory in the Webpack rules, like so:

```
{
  test: /.js$/,
  loader: 'babel-loader',
  include: [resolve('src'), resolve('test'),
resolve('node_modules/myComponent')]
},
```

The unpkg is particular of `unpkg.com`, which is a CDN. This is very nice because as soon as
we publish our project, we will have our script published at `https://unpkg.com/joke-but`
`ton`, and it will point to the `joke-button.browser.js` file that is suited for the browser.

The `prepublish` script is a special script that will be called before publishing the project to
npm with the `npm publish` command. This eliminates the possibility that you forget to
build the files before publishing your component (it happened to me many times, so I was
forced to increase the version of the software artificially, build the files manually, and
publish again).

Another interesting fact to note is the difference between `webpack.config.common.js`,
which outputs the `joke-button.common.js` file, and `webpack.config.browser.js`,
which outputs the `joke-button.browser.js` file.

The first file has the output set to the following:

```
output: {
  path: './dist',
  filename: outputFile + '.common.js',
  libraryTarget: 'commonjs2',
},
target: 'node',
```

So, it will output a library that will expose a commonJS interface; this is tailored for non-browser environments, and you will have to require or import this library to use it. On the other hand, the second file for the browser has the following output:

```
output: {
  path: './dist',
  filename: outputFile + '.browser.js',
  library: globalName,
  libraryTarget: 'umd',
},
```

A UMD will expose itself in a global scope, no need to import anything, so it's perfect for the browser because we can include the file in a Vue webpage and use the component freely. This is also possible, thanks to the index.js auto-install feature:

```
/* -- Plugin definition & Auto-install -- */
/* You shouldn't have to modify the code below */
// Plugin
const plugin = {
 /* eslint-disable no-undef */
 version: VERSION,
 install,
}
export default plugin
// Auto-install
let GlobalVue = null
if (typeof window !== 'undefined') {
 GlobalVue = window.Vue
} else if (typeof global !== 'undefined') {
 GlobalVue = global.Vue
}
if (GlobalVue) {
 GlobalVue.use(plugin)
}
```

What this code is doing is packaging the install function (which registers the component(s) with Vue) inside the plugin constant and exporting it in the meantime. Then, it checks whether there is either window or global defined, in that case, it gets hold of the Vue variable that represents the Vue library and uses the plugin API to install the component(s).

9
Advanced Vue.js – Directives, Plugins, and Render Functions

In this chapter, we will talk about the following topics:

- Creating a new directive
- Using WebSockets in Vue
- Writing a plugin for Vue
- Rendering a simple component manually
- Rendering a component with children
- Using JSX to render a component
- Creating a functional component
- Building a responsive table with higher-order components

Introduction

Directives and plugins are ways to package functionality in a reusable way and also make it easily shareable across apps and teams; you will build a few of them in this chapter. Render functions are how Vue really works under the hood to turn templates into the Vue language and then into HTML and JavaScript again; they become useful if you need to optimize the performance of your apps and work in some corner cases.

In general, you should avoid using these advanced functions when possible as they have been a little overused in the past. Usually, many problems can be solved by simply writing a good component and distributing the component itself; you should look at advanced features only when this is not true.

This chapter is for the slightly more experienced, and you probably won't find the level of step-by-step detail found in other recipes, but I have strived to make them complete nonetheless.

Creating a new directive

Directives are like mini functions that you can use to quickly drop in to your code, mainly to improve the user experience, and to add new low-level features to your graphic interface.

Getting ready

This recipe, although found in the advanced chapter, is really easy to complete. The main reason directives are *advanced* is because you should usually prefer composition to add functionality and style to your apps. When components won't cut it, use directives.

How to do it...

We will build a v-pony directive that will turn any element into a pony element. A pony element is created with a pink background and changes color when you click on it.

The HTML code for the pony element is as follows:

```
<div id="app">
  <p v-pony>I'm a pony paragraph!</p>
  <code v-pony>Pony code</code>
  <blockquote>Normal quote</blockquote>
  <blockquote v-pony>I'm a pony quote</blockquote>
</div>
```

Just to show the difference, I've included a normal blockquote element. In our JavaScript section, write the following:

```
Vue.directive('pony', {
  bind (el) {
    el.style.backgroundColor = 'hotpink'
  }
})
```

This is how you declare a new directive. The `bind` hook is called when the directive is bound to the element. The only thing we are doing now is setting the background color. We also want to make it change color after each click. To do this, you have to add this code:

```
Vue.directive('pony', {
  bind (el) {
    el.style.backgroundColor = 'hotpink'
el.onclick = () => {
    const colGen = () =>
      Math.round(Math.random()*255 + 25)
    const cols =
      [colGen() + 100, colGen(), colGen()]
    const randRGB =
      `rgb(${cols[0]}, ${cols[1]}, ${cols[2]})`
    el.style.backgroundColor = randRGB
  }
  }
})
```

Here, we are creating an `onclick` listener that will generate a random color with a bias toward red and assign it as a new background color.

At the end of our JavaScript, remember to create a `Vue` instance:

```
new Vue({
  el: '#app'
})
```

You can launch your application to see your directive in action:

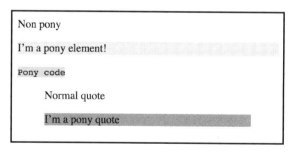

Don't forget to click on the text to change the background color!

How it works...

The syntax to declare a new directive is as illustrated:

```
Vue.directive(<name: String>, {
  // hooks
})
```

This will register a new global directive. Inside the hooks object, you can define two important functions: `bind`, which you used in this recipe, and `update`, which is triggered every time a component contained in it is updated.

Every hook function is called with at least three arguments:

- `el`: The HTML element
- `binding`: Directives can receive an argument; binding is an object that will contain the value of the argument
- `vnode`: the Vue internal representation of this element

We used the `el` parameter to edit the appearance of our element, manipulating it directly.

Using WebSockets in Vue

WebSockets are a new technology that enables two-way communication between the user and the server where the app is hosted. Before this technology, only the browser could initiate a request and, thus, a connection. If some update on the page was expected, the browser had to continuously poll the server. With WebSockets, this is no longer necessary; after the connection is established, the server can send updates only when there is a need.

Getting ready

You don't need any preparation for this recipe, just the basics of Vue. If you don't know what WebSockets are, you don't really need to, just think about them as a channel of continuous two-way communication between a server and browser.

How to do it...

For this recipe, we need a server and a browser that will act a client. We will not build a server; instead, we'll use an already existing server that just echoes whatever you send to it via WebSockets. So, if we were to send the `Hello` message, the server would respond with `Hello`.

You will build a chat app that will talk to this server. Write the following HTML code:

```
<div id="app">
  <h1>Welcome</h1>
  <pre>{{chat}}</pre>
  <input v-model="message" @keyup.enter="send">
</div>
```

The `<pre>` tag will help us render a chat. As we don't need the `<br/>` element to break a line, we can just use the n special character that means a new line.

For our chat to work, we first have to declare our WebSocket in the JavaScript:

```
const ws = new WebSocket('ws://echo.websocket.org')
```

After that, we declare our `Vue` instance that will contain a `chat` string (to contain the chat so far) and a `message` string (to contain the message we are currently writing):

```
new Vue({
  el: '#app',
  data: {
    chat: '',
    message: ''
  }
})
```

We still need to define the `send` method, which is called upon pressing *Enter* in the textbox:

```
new Vue({
  el: '#app',
  data: {
    chat: '',
    message: ''
  },
  methods: {
    send () {
      this.appendToChat(this.message)
      ws.send(this.message)
      this.message = ''
    },
```

```
    appendToChat (text) {
      this.chat += text + 'n'
    }
  }
}
```

We factored out the `appendToChat` method because we will use it to append all the messages we'll receive. To do this, we must wait for the component to be instantiated. The `created` hook is a safe place for that:

```
. . .
created () {
  ws.onmessage = event => {
    this.appendToChat(event.data)
  }
}
. . .
```

Now launch the application to chat with your personal echo chamber:

How it works...

To see the internals of what you have built, open the Chrome developer tools (⋮ | **More tools** | **Developer tools** or *Opt + Cmd + I*):

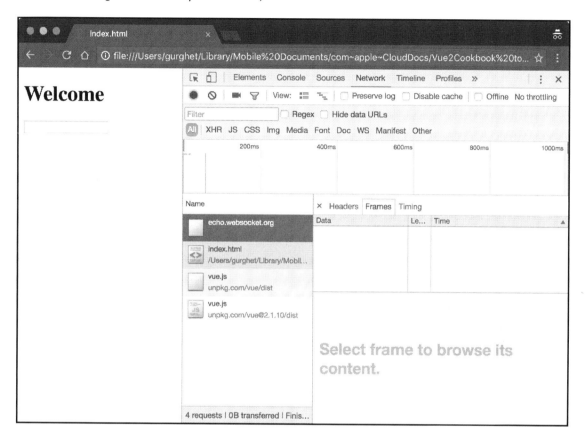

Go to the **Network** tab and reload the page; you should see the `echo.websocket.orl` WebSocket, as seen in the screenshot. Write something and messages will appear in the frame tab, like so:

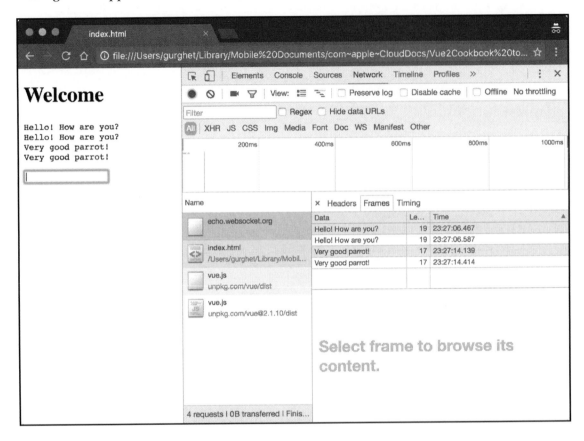

The green messages are sent from you while the white messages are the ones you receive. You can also examine the message length (in bytes) and the exact time they were sent or received.

Writing a plugin for Vue

A plugin is a collection of utilities or a global new behavior that we want in our application. Vuex and vue-router are two famous examples of Vue plugins. A plugin can really be anything, since writing one means acting at a very low level. There are different kinds of plugins you can write. For this recipe, we will concentrate on building a directive with global properties.

Getting ready

This recipe will be based on *Creating a new directive*, except that we will add some features for global coordination.

How to do it...

For this recipe, we will build a website for a kangaroo appreciation club. The layout of the home page HTML looks like this:

```
<div id="app">
  <h1>Welcome to the Kangaroo club</h1>
  <img src="https://goo.gl/FVDU1I" width="300px" height="200px">
  <img src="https://goo.gl/U1Hvez" width="300px" height="200px">
  <img src="https://goo.gl/YxggEB" width="300px" height="200px">
  <p>We love kangaroos</p>
</div>
```

You can change the link to the images of kangaroos with the one you prefer.

In the JavaScript part, we instantiate an empty Vue instance for now:

```
new Vue({
  el: '#app'
})
```

If we open the page now, we get this:

Welcome to the Kangaroo club

We love kangaroos

Now we want to add a fun note to our website. We want the elements of the page, except the title, to jump at random intervals.

To do this, the strategy you will implement is to register all the elements that will need to jump in an array, and then, periodically take a random element and make it jump.

The first thing we need to define is the jump animation in CSS:

```
@keyframes generateJump {
  20%{transform: translateY(0);}
  40%{transform: translateY(-30px);}
  50%{transform: translateY(0);}
  60%{transform: translateY(-15px);}
  80%{transform: translateY(0);}
}
.kangaroo {
  animation: generateJump 1.5s ease 0s 2 normal;
}
```

What this does is create a class named `kangaroo` that, when applied to an element, makes it jump twice by translating it along the y axis.

Next, write a function that adds this class to a specified element in the JavaScript:

```
const jump = el => {
  el.classList.add('kangaroo')
  el.addEventListener('animationend', () => {
    el.classList.remove('kangaroo')
  })
}
```

The `jump` function adds the `kangaroo` class and then removes it when the animation is finished.

We want to perform this action on a random element picked from the ones registered:

```
const doOnRandomElement = (action, collection) => {
  if (collection.length === 0) {
    return
  }
  const el =
    collection[Math.floor(Math.random()*collection.length)]
  action(el)
}
```

The `doOnRandomElement` function takes an action and a collection and applies the action to a drawn element. We then need to schedule it at random intervals:

```
const atRandomIntervals = action => {
  setTimeout(() => {
    action()
    atRandomIntervals(action)
  }, Math.round(Math.random() * 6000))
}
```

The `atRandomIntervals` function takes the specified function and calls it at random intervals shorter than 6 seconds.

We now have all the functions we need to actually build a plugin that will make our element jump:

```
const Kangaroo = {
  install (vueInstance) {
    vueInstance.kangaroos = []
    vueInstance.directive('kangaroo', {
      bind (el) {
        vueInstance.kangaroos.push(el)
      }
    })
    atRandomIntervals(() =>
      doOnRandomElement(jump, vueInstance.kangaroos))
  }
}
```

The Kangaroo plugin, when installed, creates an empty array; it declares a new directive, `kangaroo` which will register all the elements with it inside the array.

Then at random intervals, one random element is drawn from the array and the jump function is called on it.

To activate the plugin, we need one line before declaring the `Vue` instance (but after declaring `Kangaroo`):

```
Vue.use(Kangaroo)
new Vue({
  el: '#app'
})
```

We have to choose the elements that jump, that is, everything except the title:

```
<div id="app">
  <h1>Welcome to the Kangaroo club</h1>
  <img v-kangaroo src="https://goo.gl/FVDU1I" width="300px"
height="200px">
  <img v-kangaroo src="https://goo.gl/U1Hvez" width="300px"
height="200px">
  <img v-kangaroo src="https://goo.gl/YxggEB" width="300px"
height="200px">
  <p v-kangaroo>We love kangaroos</p>
</div>
```

If you run your app now, you will see that an image or the text jumps just like a kangaroo every few seconds.

How it works...

In its essence, a Vue plugin is just a way to group some functionalities. There are not many restrictions and all you have to do to create a plugin is to declare an install function. The general syntax to do that is as follows:

```
MyPlugin.install = (vueInstance, option) => {
  // ...
}
```

To use the plugin you just made, write the following:

```
Vue.use(MyPlugin, { /* any option you need */ })
```

Here, the second parameter is the optional object that gets passed to the `install` function.

Since plugins are global entities, you should use them sparsely and only for features that you foresee will affect your app throughout.

Rendering a simple component manually

Vue turns your HTML templates into render functions. Usually, you should stick to templates because they are much simpler. There are a couple of cases in which render functions become in handy. Here, we show a simple example in which render functions are useful.

Getting ready

This is the first recipe on render functions. If you already understand the basics of Vue, you will understand everything.

How to do it...

The first use case for render functions is whenever you just want a Vue instance that displays another component.

Write an empty HTML layout, as follows:

```
<div id="app"></div>
```

We have a Greeter component somewhere that we want to show as the main Vue instance. In the JavaScript part, add the following code:

```
const Greeter = {
  template: '<p>Hello World</p>'
}
```

Here, we have to imagine that we are taking the Greeter component from somewhere else and, since the component is nicely packaged, we don't want to modify it. Instead, we will pass it to the Vue main instance:

```
const Greeter = {
  template: '<p>Hello World</p>'
}
new Vue({
 el: '#app',
 render: h => h(Greeter)
})
```

If we launch the application now, we will only see the Greeter component. The main Vue instance will only act as a wrapper.

How it works...

The render function replaces the template in the Vue instance. When render is called, the passed argument is the so-called createElement function. We named it h for brevity. This function accepts three arguments, but for now, just note how the first argument we are passing (the only one we are passing) is the Greeter component.

In theory, you can write the component inline, inside the h function. In a real project, this is not always possible depending on the presence of the Vue template compiler at runtime. When you use the official Webpack template, one of the questions you are asked is whether you want to include the Vue template compiler when distributing your software.

The arguments for the `createElement` function are listed here:

1. As the first argument, the only required one, you have the option to pass three different things:
    - The options of a Vue component, like in our recipe
    - A string representing an HTML tag (such as `div`, `h1`, and `p`)
    - A function that returns an options object for a Vue component or a string representing an HTML tag
2. The second argument must be an object called **Data Object**. This object is explained in the next recipe.
3. The third argument is an array or a string:
    - The array represents a list of elements, text, or components to put inside the component
    - You can write a string that will be rendered to text

Rendering a component with children

In this recipe, you will build a simple web page with a few elements and components completely using render functions. This will give you a close-up view of how Vue compiles your templates and components. It may be useful if you want to build an advanced component and you want a full example to kick start.

Getting ready

This is a complete recipe on how to build components through render functions. Usually, you don't need to do this in practice; it's recommended only for advanced readers.

How to do it...

You will build a page for a plumber club. The page will look like this:

The plumber club page

Your name is Andrea

Hello Andrea!

Here you will find *a flood* of plumbers.

Whenever we write a name inside the name textbox, it will be written in the greeting exactly like the `v-model` directive.

For this recipe, we are starting from the end instead of the beginning because usually when you have to resort to the `render` function, you have a pretty clear idea of what you are trying to get.

In the HTML side of our app, let's start with an empty tag:

```
<div id="app"></div>
```

In the JavaScript, write an empty `<div>` element in the `render` function:

```
new Vue({
  el: '#app',
  render: h => h('div')
})
```

The first thing we'll put inside is the title, like so:

```
new Vue({
  el: '#app',
  render: h => h(
    'div',
[
      h('h1', 'The plumber club page')
    ]
  )
})
```

All the other elements and components will fit inside the array we have just created for the title.

We need an `<input>` element that will take the value and display a greeting. For this, we can build a `Vue` component.

In the following code, we are using a regular JavaScript function instead of an arrow function; this is because we want a reference to the component itself. Arrow functions don't allow you to modify the scope of `this`, while `this` depends on how the function is called and can be optionally bound to any variable in regular functions. In our case, it will be bound to the instance component.

After the title of the page, we add the following component in the same array:

```
h(
  {
    render: function (h) {
      const self = this
      return h('div', [
        'Your name is ',
        h('input', {
          domProps: {
            value: self.name
          },
          on: {
            input (event) {
              self.name = event.target.value
            }
          }
        }),
        h(
          'p',
          'Hello ' + self.name +
            (self.exclamation ? '!' : ''))
      ])
    },
    data () { return { name: '' } },
    props: ['exclamation']
  },
  {
    props: {
      exclamation: true
    }
  }
)
```

The component has three options: the `render`, `data`, and `props` functions.

The second parameter of the `createElement` function is to actually assign values to our props:

```
{
  props: {
    exclamation: true
  }
}
```

This will be equivalent to writing `:exclamation="true"` when declaring the component.

You can easily understand the `data` and `props` options of the component. Let's examine what we wrote in the `render` function.

In the first line of the function, we set `self = this` as a convenient way to refer to the component were we to add any nested functions. Then, we return the result of a `createElement` function (h) that, inside a div tag, places three things in the DOM. The first is the raw text `Your name is` and then two elements: an input and a paragraph.

We don't have a direct equivalent of the `v-model` directive when working with render functions. Instead, we implement it manually. We bind the value to the name, and then we add a listener to the input event that will set the value of the state variable, `name`, to whatever is inside the textbox.

We then insert a paragraph element that will compose the greeting phrase, adding an exclamation point based on the value of the `exclamation` prop.

After the component, we can add the following, as illustrated, in the same array:

```
'Here you will find ', h('i', 'a flood '), 'of plumbers.'
```

If you have done things right, you should be able to run the application and see the whole page.

How it works...

In this example, we've seen a glimpse of what happens behind the curtains when Vue compiles our templates; again, you are not advised to do this with regular components. Most of the time, the result will be just more verbose with little or no gain. On the other hand, there are a couple of cases in which writing the render function may actually result in better or more robust code and cover some functionality that is difficult to express with templates.

Using JSX to render a component

JSX is very popular in the React community. In Vue, you don't have to use JSX to build templates for your components; you can use the much more familiar HTML. JSX, however, is the next best thing you can do if you are forced to write a lot of render functions.

Getting ready

Before venturing into this recipe, you better play a little with the render function. The previous recipes provide some exercises.

How to do it...

JSX needs a Babel plugin to work. For this recipe, I will assume that you are working within the webpack template.

To install the babel plugin, you can run the following command:

```
npm install
  babel-plugin-syntax-jsx
  babel-plugin-transform-vue-jsx
  babel-helper-vue-jsx-merge-props
  --save-dev
```

Inside the `.babelrc` file, add the following in the `plugins` array:

```
"plugins": [
  ...
  "transform-vue-jsx"
]
```

Run `npm install` as usual to actually install all the dependencies.

Now, open the `main.js` and delete everything inside. Replace it with the following code:

```
import Vue from 'vue'

/* eslint-disable no-new */
new Vue({
  el: '#app',
  render (h) {
    return <div>{this.msg}</div>
  },
  data: {
```

```
      msg: 'Hello World'
    }
})
```

The highlighted line is the weird bit if you have never seen JSX. Just note that we didn't use the arrow function in the `render` option in the preceding code. That's because we are using `this` inside and we want it to be bound to the component.

You can already see your page working using the `npm run dev` command.

How it works...

The babel plugin will turn the JSX code into a JavaScript `render` function.

I wouldn't recommend using JSX with Vue. The only time I can see it being useful is whenever you need to intermix `render` functions with JavaScript and you need a quick and readable way of defining templates. Other than that, there are not many advantages to using JSX.

There's more...

Let's complicate the code a little bit to at least have a flavor of how JSX plays with props.

Define a new component before the main `Vue` instance:

```
const myComp = {
  render (h) {
    return <p>{this.myProp}</p>
  },
  props: ['myProp']
}
```

Let's use this component in our `Vue` instance and pass the `msg` variable via props:

```
new Vue({
  el: '#app',
  render (h) {
    return <div>
      <myComp myProp={this.msg}/>
    </div>
  },
  data: {
    msg: 'Hello World'
  },
```

```
  components: {
    myComp
  }
})
```

The syntax is slightly different from an HTML template. In particular, note how props are passed and how we can use camelCase and self-closing tags.

Creating a functional component

A lighter version of a component is a functional component. The functional component doesn't have instance variables (so no `this`) and has no state. In this recipe, we will write a simple functional component that takes some instructions via HTML and turns them into a drawing.

Getting ready

Before attempting this recipe, you should at least become familiar with the render function in Vue. You can use the previous recipes to do that.

How to do it...

When you are writing an `<svg>` element, you usually have to put data in the attributes of elements inside it to actually draw shapes. For example, if you want to draw a triangle, you have to write the following:

```
<svg>
  <path d="M 100 30 L 200 30 L 150 120 z"/>
</svg>
```

The text inside the d attribute is a series of instructions that make a virtual cursor move to draw: M moves the cursor to the (100, 30) coordinate inside the `<svg>`, then L traces a line up until (200, 30) and then again to the (150, 120) coordinate. Finally, z closes the path we are drawing, and the result is always a triangle.

We would like to write a triangle with a component, but we don't like attributes and we want to write in our own language, so we would write the following to get the same result:

```
<orange-line>
  moveTo 100 30 traceLine 200 30 traceLine 150 120 closePath
</orange-line>
```

This is a perfect job for a functional component because there is no state to manage, only a translation from one component to one element.

Your HTML layout will simply look like this:

```
<div id="app">
  <orange-line>
    moveTo 100 30 traceLine 200 30 traceLine 150 120 closePath
  </orange-line>
</div>
```

Then, lay out your functional component in your JavaScript:

```
const OrangeLine = {
  functional: true,
  render (h, context) {
    return h('svg',
      []
    )
  }
}
```

You have to specify that the component will be functional with `functional: true`; then the render function is slightly different than usual. The first argument is still the `createElement` function, but the second passed is the context of our component.

We can access the text written inside the HTML of our component (the commands to draw) through `context.children`.

You can see that I already added an empty `<svg>` element. Inside this, there is an empty array of children; we will put only the `<path>` element there, which is as follows:

```
render (h, context) {
  return h('svg',
    [
  h('path', {
        attrs: {
          d: context.children.map(c => {
            return c.text
              .replace(/moveTo/g, 'M')
```

```
                .replace(/traceLine/g, 'L')
                .replace(/closePath/g, 'z')
            }).join(' ').trim(),
            fill: 'black',
            stroke: 'orange',
            'stroke-width': '4'
        }
      })
    ]
  )
}
```

The highlighted code creates a path element and then sets some attributes, such as `fill` and `stroke`. The `d` attribute takes the text from inside the component, makes some substitutions, and then returns it.

We just need to create the `Vue` instance in the JavaScript:

```
new Vue({
  el: '#app',
  components: {
    OrangeLine
  }
})
```

Now, loading the app, we should see a triangle, which is shown in the following screenshot:

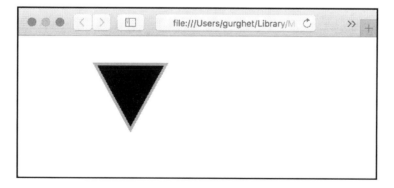

How it works...

Vue lets you create components that are very lightweight as they don't have any internal state. With this come some limitations, for example, the only place where we can put some logic to process user input (in the form of children of the element or props) is in the render function.

The context we passed contains the following properties:

- `props`: This is passed by the user.
- `children`: This is really an array of virtual nodes, children of our component in the template. We don't have the actual HTML element here but only a representation of it by Vue.
- `slots`: This is a function returning the slots (can be used instead of children in some cases).
- `data`: This is the entire data object passed to the component.
- `parent`: This is a reference to the parent component.

In our code, we extracted the text inside the component by doing the following:

```
context.children.map(c => {
  return c.text
    .replace(/moveTo/g, 'M')
    .replace(/traceLine/g, 'L')
    .replace(/closePath/g, 'z')
}).join(' ').trim()
```

We are taking the array of virtual nodes contained in children and mapping each node to its text. Since we put only some text in our HTML, the array of nodes will be a singleton, with only one node: the text we entered. Therefore, in this particular case, doing `var a = children.map(c => someFunction(c))` is then equivalent of doing `var a = [someFunction(children[0])]`.

We are not only extracting the text though, we are replacing some terms I invented to describe `svg` commands, with the real commands. The `join` function will sew together all the strings in the array (just one in our case) and `trim` will remove all the white spaces and line breaks.

Building a responsive table with higher-order components

Functional components are very good wrappers when we have to decide which component to actually wrap. In this recipe, you'll write a responsive table that will display different columns depending on the browser width.

Getting ready

This recipe is about functional components. If you want to warm up, you can try and complete the previous recipe.

How to do it...

For this recipe, we will use the excellent semantic UI CSS framework. To use it, you have to include the CSS library as a dependency or as a `<link>` tag. For example, you can put the following code in the `<head>` of your HTML:

```
<link rel="stylesheet"
href="https://cdnjs.cloudflare.com/ajax/libs/semantic-ui/2.2.7/semantic.css
" />
```

If you are using JSFiddle, the link inside should be sufficient.

Another tag you have to add to your page for it to look good on mobile is this:

```
<meta name="viewport" content="width=device-width">
```

This tells the mobile browser that the width of the page is equal to the width of the device. If you don't put this, the mobile may assume that the page is much larger than the phone and, trying to display all of it, show a miniaturized version of your app.

We will design a table of cat breeds. You can see all the data in the Vue instance status. Write it in your JavaScript:

```
new Vue({
  el: '#app',
  data: {
    width: document.body.clientWidth,
    breeds: [
      { name: 'Persian', colour: 'orange', affection: 3, shedding: 5 },
      { name: 'Siberian', colour: 'blue', affection: 5, shedding: 4 },
```

```
      { name: 'Bombay', colour: 'black', affection: 4, shedding: 2 }
    ]
    },
    created() {
      window.onresize = event => {
        this.width = document.body.clientWidth
      }
    },
    components: {
      BreedTable
    }
})
```

We are declaring the `width` variable to change the layout of the page and since the width of the page is not reactive by nature, we're also installing a listener on `window.onresize`. For a real project, you'll probably want something a bit more sophisticated, but for this recipe, this will suffice.

Also, note how we are using the `BreedTable` component, which we write like this:

```
const BreedTable = {
  functional: true,
  render(h, context) {
    if (context.parent.width > 400) {
      return h(DesktopTable, context.data, context.children)
    } else {
      return h(MobileTable, context.data, context.children)
    }
  }
}
```

What our component is doing is just passing all the `context.data` and `context.children` to another component, which will be `DesktopTable` or `MobileTable`, depending on the resolution.

Our HTML layout is the following:

```
<div id="app">
  <h1>Breeds</h1>
  <breed-table :breeds="breeds"></breed-table>
</div>
```

The `breeds` props will be passed on to the selected component in the `context.data`.

Our desktop table will look pretty regular for a table:

```
const DesktopTable = {
  template: `
    <table class="ui celled table unstackable">
      <thead>
        <tr>
          <th>Breed</th>
          <th>Coat Colour</th>
          <th>Level of Affection</th>
          <th>Level of Shedding</th>
        </tr>
      </thead>
      <tbody>
        <tr v-for="breed in breeds">
          <td>{{breed.name}}</td>
          <td>{{breed.colour}}</td>
          <td>{{breed.affection}}</td>
          <td>{{breed.shedding}}</td>
        </tr>
      </tbody>
    </table>
  `,
  props: ['breeds']
}
```

The classes at the top are part of semantic UI and they will make our table look much better. The `unstackable` class, in particular, disables the automatic stacking performed by CSS. We will cover more on this in the next section.

For the mobile table, we'd like to edit not only the styling, but we'd also like to group the columns themselves. The breed will go along with the color and the affection with the shedding. Also, we want to express them in a compact style. The table head will look like this:

```
const MobileTable = {
  template: `
    <table class="ui celled table unstackable">
      <thead>
        <tr>
          <th>Breed</th>
          <th>Affection & Shedding</th>
        </tr>
      </thead>
    ...
```

Instead of just spelling the coat color, we draw a little circle of that color:

```
...
<tbody>
  <tr v-for="breed in breeds">
    <td>{{breed.name}}
      <div
        class="ui mini circular image"
        :style="'height:35px;background-color:'+breed.colour"
      ></div>
    </td>
  ...
```

Also, instead of using numbers like in the desktop table for the affection and shedding level, we put a heart and star rating:

```
    ...
    <td>
      <div class="ui heart rating">
        <i
          v-for="n in 5"
          class="icon"
          :class="{ active: n <= breed.affection }"
        ></i>
      </div>
      <div class="ui star rating">
        <i
          v-for="n in 5"
          class="icon"
          :class="{ active: n <= breed.shedding }"
        ></i>
      </div>
    </td>
  </tr>
</tbody>
</table>
```

Also, don't forget to declare the `breeds` prop like in the `DesktopTable` component.

Now launch your application in a browser. You can see how the table groups the column when squished enough:

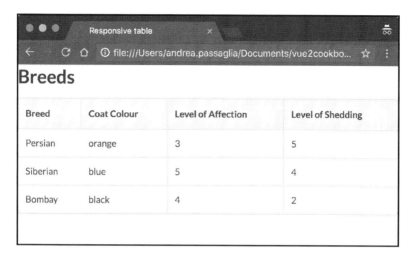

The following screenshot shows that numbers are replaced by hearts and star rating:

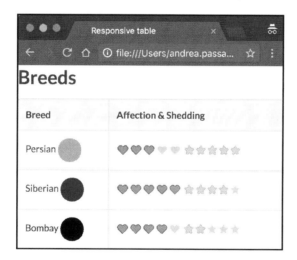

How it works...

A responsive page changes its layout according to the width of the browser and this is very important when the user is using a tablet or smartphone to browse the website.

Most of the components have to be developed only once for a responsive page, and only the styling is done multiple times according to different sizes. This can save a lot of development time if compared to having a separate site optimized for mobile.

Normally, in a responsive page table, go from columnar to stacked, as shown in the following illustration:

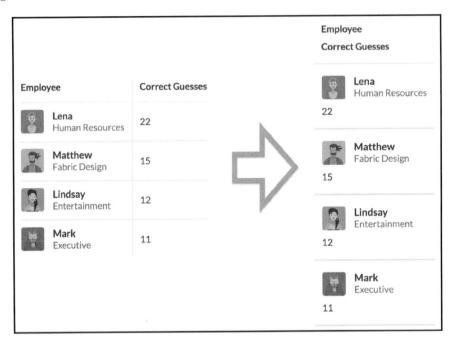

I never liked this approach, but the objective disadvantage is that if you make your table look good on one side, it will look not so good on the other. This is because you have to style the cells in the same way and what the responsiveness does is that it stacks them up.

What our `BreedTable` component does is to dynamically switch between the two components instead of simply relying on the CSS. Since it's a functional component, it has the advantage of being very lightweight compared to a full-fledged component.

In a real application, using the `onresize` event is questionable, mainly because of the performance hit. In a production system, the solutions for responsiveness via JavaScript need to be more structured. For example, consider using a timer or using `matchMedia`.

As a last thing, note how the Vue instance never registers the two subcomponents; this is because they never appear in a template but are referenced directly in the code as objects.

10
Large Application Patterns with Vuex

In this chapter, we'll cover the following recipes:

- Dynamically loading pages in your vue-router
- Building a simple storage for the application state
- Understanding Vuex mutations
- Listing your actions in Vuex
- Separating concerns with modules
- Building getters to help retrieve your data
- Testing your store

Introduction

In this chapter, you will learn how Vuex works and how to use it to support a scalable application. Vuex implements a pattern that is popular in frontend frameworks and consists of dividing the different concerns to manage a big global application state. The mutations are the only things that can change the state, so you have only one place to look for that. Much of the logic, along with all the asynchronous logic, is contained in the actions; finally, getters and modules further help to spread the cognitive load when it comes to computing the derived state and splitting your code into different files.

Along with recipes, you will find grains of wisdom that I found useful when developing real large applications; some have to do with naming conventions and others with little tricks to avoid bugs.

If you complete all the recipes, you will be ready to develop big frontend applications with fewer bugs and seamless collaboration.

Dynamically loading pages in your vue-router

Soon, you will build huge Vue websites with loads of components. Loading a lot of JavaScript may generate wasteful and useless upfront delay. In the *Loading your components asynchronously* recipe in `Chapter 4`, *All About Components*, we already saw a hint of how to retrieve our components remotely. Here we will apply a similar technique to components loaded by a route in vue-router.

Getting ready

This recipe requires knowledge of vue-router. If you want, you can go through *Loading your components asynchronously* in `Chapter 4`, *All About Components*, to get a better idea of what is happening.

How to do it...

Create a new project with `vue-cli` by making a new directory and running the following command:

```
vue init webpack
```

You can answer the question as you prefer, as long as you add the `vue-router` to the template when asked.

We will create two components: one will be our home page and it will be small and light, the other component will be very big and very slow to load. What we want to achieve is to load the home page immediately, without having to wait for the huge component to be downloaded by the browser.

Open the `Hello.vue` file in the `components` folder. Delete everything and only leave the following:

```
<template>
  <div>
    Lightweight hello
```

```
    </div>
</template>
```

In the same folder, create another file named `Massive.vue` and write the following inside it:

```
<template>
  <div>
   Massive hello
  </div>
</template>

<script>
/* eslint-disable no-unused-vars */
const a = `
```

Leave an open back tick at the last line because we have to bloat the file with a lot of useless data. Save and close `Massive.vue`.

In a console, go to the same directory where the file is stored and use the following file to put a lot of garbage into it:

```
yes "XXX" | head -n $((10**6)) >> Massive.vue
```

What this command does is append the XXX line to the file repeatedly 10^6 times; this will add 4 million bytes to the file, making it too huge for a fast browsing experience.

Now we need to close the back tick we opened. Don't try to open the file now, as your text editor may not be capable of opening such a big file; instead, use the following command:

```
echo '`</script>' >> Massive.vue
```

Our `Massive` component is now complete.

Open the `index.js` inside the `router` folder and add the component and its route:

```
import Massive from '@/components/Massive'
...
export default new Router({
  routes: [
    {
      path: '/',
      name: 'Hello',
      component: Hello
    },
    {
      path: '/massive',
      name: 'Massive',
```

```
        component: Massive
    }
  ]
})
```

After installing all the dependencies with `npm install`, we are now ready to launch our very large app with the `npm run dev` command.

The app will load quite fast, but that's because it's loading directly from your local storage; to simulate a more realistic scenario, open the developer tools at the **Network** tab and select network throttling. Pick something slow, such as GPRS or maybe good 3G, which most of us may have:

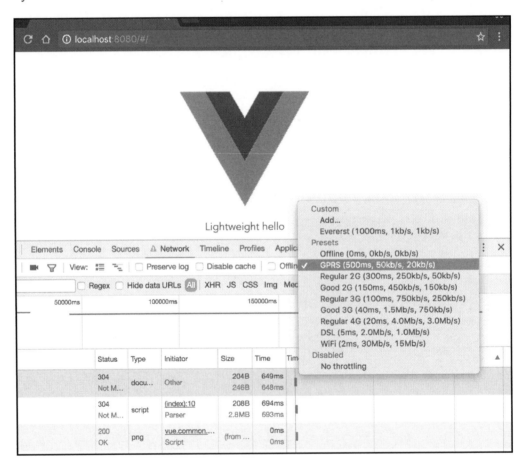

Now right-click on the refresh button and select **Hard Reload** to bypass the cache (or press *Shift + Cmd + R*):

You will notice that the page doesn't load for a few minutes. You can stop the loading of the page by clicking on the refresh button again when it becomes an X.

To fix this, go back to the `index.js` file in the `router` folder. Delete the following line, where you import the `Massive` component:

```
import Massive from '@/components/Massive'
```

The preceding line is telling Webpack to include all the code contained in the `Massive` component in a single js bundle. Instead, we want to tell Webpack to keep the `Massive` component as a separate bundle and to load it only when necessary.
Instead of directly importing the component, declare `Massive` with the following code:

```
const Massive = resolve =>
  require(['../components/Massive.vue'], resolve)
```

Webpack will turn this special syntax into a separate file that will be loaded lazily. Save and do another hard refresh with the throttling still set to slow speed (like GPRS to good 3G). After a few seconds, you should be able to see the hello page. If you want to load the `Massive` component, just add `massive` to the URL, but you'll be in for some waiting.

How it works...

Now you obviously won't have such a big component in a real application, but you can easily see that if the `Massive` component represents all the other components of your app, they can quickly amount to such a big size.

The trick here is to load them asynchronously; Webpack will help you separate them into smaller bundles so that they will be loaded only if and when required.

There's more...

There is an alternative syntax to import components lazily. It may become an ECMA standard in the future, so you should be aware of it. Open `index.js` inside the `router` directory and completely remove the import of the `Massive` component or the `Massive` constant line we added in this recipe.

Inside the routes, try the following when specifying the component for the `/massive` route:

```
routes: [
  {
    path: '/',
    name: 'Hello',
    component: Hello
  },
  {
    path: '/massive',
    name: 'Massive',
    component: import('@/components/Massive')
  }
]
```

This will be equivalent to what we have done before, because Webpack will take the line and instead of directly importing the code of the Massive component, it will create a different js file, loaded lazily.

Building a simple storage for the application state

In this recipe, you will understand the fundamentals of Vuex when building a big application. This recipe is a little unorthodox because to understand how Vuex's store work, we will manipulate it directly; you should never do that in a real application.

Getting ready

Before trying this recipe, you should complete **Making two components talk with Vuex** in `Chapter 4`, *All About Components*.

How to do it...

Create a new project based on the Webpack template with the following command run in a new directory:

```
vue init webpack
```

How you answer the question is not relevant. Run `npm intall` and install Vuex with `npm install vuex --save` or `yarn add vuex` if you use yarn.

Open the `main.js` file inside the `src` folder and add the following highlighted lines to finish installing Vuex:

```
import Vue from 'vue'
import App from './App'
import router from './router'
import store from './store'

/* eslint-disable no-new */
new Vue({
 el: '#app',
 router,
 store,
 template: '<App/>',
 components: { App }
})
```

Of course, there is no `store` module right now, so you need to create one. To do this, create a folder just under the `src` folder and call it `store`. Inside it, create a file named `index.js`. In the `main.js` file, we didn't specify to use the `index.js` file, but that's the default behavior when no file is specified but only the folder.

What we will implement is a simplified stock market. We have three assets: stars (STAR), lamps (LAMP), and diamonds (DIAM). We will define two routes: one for the STAR/LAMP market and another for the LAMP/DIAM market.

Inside the `index.js` file in the store folder, write the following:

```
import Vue from 'vue'
import Vuex from 'vuex'
Vue.use(Vuex)
const store = new Vuex.Store({
  state: {
    STAR: 100,
    LAMP: 100,
    DIAM: 100,
```

```
      rate: {
        STAR: {
          LAMP: 2
        },
        LAMP: {
          DIAM: 0.5
        }
      }
    }
  })
  export default store
```

We are creating a new Vuex store that will hold our balance. Initially, we have 100 of each asset; in the store, the exchange rate between stars and lamps and between lamps and diamonds is also fixed.

Create a new component under the components directory, named Market.vue. It will have the following template:

```
<template>
  <div class="market">
    <h2>{{symbol1}}/{{symbol2}} Stock Exchange</h2>
    <div class="buy-sell">
      <input v-model.number="amount">{{symbol1}}
      <button @click="buy">
        Buy for {{rate*amount}} {{symbol2}}
      </button>
      <button @click="sell">
        Sell for {{rate*amount}} {{symbol2}}
      </button>
    </div>
  </div>
</template>
```

symbol1 and symbol2 represent the two assets traded. In the JavaScript of this component, where we define the sell and buy methods, we operate directly on the global Vuex store:

```
<script>
export default {
  name: 'market',
  data () {
    return {
      amount: 0
    }
  },
  computed: {
    rate () {
```

```
        return this.$store.state.rate[this.symbol1][this.symbol2]
      }
    },
    props: ['symbol1', 'symbol2'],
    methods: {
      buy () {
        this.$store.state[this.symbol1] += this.amount
        this.$store.state[this.symbol2] -= this.amount * this.rate
      },
      sell () {
        this.$store.state[this.symbol1] -= this.amount
        this.$store.state[this.symbol2] += this.amount * this.rate
      }
    }
  }
}
</script>
```

 You should never touch the state directly like I've done here. You should always use mutations. Here, we are skipping the middleman to keep the recipe minimalistic. There's more on mutations in the next recipe.

You have to use this component in `index.js`, inside the `router` folder, in the following way:

```
import Vue from 'vue'
import Router from 'vue-router'
import Market from '@/components/Market'
Vue.use(Router)
export default new Router({
  routes: [
    {
      path: '/',
      redirect: '/STAR/LAMP'
    },
    {
      path: '/:symbol1/:symbol2',
      component: Market,
      props: true
    }
  ]
})
```

In the preceding code, we are using the `Market` component for any route that contains a couple of trade symbols. As a home page, we are using the STAR/LAMP market.

To display some navigation links to a different market and our current balance, we can edit the `App.vue` component with the following template:

```
<template>
  <div id="app">
    <nav>
      <ul>
        <li>
          <router-link to="/STAR/LAMP">STAR/LAMP Market</router-link>
        </li><li>
          <router-link to="/LAMP/DIAM">LAMP/DIAM Market</router-link>
        </li>
      </ul>
    </nav>
    <router-view></router-view>
    <div class="balance">
      Your balance is:
      <ul>
        <li>{{$store.state.STAR}} stars</li>
        <li>{{$store.state.LAMP}} lamps</li>
        <li>{{$store.state.DIAM}} diamonds</li>
      </ul>
    </div>
  </div>
</template>
```

We don't need any JavaScript for this component, so you can delete the `<script>` tag.

Our app is now ready; launch it and start trading with it. The following image is our completed app without the styles contained in `App.vue`:

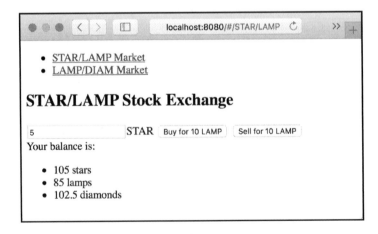

How it works...

The balance in the bottom is like a summary of the global state. With Vuex, we were able to affect other components by accessing the `$store` variable that gets injected in every component by the Vuex plugin. You can easily imagine how to use this strategy in a big application when you want to basically expand the scope of a variable beyond the component itself.

Some of the states may be local, for example if you need some animations or you need some variables to show modal dialogs for the component; it's perfectly okay to not put these values in the store. Otherwise, having a structured centralized state in one place helps a lot. In the subsequent recipes, you'll use more advanced techniques to exploit the power of Vuex better.

Understanding Vuex mutations

The proper way to mutate the state in a Vuex application is with the help of mutations. Mutations are a very useful abstraction to decompose state changes in the atomic unit. In this recipe, we will explore just that.

Getting ready

This recipe can be completed without knowing too much about Vuex, but completing the previous recipe first is suggested.

How to do it...

Add Vuex as a dependency to your project (the CDN address is `https://unpkg.com/vuex`). I will assume that you are using JSFiddle to follow along; otherwise, just remember to put `Vue.use(Vuex)` before the store code.

The sample application we will build is to broadcast notifications to the users of the website.

The HTML layout looks as shown:

```
<div id="app">
  <div v-for="(message, index) in messages">
    <p style="cursor:pointer">{{message}}
      <span @click="close(index)">[x]</span>
    </p>
  </div>
  <input v-model="newMessage" @keyUp.enter="broadcast">
  <button @click="broadcast">Broadcast</button>
</div>
```

The idea is to have a textbox to write messages and the broadcasted messages will be displayed on the top with the most recent appearing first. The messages can be dismissed by clicking on the little **x**.

First, let's build a store that will hold the list of broadcasted messages and enumerate the possible mutations we can make to said list:

```
const store = new Vuex.Store({
  state: {
    messages: []
  },
  mutations: {
    pushMessage (state, message) {
      state.messages.push(message)
    },
    removeMessage (state, index) {
      state.messages.splice(index, 1)
    }
  }
})
```

So, we have a list of messages; we can push one to the top of the list or we can remove a message by knowing its index.

Next, we need to write the logic of the application itself:

```
new Vue({
  store,
  el: '#app',
  data: {
    newMessage: ''
  },
  computed: Vuex.mapState(['messages']),
  methods: {
    broadcast () {
      store.commit('pushMessage', this.newMessage)
```

```
      this.newMessage = ''
    },
    close (index) {
      store.commit('removeMessage', index)
    }
  }
})
```

You can now launch the app and start broadcasting messages to our imaginary users:

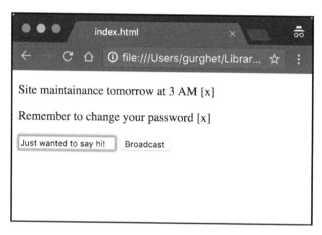

How it works...

I think it's important to note the names of the mutations; they are called `pushMessage` and `removeMessage`, but what they really do in this application is show the message in a stack on the screen and (fictionally) broadcast messages to users. Would it be better to call them `showMessage`, or `broadcastMessage` and `hideMessage`? No, that's because there has to be a clear separation of intent between the mutation itself and the particular effects of that mutation. The problem becomes clear when, for example, we decide to give users the ability to ignore these notifications or we introduce a delay before actually broadcasting the notifications. Then we will have a `showMessage` mutation that does not actually show a message.

The computed syntax we have used is as illustrated:

```
computed: Vuex.mapState(['messages'])
```

You don't have to explicitly use Vuex in your expression when you are importing Vuex as an ES6 module. You just need to write `import { mapState } from 'Vuex'`.
Then, the `mapState` function will be available.

The `mapState` method takes an array of strings as a parameter, looks for a `state` variable in the store with the same name as the string, and creates a computed property with the same name. You can do this with as many variables as you want.

There's more...

If you followed along on a local npm project, open the Vue developer tools (unfortunately Vue developer tools is not available when using JSFiddle) and you will see that a new mutation is issued with each message. Consider that you click on the little clock:

You can actually undo the mutation with that, as shown in the following illustration:

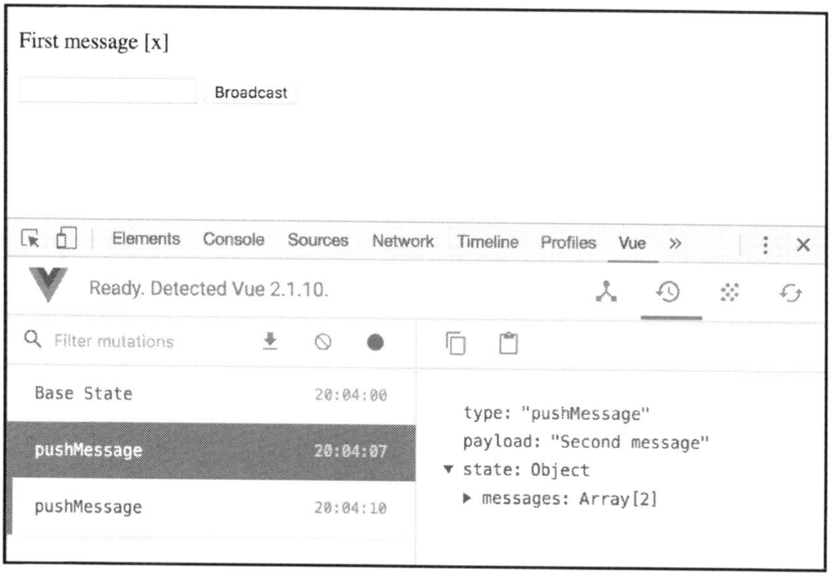

Note how the state didn't change when clicking the time travel option; that's because the purple ribbon is still at the last state. To examine a different state, just click on the name of the mutation itself.

This debug mechanism is possible because mutations are always synchronous; this means that it's possible to take a snapshot of the state before and after the mutation and navigate through time. In the next recipe, you will learn how to use Vuex to perform asynchronous actions.

Listing your actions in Vuex

All your mutations must be synchronous, so how do you do things such as waiting for a timeout or using Axios for an AJAX request? Actions are the next level of abstraction that will help you with this. Inside an action, you can commit multiple mutations and make asynchronous operations.

Getting ready

Mutations are the building blocks of actions, so it's highly suggested you complete the preceding recipe before trying this.

We will be using the setup from the *Building a simple storage for the application state* recipe; you can use your own as well, but in any case this recipe is based on a slight modification of the official Webpack template.

How to do it...

You will build a clone of the popular Xkcd website. Actually, it will be a wrapper more than a real clone, since we will reuse the panels from the website.

Create a Vue project based on the Webpack template with `vue init webpack`. The first thing we will do is wire up the API to the Xkcd website in the `index.js` inside the `config` folder. Put the following lines inside the `proxyTable` object:

```
module.exports = {
  ...
  dev: {
    proxyTable: {
      '/comic': {
        target: 'https://xkcd.com',
        changeOrigin: true,
        pathRewrite: (path, req) => {
          const num = path.split('/')[2]
          return `/${num}/info.0.json`
        }
      }
    },
  ...
```

This will redirect all the requests we make to `/comic` to the Xkcd website.

Inside `src`, make a new `store` directory and an `index.js` inside it; here, start building the application store:

```
import Vue from 'vue'
import Vuex from 'vuex'

Vue.use(Vuex)

const store = new Vuex.Store({
  state: {
```

```
      currentPanel: undefined,
      currentImg: undefined,
      errorStack: []
    },
    actions: {},
    mutations: {}
  }

  export default store
```

You should import this inside `main.js` like in previous recipes. We want to trace the current panel number, the link to the panel image, and the possible errors. The only way to modify the state is through mutations, while actions can perform asynchronous work.

When the app is loaded, we plan to display the latest comic. For this, we create an action:

```
  actions: {
    goToLastPanel ({ commit }) {
      axios.get(endpoint)
        .then(({ data }) => {
          commit('setPanel', data.num)
          commit('setImg', data.img)
        }).catch(error => {
          commit('pushError', error)
        })
    }
    ...
```

For this code to work, we need to declare the endpoint and install Axios:

```
  ...
  import axios from 'axios'
  ...
  const endpoint = '/comic/'
```

It should be easy for you to write the corresponding mutations:

```
  mutations: {
    setPanel (state, num) {
      state.currentPanel = num
    },
    setImg (state, img) {
      state.currentImg = img
    },
    pushError (state, error) {
      state.errorStack.push(error)
    }
  }
```

We'll recycle the `Hello.vue` component and put the following template inside it:

```
<template>
  <div class="hello">
    <h1>XKCD</h1>
    <img :src="currentImg">
  </div>
</template>
```

To make the last panel appear on loading you can use the following JavaScript in the component:

```
<script>
import { mapState } from 'vuex'
export default {
  name: 'hello',
  computed: mapState(['currentImg']),
  created () {
    this.$store.dispatch('goToLastPanel')
  }
}
</script>
```

Also, you can delete most of the `App.vue` template and leave only the following:

```
<template>
  <div id="app">
    <router-view></router-view>
  </div>
</template>
```

How it works...

The `proxyTable` object will configure the `http-proxy-middleware`. This is useful every time we are developing the UI of a bigger web application and we launch our developer server on `localhost`, but our API responds to another web server. This is especially relevant when we want to use CORS and we don't allow other websites to use our API. The Xkcd API doesn't allow `localhost` to consume the web service. This is why, even if we try to use the Xkcd API directly, our browser won't let us. The `changeOrigin` option will send the request with Xkcd as host, making CORS unnecessary.

To call an action from a component, we used the `dispatch` function. It's also possible to pass the second argument, the first being the name of the action itself. The second argument is then passed when you define the action as the second parameter.

A last note on the naming--it being implicit that actions are asynchronous while mutations are synchronous, there is no need, in my opinion, to make the asynchronicity in the name of the actions explicit.

Separating concerns with modules

When building big applications, the Vuex store can become crowded. Luckily, it's possible to divide the different concerns of the applications into separate compartments with modules.

Getting ready

This recipe can be a reference if you want to use modules. You are expected to already know enough about Vuex.

For this recipe, you will have to be a little familiar with Webpack.

How to do it...

In this recipe, we will model a fully functional human body in a slightly simplified manner. Every organ will have a separate module.
Create a new Webpack template with `vue init webpack` and `npm install vuex`. Create a new directory with the `src/store/index.js` file in it. Inside, write the following:

```
import Vue from 'vue'
import Vuex from 'vuex'

Vue.use(Vuex)

const store = new Vuex.Store({
  modules: {
    brain,
    heart
  }
})

export default store
```

The `heart` module is like this; put it before the store declaration:

```
const heart = {
  state: { loves: undefined },
  mutations: {
    love (state, target) {
      state.loves = target
    },
    unlove (state) {
      state.loves = undefined
    }
  }
}
```

Note how the state passed inside the mutations is not the root state, but the local state of the module.

Then comes the brain, which is divided into the left and right lobes; write the following before the store:

```
const brain = {
  modules: {
    left: leftLobe,
    right: rightLobe
  }
}
```

You can implement them as simple Boolean states (write them before the brain on which they depend):

```
const leftLobe = {
  namespaced: true,
  state: { reason: true },
  mutations: {
    toggle (state) { state.reason = !state.reason }
  }
}
const rightLobe = {
  namespaced: true,
  state: { fantasy: true },
  mutations: {
    toggle (state) { state.fantasy = !state.fantasy }
  }
}
```

Setting `namespaced` to true modifies the way you can call the mutator. Since they are both called `toggle`, now you can specify which lobe, for example, for the left lobe the mutation string becomes `left/toggle`, where `left` says it is the key used in the brain to refer to the left lobe.

To see your store in action, you can create a component that uses all the mutations. For the brain, we can have two pictures of the lobes, like so:

```
<img
  :class="{ off: !$store.state.brain.left.reason }"
  src="http://i.imgur.com/n8B6wuY.png"
  @click="left"><img
  :class="{ off: !$store.state.brain.right.fantasy }"
  src="http://i.imgur.com/4BbfVur.png"
  @click="right">
```

This will create two drawings of brain lobes in red pencil; note the use of the name of the modules in a nested way. The following `off` CSS rule grays the lobes out:

```
.off {
  filter: grayscale(100%)
}
```

To call the mutations, we use the aforementioned strings in the right methods:

```
methods: {
  left () {
    this.$store.commit('left/toggle')
  },
  right () {
    this.$store.commit('right/toggle')
  }
}
```

You can also create an input textbox and call the other two mutations, as follows:

```
...
love () {
  this.$store.commit('love', this.partner)
},
clear () {
  this.$store.commit('unlove')
  this.partner = undefined
}
...
```

This was very easy, but how do you retrieve the loved name? You can put these mustachios in your template:

```
<p>♥ loves: {{$store.state.heart.loves}}</p>
<input v-model="partner" @input="love">
<button @click="clear">Clear</button>
```

You obviously have to declare the `partner` variable on your Vue instance:

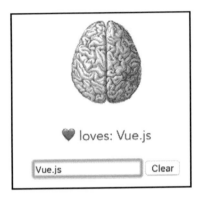

How it works...

We have seen how to use modules to split your application concerns into different units. This ability may become important as the project grows in size.

The common pattern is that while inside a mutation, you have direct access to the local state:

```
const leftLobe = {
  namespaced: true,
  state: { reason: true },
  mutations: {
    toggle (state) {
      // here state is the left lobe state
      state.reason = !state.reason
    }
  }
}
```

In a mutation, it makes sense to have access only to the local state. The brain, for example, cannot change the heart and vice versa, but what about actions? If we declare an action inside a module, we are passed an object called context that looks like this:

```
{
  "getters":{},
  "state":{
    "reason":true
  },
  "rootGetters":{},
  "rootState":{
    "brain":{
      "left":{
        "reason":true
      },
      "right":{
        "fantasy":false
      }
    },
    "heart":{
      "loves": "Johnny Toast"
    }
  }
}
```

So, if we want to declare an action in the left lobe and we want to affect the heart, we have to do something like the following:

```
actions: {
  beNerd ({ rootState }) {
    rootState.heart.loves = 'Math & Physics'
  }
}
```

Building getters to help retrieve your data

You don't want to keep too much data in your state. It can be especially dangerous to keep duplicate or derivative data because it can be brought out of sync very easily. Getters help you with this without shifting the burden onto the components by keeping all the logic in one place.

Getting ready

This recipe is for you if you already have some Vuex knowledge and want to expand your horizons.

How to do it...

Imagine that you are building a Bitcoin wallet. You want to give your users an overview of their balance, and you want them to see how many Euros it corresponds to.

Create a new Webpack template with `vue init webpack` and `npm install vuex`. Create a new `src/store/index.js` file and write the following inside it:

```
import Vue from 'vue'
import Vuex from 'vuex'

Vue.use(Vuex)

const store = new Vuex.Store({
  state: {
    bitcoin: 600,
    rate: 1000,
    euro: 600000
  }
})

export default store
```

This code is prone to errors. The first error can be a miscalculation of the Euro amount if we don't get the multiplication right. The second kind of error can be that we tell the user the `bitcoin` and `euro` balance during a transaction, resulting in a stale and wrong amount for one of the two.

To tackle these issues, we use `getters`:

```
const store = new Vuex.Store({
  state: {
    bitcoin: 600,
    rate: 1000
  },
  getters: {
    euro: state => state.bitcoin * state.rate
  }
})
```

This way the `euro` amount is never in the state but always computed. Moreover, it is centralized in the store, so we don't need to add anything to our components.

Now, it's easy to retrieve the two amounts from a template:

```
<template>
  <div>
    <h1>Balance</h1>
    <ul>
      <li>{{$store.state.bitcoin}}฿</li>
      <li>{{$store.getters.euro}}&euro;</li>
    </ul>
  </div>
</template>
```

Here, `&#3647 ;` is the HTML entity for the Bitcoin symbol.

How it works...

Having a `getter` for derived data is always a good idea if we are not talking about input data. A notable feature of getters we have not yet discussed is their ability to interact with other getters and take an argument.

Accessing other getters

The second argument passed to a getter when called is the object that contains the other getters:

```
getters: {
  ...
  getCatPictures: state => state.pictures.filter(pic => isCat(pic))
  getKittens: (state, getters) => {
    return getters.getCatPictures().filter(cat => !isAdult(cat))
  }
}
```

In our recipe, we could call the `euro` getter to have some more derived data, like roughly how many houses we can buy with our Bitcoin given an average price of 150,000 euros:

```
const store = new Vuex.Store({
  state: {
    bitcoin: 600,
    rate: 1000
  },
```

```
  getters: {
    euro: state => state.bitcoin * state.rate,
  houses: (state, getters) => getters.euro() / 150000
})
```

Passing an argument

If a getter returns a function with an argument, that argument will be the argument of the getter:

```
getters: {
  ...
  getWorldWonder: state => nth => state.worldWonders[nth]
}
```

In our recipe, a practical example could specify the average cost of a house in the getter from the previous paragraph:

```
const store = new Vuex.Store({
  state: {
    bitcoin: 600,
    rate: 1000
  },
  getters: {
    euro: state => state.bitcoin * state.rate,
  houses: (state, getters) => averageHousePrice => {
      return getters.euro() / averageHousePrice
    }
})
```

Testing your store

As you know from *Chapter 7, Unit Testing and End-To-End Testing*, testing is the most important part of professional software. As the store often defines the business logic of your application, testing it may be vital for your application. In this recipe, you will write tests for a Vuex store.

Getting ready

This recipe requires knowledge from *Chapter 7, Unit Testing and End-To-End Testing* and familiarity with Vuex; you can get it from the earlier recipes of this chapter.

How to do it...

First, I'll define some features that our store must implement; then you will write tests that prove that the features are present and working.

Software requirements

Our store consists of items in a to-do list, like the following:

```
state: {
  todo: [
    { id: 43, text: 'Buy iPhone', done: false },
    ...
  ],
  archived: [
    { id: 2, text: 'Buy gramophone', done: true },
    ...
  ]
}
```

We have two requirements:

- We must have an `MARK_ITEM_AS_DONE` mutation that changes the `done` field from false to true
- We must have a `downloadNew` action that downloads the latest items from our server and adds them to the list

Testing mutations

To be able to test your mutations, you have to make them available for your test files. To do this, you have to extract the mutation object from your store. Consider something like this:

```
import Vuex from 'vuex'
import Vue from 'vue'

Vue.use(Vuex)

const store = new Vuex.Store({
  ...
  mutations: {
    ...
    MARK_ITEM_AS_DONE (state, itemId) {
      state.todo.filter(item => {
        return item.id === itemId
```

```
    }).forEach(item => {
      item.done = true
    })
    state.archived.filter(item => {
      return item.id === itemId
    }).forEach(item => {
      item.done = true
    })
  }
 }
})
```

```
export default store
```

You have to extract it to something similar to this:

```
export const mutations = { ... }

const store = new Vuex.Store({ ... })

export default store
```

This way, you can import the mutations in your test files with the following line:

```
import { mutations } from '@/store'
```

The test for requirement number 1 can be written as follows:

```
describe('mutations', () => {
  it(`MARK_ITEM_AS_DONE mutation must change the
        done field from false to true for a todo`, () => {
    const state = {
      todo: [
        { id: 43, text: 'Buy iPhone', done: false }
      ],
      archived: [
        { id: 40, text: 'Buy cat', done: false }
      ]
    }
    mutations.MARK_ITEM_AS_DONE(state, 43)
    expect(state.todo[0].done).to.be.true
  })
})
```

If you are using the official Webpack template, you can run your tests with `npm run unit`. This uses PhantomJS by default, which doesn't implement some features. You can either use Babel polyfills or simply go into `karma.conf.js` and write `Chrome` instead of `PhantomJS` in the `browsers` array. Remember to install the Chrome launcher with `npm install karma-chrome-launcher --save-dev`.

Testing actions

Testing actions means testing that the action commits the expected mutations. We are not interested in the mutations themselves (not in unit tests at least) because they are already tested separately. We might, though, need to mock some dependencies.

To avoid any dependencies from Vue or Vuex (since we don't need them and they may pollute the tests), we create a new `actions.js` file inside the `store` directory. Install Axios with `npm install axios`. The `actions.js` file can look like the following:

```
import axios from 'axios'

export const actions = {
  downloadNew ({ commit }) {
    axios.get('/myNewPosts')
      .then(({ data }) => {
        commit('ADD_ITEMS', data)
      })
  }
}
```

To test for requirement number 2, we start by mocking the call to the server that should download the new to-do items:

```
describe('actions', () => {
const actionsInjector =
  require('inject-loader!@/store/actions')
const buyHouseTodo = {
  id: 84,
  text: 'Buy house',
  done: true
}
const actions = actionsInjector({
  'axios': {
    get () {
      return new Promise(resolve => {
        resolve({
          data: [buyHouseTodo]
```

```
          })
        })
      }
    }
  }).default
  }
```

This will ensure that any call to the get method of `axios` will always return a new to-do item.

Then, we want to ensure that the `ADD_ITEMS` mutation is called upon dispatch:

```
describe('actions', () => {
  const actionsInjector =
    require('inject-loader!@/store/actions')
    const buyHouseTodo = {
      id: 84,
      text: 'Buy house',
      done: true
    }
    const actions = actionsInjector({
      'axios': {
        get () {
          return new Promise(resolve => {
            resolve({ data: [buyHouseTodo] })
          })
        }
      }
    }).default
    it(`downloadNew should commit ADD_ITEMS
    with the 'Buy house' todo when successful`, done => {
    const commit = (type, payload) => {
      try {
        expect(type).to.equal('ADD_ITEMS')
        expect(payload).to.deep.equal([buyHouseTodo])
        done()
      } catch (error) {
        done(error)
      }
    }
  actions.downloadNew({ commit })
  })
})
```

How it works...

While the testing of the mutations is pretty straightforward, I think the testing of the actions deserves some more explaining.

Since we didn't want to depend on external services for actions, we had to mock the `axios` service. We used the `inject-loader`, which takes the original library and mocks the parts we specify with arbitrary code (the @ symbol is a shorthand for `src`); in our case, we mocked the `axios` library and, precisely, the `get` method. We had to use the CommonJS syntax (with the `require`) because that's the only way to tell Webpack to use loaders in imports.

What we have done in the test is that we also mocked the `commit` function. Normally, this function calls a mutation that modifies the state. We just want to know if the correct mutation is called and with the right arguments. Moreover, we had to wrap everything in a `try` block; without it, the test would fail over a timeout and we'd lose the error. Instead, now we fail immediately and we can read, from the console, what error caused the test to fail.

11
Integrating with Other Frameworks

In this chapter, we'll explore the following topics:

- Building universal applications with Electron
- Using Vue with Firebase
- Creating a real-time app with Feathers
- Creating a reactive app with Horizon

Introduction

Vue is powerful, but if you need a backend, it can't do much alone; at a minimum you will need a server to deploy your software. In this section, you will actually build small, but complete and working, applications with popular frameworks. Electron is used to bring Vue apps to the desktop. Firebase is a modern cloud backend and, finally, FeatherJS is a minimalistic but full-featured JavaScript backend. When you are finished with these, you will have all the tools required to interact with them and quickly build professional applications.

Building universal applications with Electron

Electron is a framework for creating universal applications that run on Mac, Linux, and Windows. At it's core is a stripped down version of a web browser. It has been used to create widely used applications such as Slack and Visual Studio Code, among others. In this recipe, you'll build a simple app with Electron.

Getting ready

To build this app, we will use only basic Vue functionalities. Electron is out of scope for this book, but for this recipe no knowledge of Electron is required; in fact, this is a good starting point to learn more about Electron.

How to do it...

In this recipe, we will build a small but complete app--a pomodoro application. A pomodoro is an interval of about 25 units of time, in which you should concentrate on doing work. It's called this because you usually use a tomato-shaped kitchen timer to measure that. This app will track the time instead, so you don't have to buy an expensive kitchen timer.

The best way to spin up a Vue project with Electron is to use the Electron-Vue boilerplate (you don't say!). This can be easily achieved with the following command:

```
vue init simulatedgreg/electron-vue pomodoro
```

You can answer with the default values, but when asked which plugin to install, just select `vue-electron`. Install all the dependencies with `npm intall` and, if you like, you can keep the application open with hot-reloading while you make the necessary modifications with `npm run dev`. You can hide the dev tools by just clicking on the *x* in the corner:

```
  vue init simulatedgreg/electron-vue

? Generate project in current directory? Yes
? Application Name pomodoro
? Project description A pomodoro app
? Select which Vue plugins to install
 ● vue-electron
 ○ vue-resource
 ○ vue-router
)○ vuex
```

First of all, we want our app to be small-ish. Let's go to the `app/src/main/index.js` file; this file controls the life cycle of our application. Change the window size to the following:

```
mainWindow = new BrowserWindow({
  height: 200,
  width: 300
})
```

Then, we don't really want the boilerplate components in the
app/src/render/components folder, so you can delete everything. Instead, create a
Pomodoro.vue file and put this template inside:

```
<template>
  <div class="pomodoro">
    <p>Time remaining: {{formattedTime}}</p>
    <button v-if="remainingTime === 1500" @click="start">Start</button>
    <button v-else @click="stop">Stop</button>
  </div>
</template>
```

To make it work, we also have to write the JavaScript part, as follows:

```
<script>
export default {
  data () {
    return {
      remainingTime: 1500,
      timer: undefined
    }
  },
  methods: {
    start () {
      this.remainingTime -= 1
      this.timer = setInterval(() => {
        this.remainingTime -= 1
        if (this.remainingTime === 0) {
          clearInterval(this.timer)
        }
      }, 1000)
    },
    stop () {
      clearInterval(this.timer)
      this.remainingTime = 1500
    }
  }
}
</script>
```

This way, clicking on the start button in the program will subtract 1 second every second.
Clicking on the stop button will clear the timer and reset the remaining time to 1500 seconds
(25 minutes). The timer object is basically the result of the setInterval operation, and
clearInterval just stops whatever the timer was doing.

In our template, we want a `formattedTime` method in the sense that we'd like to see the time in `mm:ss` format, which is much more human-readable than just the number of remaining seconds (even if that's more geeky), so we need to add the computed function:

```
computed: {
  formattedTime () {
    const pad = num => ('0' + num).substr(-2)
    const minutes = Math.floor(this.remainingTime / 60)
    const seconds = this.remainingTime - minutes * 60
    return `${minutes}:${pad(seconds)}`
  }
}
```

To add this component to the app, go to the `App.vue` file and edit the following lines, replacing the `landingPage` placeholder element:

```
<template>
  <div id="#app">
    <pomodoro></pomodoro>
  </div>
</template>

<script>
  import Pomodoro from 'components/Pomodoro'
  export default {
    components: {
      Pomodoro
    }
  }
</script>
```

Launching the app with `npm run dev`, you should now be able to track the time while working or studying:

You can even build a distributable version of the application with the `npm run build` command.

How it works...

The way we implemented the timer is not particularly accurate for time tracking. Let's review the code:

```
this.timer = setInterval(() => {
  this.remainingTime -= 1
  if (this.remainingTime === 0) {
    clearInterval(this.timer)
  }
}, 1000)
```

This means that we decrease the remaining time every second. The problem is that the `setInterval` function itself is not 100% accurate and may fire the function a bit before or after 1000 milliseconds, depending on the machine's computational load; this way, the margin of error can accumulate and become a considerable amount. A better approach would be to check the clock every time the function gets called and adjust for the error at each loop, though we won't cover that here.

Using Vue with Firebase

Using Vue with Firebase as a backend is very easy, thanks to VueFire--a plugin that contains bindings for Firebase. In this recipe, you will develop a fully functional database of smells.

Getting ready

Firebase is out of the scope of this book, but I will assume, for this recipe, that you have a familiarity with the basic concepts. Except for this, there is really not much you need to know, as we will build a very basic Vue application on top of that.

How to do it...

Before starting to write code, we need to create a new Firebase application. To do this, you have to log in at `https://firebase.google.com/` and create a new application. In our case, it will be called `smell-diary`. You will also need to take note of your API key, which is found in the project settings:

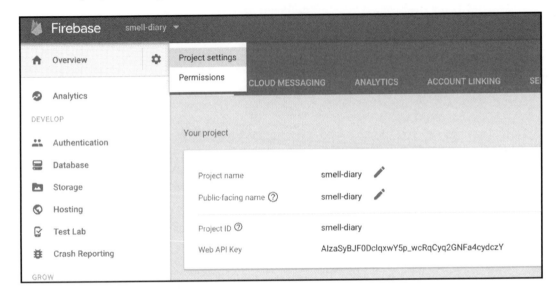

Also, you will need to disable authentication; go to the **Database** section and, in the **Rules** tab, set both read and write to true:

```
{
  "rules": {
    ".read": true,
    ".write": true
  }
}
```

We are finished with the Firebase configuration.

Open a clean HTML5 boilerplate or JSFiddle, with `Vue` as a library. We will need the following dependencies expressed as script tags inside the head of the file:

```
<script src="https://unpkg.com/vue/dist/vue.js"></script>
<script
src="https://www.gstatic.com/firebasejs/3.6.9/firebase.js"></script>
<script src="https://unpkg.com/vuefire/dist/vuefire.js"></script>
```

VueFire will automatically detect Vue (so the order is important) and install itself as a plugin. We will build a very simple database to keep track of the odor of things that surround us. The following is the HTML layout of our app:

```
<div id="app">
  <ul>
    <li v-for="item in items">
      {{item.name}}: {{item.smell}}
      <button @click="removeItem(item['.key'])">X</button>
    </li>
  </ul>
  <form @submit.prevent="addItem">
    <input v-model="newItem" />
    smells like
    <input v-model="newSmell" />
    <button>Add #{{items.length}}</button>
  </form>
</div>
```

In the JavaScript part of our app, we need to specify the API key to authenticate with Firebase, write the following:

```
const config = {
  databaseURL: 'https://smell-diary.firebaseio.com/'
}
```

Then, we feed the configuration to Firebase and get a hold of the database:

```
const firebaseApp = firebase.initializeApp(config)
 const db = firebaseApp.database()
```

This can be done outside the Vue instance. The VueFire plugin installs a new option in the Vue instance, named `firebase`; we have to specify that we want to access the /items in the Firebase app with the `item` variable:

```
new Vue({
  el: '#app',
  firebase: {
    items: db.ref('/items')
  }
})
```

The `newItem` and `newSmell` variables will temporarily hold the values we entered in the input boxes; then, the `addItem` and `removeItem` methods will publish and remove data from our database:

```
data: {
  newItem: '',
  newSmell: ''
},
methods: {
  addItem () {
    this.$firebaseRefs.items
      .push({
        name: this.newItem,
        smell: this.newSmell
      })
    this.newItem = ''
    this.newSmell = ''
  },
  removeItem (key) {
    this.$firebaseRefs.items
      .child(key).remove()
  }
}
```

If you launch your app now, you'll already be able to add your favorite scents and what to sniff to find them:

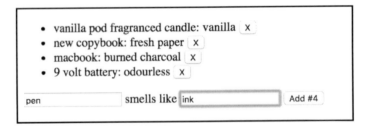

How it works...

Firebase works as a simple key value store. In our case, we are never storing values but always adding children; you can take a look at what you've created in the Firebase console:

The keys are created automatically and they contain empty values and 32 levels of nested data. We are using one level of nesting to insert the name and the smell for each object.

Creating a real-time app with Feathers

Most modern applications are real time, not in the traditional sense, but in the sense that they don't need the page to reload for them to be updated. The most common way to implement this is through WebSockets. In this recipe, we will leverage Feathers and Socket.io to build a cat database.

Getting ready

There is no prerequisite for this recipe, but you can complete the *Createing a REST client (and server!)* recipe before starting this one if you want to have more context.

How to do it...

To complete this recipe, you'll need the Feathers' command line; install it with the following command:

```
npm install -g feathers-cli
```

Now, run `feathers generate`, which will create all the boilerplate for you. When asked about the API, select **Socket.io**:

```
 ▶ feathers generate
local@Gorilla~$

? Description Funny cats
? What type of API are you making?
  ○ REST
 )● Realtime via Socket.io
  ○ Realtime via Primus
```

All the other questions can be left to the default value. While still in the Feather console, type `generate service` to create a new service. You can call it cats and leave the other questions to their default values.

Inside the `public` folder, open `index.html` and delete everything except a HTML5 boilerplate. You will need three dependencies in the head:

```
<script src="//cdnjs.cloudflare.com/ajax/libs/vue/2.1.10/vue.js"></script>
<script
src="//cdnjs.cloudflare.com/ajax/libs/socket.io/1.7.3/socket.io.js"></scrip
t>
<script src="//unpkg.com/feathers-
client@^1.0.0/dist/feathers.js"></script>
```

Write the HTML layout, as follows, in the body tag:

```
<div id="app">
  <div v-for="cat in cats" style="display:inline-block">
    <img width="100" height="100" :src="cat.url" />
    <p>{{cat.name}}</p>
  </div>
  <form @submit.prevent="addCat">
    <div>
      <label>Cat Name</label>
      <input v-model="newName" />
    </div>
    <div>
      <label>Cat Url</label>
      <input v-model="newUrl" />
    </div>
    <button>Add cat</button>
    <img width="30" height="30" :src="newUrl" />
  </form>
</div>
```

The first <div> tag is a gallery of cats. Then, build a form to add new images of the cats you collect.

In the body tag, you can always configure the Feathers service with the following lines:

```
<script>
  const socket = io('http://localhost:3030')
  const app = feathers()
    .configure(feathers.socketio(socket))
  const catService = app.service('cats')
```

This is for configuring the client for the browser that will connect to the WebSockets. The catService method is a handle to the cat database. Next, we write the Vue instance:

```
new Vue({
  el: '#app',
  data: {
    cats: [],
    newName: '',
    newUrl: ''
  },
  methods: {
    addCat () {
      catService.create({
        name: this.newName,
        url: this.newUrl
      })
      this.newName = ''
      this.newUrl = ''
    }
  },
```

Finally, we need to ask for all the cats in the database on startup, while installing a listener in case new cats are created (even by other users):

```
  mounted () {
    catService.find()
      .then(page => {
        this.cats = page.data
      })
    catService.on('created', cat => {
      this.cats.push(cat)
    })
  }
})
</script>
```

If you run your application with `npm start`, you can navigate to the URL written in the console to view your new app. Open another browser window and see how it changes in real-time:

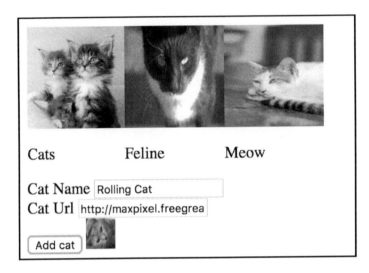

How it works...

Seeing the cats added in real time is clearly the way to go for modern applications. Feathers lets you create them in a snap and with a fraction of the code, thanks to the underlying Socket.io, which in turn uses WebSockets.

WebSockets are really not that complex and what Feathers does in this case is just listen for messages in the channel and associate them with actions like adding something to the database.

The power of Feathers is visible when you can just swap database and WebSocket provider, or switch to REST, without even touching your Vue code.

Creating a reactive app with Horizon

Horizon is a platform to build reactive, real-time scalable apps. It uses RethinkDB internally and is immediately compatible with Vue. In this recipe, you'll build an automatic personal diary.

Getting ready

This recipe just requires a bit of Vue fundamentals, but really not much else.

Before starting though, ensure that you install RethinkDB. You can find more info on this on their website (`https://www.rethinkdb.com/docs/install/`). If you have Homebrew, you can install it with `brew install rethinkdb`.

Also, you will need a Clarifai token. To get one for free, go to `https://developer.clarifa` `i.com/` and sign up. You'll be presented with the code you are supposed to write in your application, like in the following image:

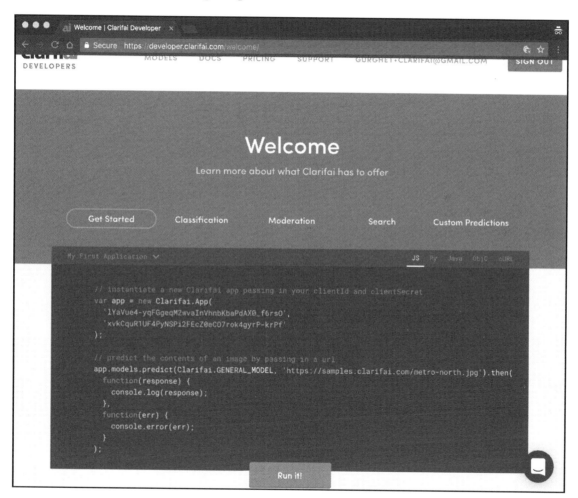

In particular, you will need the `clientId` and the `clientSecret`, which are displayed in this fashion:

```
var app = new Clarifai.App(
  'your client id would be printed here',
  'your client secret would be here'
);
```

Take note of this code or be ready to copy and paste it in to your application.

How to do it...

Writing a journal is a difficult task, you have to write a lot every day. In this recipe, we'll build an automatic journal that will write for us, based on pictures we take during the day.

Horizon will help us to memorize everything and to sync the diary between our devices. After installing RethinkDB, install Horizon with the following command:

```
npm install -g horizon
```

Now, you'll have the new command, `hz`, available. Check it by typing `hz -h`; you should see something like the following:

```
▸ gurghet@Gorilla   ~/Documents   hz -h
Usage: hz subcommand [args...]
Available subcommands:
  init - Initialize a horizon app directory
  serve - Serve a Horizon app
  version - Print the version number of horizon
  create-cert - Generate a certificate
  make-token - Generate a token to log in as a user
  schema - Apply and save the schema from a horizon database
  migrate - migrate an older version of horizon to a newer one
▸ gurghet@Gorilla   ~/Documents   ▮
```

To create the directory that will host our new app, type the following:

```
hz init vue_app
```

Then, enter the newly create `vue_app` directory and take a look at the `index.html` in the `dist` folder. This is the file that will be the entry point to our server, open it with an editor. You can clear everything and leave only an empty HTML5 boilerplate with an empty `<head>` and `<body>`. In the head section, we need to declare dependencies on Vue, Horizon, and Clarifai, as illustrated:

```
<script src="https://unpkg.com/vue"></script>
<script src="/horizon/horizon.js"></script>
<script src="https://sdk.clarifai.com/js/clarifai-latest.js"></script>
```

Just note how Horizon doesn't come from a CDN but from a local dependency.

We start by laying out a template for our journal. We have two parts. In the first, we will list what we did in the past. Write the following in the body of the HTML:

```
<div id="app">
  <div>
    <h3>Dear diary...</h3>
    <ul>
      <li v-for="entry in entries">
        {{ entry.datetime.toLocaleDateString() }}:
        {{ entry.text }}
      </li>
    </ul>
  </div>
...
```

In the second part, we will enter new entries:

```
  ...
  <h3>New Entry</h3>
  <img
    style="max-width:200px;max-height:200px"
    :src="data_uri"
  />
  <input type="file" @change="selectFile" ref="file">
  <p v-if="tentativeEntries.length">Choose an entry</p>
  <button v-for="tentativeEntry in tentativeEntries"
@click="send(tentativeEntry)">
    {{tentativeEntry}}
  </button>
</div>
```

After this, open a `<script>` tag in which we'll write all of the following JavaScript.

First, we need to log in to Clarifai:

```
var app = new Clarifai.App(
  '7CDIjv_VqEYfmFi_ygwKsKAaDe-LwEzc78CcW1sA',
  'XCOS9GHxS0iONFsAdiA2xOUuBsOhATOjZWQTx4h1'
  )
```

Obviously, you want to enter your `clientId` and `clientSecret` from Clarifai.

Then, we need to spin up Horizon and have a handle to the `entries` collection that we will create:

```
const horizon = new Horizon()
const entries = horizon('entries')
```

Now, we finally write our `Vue` instance with three state variables:

```
new Vue({
  el: '#app',
  data: {
    tentativeEntries: [],
    data_uri: undefined,
    entries: []
  },
  ...
```

The `tentativeEntries` array will contain a list of possible entries for the diary we can choose from; `data_uri` will contain the (base64 code of the) image we want to use as a reference for what we did today; `entries` are all the past entries.

When we load an image, we ask Clarifai to come up with possible entries:

```
  ...
  methods: {
    selectFile(e) {
    const file = e.target.files[0]
    const reader = new FileReader()
    if (file) {
      reader.addEventListener('load', () => {
        const data_uri = reader.result
        this.data_uri = data_uri
        const base64 = data_uri.split(',')[1]
        app.models.predict(Clarifai.GENERAL_MODEL, base64)
          .then(response => {
            this.tentativeEntries =
              response.outputs[0].data.concepts
              .map(c => c.name)
          })
```

```
      })
    reader.readAsDataURL(file)
  }
},
...
```

Then when we press the send button, we tell the Horizon collection of entries to store this new one:

```
    ...
    send(concept) {
      entries.store({
        text: concept,
         datetime: new Date()
      }).subscribe(
        result => console.log(result),
        error => console.log(error)
      )
      this.tentativeEntries = []
      this.$refs.file.value = ''
      this.data_uri = undefined
    }
  }
})
```

Finally, we want to ensure that we have the last ten entries on the screen when the page loads and that every time a new entry is added, it pops up in real time. Add the following hook inside the Vue instance, after the methods:

```
created() {
  entries.order('datetime', 'descending').limit(10).watch()
    .subscribe(allEntries => {
      this.entries = [...allEntries].reverse()
  })
}
```

To run the Horizon server, use the following command:

```
hz serve --dev
```

The output for the preceding code is as follows:

Go to the specified address (the first line, not the admin interface), and you will see the following:

You will note that if you have other browser windows open, they will be updated in real time. Now you can finally write a journal every day without typing!

How it works...

Our application uses a pattern called reactive. Its core can be clearly seen in the handle created:

```
entries.order('datetime', 'descending').limit(10).watch()
  .subscribe(allEntries => {
    this.entries = [...allEntries].reverse()
  })
```

The first line returns what is called an observable in reactive. An observable can be thought of as a source of events. Every time an event is fired, the subscriber to that source will process it. In our case, we are taking the whole entries collection and the events thrown are modifications to that collection. Every time we receive an event of this type, we update the entries array.

I will not provide a deep explanation of reactive programming here, but I would like to highlight that this pattern is very helpful for scalability because of the ease with which you can implement controls for your data flow; limit(10) is an example this.

Index